Crafting Policies to End Poverty in Latin America
The Quiet Transformation

This book provides a theory and evidence to explain the initial decision of governments to adopt a conditional cash transfer program (the most prominent type of antipoverty program currently in operation in Latin America) and whether such programs are insulated from political manipulations or not. Ana Lorena De La O shows that whether presidents limit their own discretion or not has consequences for the survival of policies, their manipulation, and how effective they are in improving the lives of the poor. These policy outcomes, in turn, affect the quality of democracy. This book is the first of its kind to present evidence from all Latin American conditional cash transfers.

Ana Lorena De La O is an associate professor of political science at Yale University, where she is affiliated with the MacMillan Center for International and Area Studies, the Institution for Social and Policy Studies, and the Jackson Institute for Global Affairs. Her research relates to the political economy of poverty alleviation, clientelism, and the provision of public goods. Her work has appeared in the *American Journal of Political Science*, the *Journal of Politics*, *Comparative Political Studies*, the *Quarterly Journal of Political Science*, and the *Annals of the American Academy of Political and Social Sciences*. She earned her Ph.D. in Political Science from the Massachusetts Institute of Technology.

Crafting Policies to End Poverty in Latin America

The Quiet Transformation

ANA LORENA DE LA O
Yale University

CAMBRIDGE
UNIVERSITY PRESS

32 Avenue of the Americas, New York, NY 10013-2473, USA

Cambridge University Press is part of the University of Cambridge.

It furthers the University's mission by disseminating knowledge in the pursuit of education, learning, and research at the highest international levels of excellence.

www.cambridge.org
Information on this title: www.cambridge.org/9781107089488

© Ana Lorena De La O 2015

This publication is in copyright. Subject to statutory exception and to the provisions of relevant collective licensing agreements, no reproduction of any part may take place without the written permission of Cambridge University Press.

First published 2015

A catalog record for this publication is available from the British Library.

Library of Congress Cataloging in Publication Data
De La O, Ana L.
Crafting policies to end poverty in Latin America : the quiet transformation / Ana De La O.
    pages cm
Includes bibliographical references and index.
ISBN 978-1-107-08948-8 (hardback : alk. paper)
 1. Poverty – Latin America. 2. Public welfare – Latin America. 3. Latin America – Economic policy. 4. Latin America – Social policy. I. Title.
HC130.P6.O22   2015
362.5'82098–dc23   2014043959

ISBN 978-1-107-08948-8 Hardback

Cambridge University Press has no responsibility for the persistence or accuracy of URLs for external or third-party Internet Web sites referred to in this publication and does not guarantee that any content on such Web sites is, or will remain, accurate or appropriate.

To my family

Contents

List of Figures		*page* ix
List of Tables		xi
Acknowledgments		xiii
1	Introduction	1
2	The Universe of Cash Transfer Programs	24
3	Politics of Fighting Poverty	44
4	Explaining Policy Adoption and Design	57
5	Explaining Policy Outcomes	96
6	Conditional Cash Transfers and Clientelism	112
7	The Electoral Bonus of Conditional Cash Transfers	134
8	Conclusions	150
Appendix		159
References		161
Index		175

List of Figures

1.1	Average strictness in program design	page 21
2.1	Child labor in Latin America	26
2.2	Average design and implementation of CCTs in Latin America	41
2.3	CCTs' design, implementation, and checks to presidential power	42
3.1	The political game	49
5.1	Effects of divided government and checks on CCTs' duration	106

List of Tables

2.1	Conditional Cash Transfers in Latin America	*page* 28
4.1	Effects of Divided Government on the Adoption of an Above-Average CCT, a Below-Average CCT, and Design Score	63
4.2	Effects of Checks on the Executive on the Adoption of an Above-Average CCT, a Below-Average CCT, and Design Score	66
4.3	Robustness Check: Effects of Divided Government and Checks, Controlling for Diffusion	68
4.4	Regression Discontinuity Design	69
4.5	Effects of President's Party Legislative Majority on the Adoption of an Above-Average CCT, a Below-Average CCT, and Design Score	71
5.1	Effects of Divided Government and Checks on CCTs' Implementation	100
5.2	Political Determinants of Program Expansion	103
5.3	Program Survival: Descriptive Statistics	105
5.4	What People Value in a Poverty Relief Program (by Income Groups)	107
6.1	Survey Participants' Knowledge of Program Sources	116
6.2	Education, Income, and Party Identification of Survey Sample	125
6.3	*Oportunidades* and Clientelism (Survey Data)	129
6.4	List Experiment (Comparison of Means)	132
7.1	Descriptive Statistics of Experimental Villages and Electoral Precincts	140

7.2	Baseline Characteristics (Means and Standard Deviations)	141
7.3	Impact of *Progresa* on Turnout and Party Vote Shares	144
7.4	Impact of Assignment to Early and Late Treatment on Number of Party Observers	147

Acknowledgments

I owe an enormous debt of gratitude to family, friends, and colleagues. The help of Chappell Lawson, Jim Snyder, Jonathan Rodden, and Michael Piore was crucial to getting this project off the ground. I profited greatly from conversations with Sue Stokes, whose support and plentiful good advice are noted with appreciation. In Mexico, the Center of Research for Development provided a stimulating environment. Thanks to Edna Jaime and Luis Rubio for their generous hospitality. I am also grateful to Juan E. Pardinas, Jimena Otero, Mónica Miguel, and Rosalva Miguel for leading me to Santa María Citendejé, where this project began. Oliver Azuara, Santiago Levy, Daniel Hernández, Mónica Orozco, Mario García, Cuauhtémoc Cárdenas, Carlos Rojas Gutiérrez, and Rogelio Gómez Hermosillo took time from their incredibly busy schedules to talk with me and help me understand the dynamics of conditional cash transfers, for which I thank them. I owe a great debt to Luis Ruvalcaba Pérez, from what was then called the Federal Electoral Institute, who gave me access to crucial data for Chapter 7. David Nickerson and I pooled resources to collect the survey in Chapter 6. I am sincerely grateful that he allowed me to use his list experiment. Thanks to Kyla Russell, Linette Lecussan, and Carolina Orellana for providing excellent research assistance.

Many people commented helpfully on parts, or the entire book; special thanks to Sue Stokes for reading the manuscript multiple times. Thanks also to Rebecca Weitz-Shapiro, Valerie Frey, Thad Dunning, Ellie Powell, Dan Butler, Paulina Ochoa, John Roemer, Adria Lawrence, Libby Wood, Alex Debs, Sigrun Khal, Tariq Tachil, Robert Kaufman, Evelyn Huber, Gwyneth McClendon, Elizabeth Carlson, Jennifer Bussell, Victoria Murillo, Isabela Mares, Michiko Ueda, Neil Ruiz, Adam Ziegfeld, and Jon Berlin.

This project also benefited from insightful conversations with Alejandro Poiré, Beatriz Magaloni, Alberto Díaz-Cayeros, Jorge Domínguez, Ernesto Zedillo, Abhijit Banerjee, Kanchan Chandra, Richard Locke, Adam Berinsky,

Roger Peterson, Ken Scheve, Ian Shapiro, Don Green, Stathis Kalyvas, Alan Gerber, Greg Huber, Jacob Hacker, Susan Hyde, Ellen Lust, and Steven Wilkinson. Thanks also to Rohini Pande, Sarah Brooks, Karen Jusko, Stuti Khemani, Juan Pablo Luna, Guillermo Rosas, Lorena Becerra, Claudia Maldonado, Leonard Wantchekon, Chris Berry, Richard Snyder, Cesar Zucco, José Antonio Ocampo, Scott Martin, Ernesto Calvo, Mariela Szwarcberg, Jennifer Tobin, James Vreeland, Ken Green, Alejandro Moreno, Alberto Simpser, Rodrigo Canales, and Gabriela Pérez Yarahuán. Over the years, I also benefited from the feedback of numerous participants at conferences and seminars, including Stanford University, University of Manchester, Yale University, Harvard University, University of Chicago, Columbia University, Brown University, Georgetown University, University of Maryland, and conferences organized by the American Political Science Association, the Midwest Political Science Association, and the Latin American Studies Association.

I am grateful for the institutional support of MIT and Yale University. At Yale, I note with appreciation the support from a Junior Faculty Fellowship in the Social Sciences, from the MacMillan Center for International Studies, from the Institute for Social and Policy Studies, and from the Leitner Program in Comparative Political Economy. The Harris School of Public Policy at the University of Chicago and the Government Department at Georgetown kindly hosted me during my academic leaves.

At Cambridge University Press, I would like to thank my editor, Lew Bateman, for his interest in this book and Shaun Vigil, Pooja Bhandari, and Kristin Landon for their help in the production process. Three anonymous reviewers provided very constructive criticism, for which I thank them.

Last but not least, writing this book was possible only because my parents, José Luis and Julieta, and my sister, Paty, made me feel close to my dear Mexico at all times. Thank you. My most heartfelt thanks are to my husband, Oliver Azuara, for the innumerable ways he helped me in this project and for his unconditional support of my academic career. For the love of my family and their support, I am grateful beyond words. This book is dedicated to them.

1

Introduction

Since the early 1990s, governments in Latin America have been experimenting with innovative approaches to poverty alleviation. The programs that have been created in the region have garnered the attention of scholars and policymakers worldwide. During this wave of social policy reform, the uncelebrated breakthrough in the fight against poverty is that some presidents in the region have adopted programs whose operational guidelines – such as fixed eligibility criteria, monitoring systems, and independent program evaluations – limit governments' ability to manipulate programs for political gain. Yet not all presidents in Latin America have adopted such programs. Why did some governments pursue poverty relief programs insulated from politics, while others pursued manipulable programs, and yet others did not reform their policies at all? What are the implications of this variation for the prospects of eradicating poverty in the region?

This book examines the political processes that led some governments to tie their own hands in crafting antipoverty programs. The degree to which executives limited their discretion had implications for various policy outcomes, including the life span of programs, the extent to which antipoverty policies were used as political instruments, and, ultimately, the degree to which programs improved the lives of the poor.

I argue that while economic crises create the conditions for a new pro-poor social coalition, the governments of young democracies adopt poverty alleviation programs whose operational rules suppress political discretion when they face an antagonistic legislature. Such a decision improves the programs' effectiveness in promoting social development. These policy outcomes, in turn, strengthen democratic systems by eroding clientelism and promoting the electoral participation of program recipients.[1] Conversely, when governments' interests are aligned with those of legislators, poverty relief programs do not include such provisions, politicians have more opportunities to politicize a program, and efforts to fight poverty are less effective. These policy outcomes are deleterious to democracy because they reinforce clientelism, and thus hinder the ability of poor voters to hold politicians accountable.[2] Economic crises, as well as conflict and compromise between the executive and legislative branches, determine the kinds of poverty relief programs that a government pursues, with direct consequences for the economic and political capabilities of the poor.[3]

That politics help explain governments' efforts to eradicate poverty is a well-accepted idea. Yet our understanding of the mechanisms through which politics matter is incomplete. Scholarly work on the welfare state has provided an extensive analysis of social protection systems, but the emphasis has been disproportionately on pensions and, to a lesser extent, on aggregate spending on education and health. For these two areas of the welfare state, scholars find that as democracy became more consolidated toward the end of the twentieth century, governments in Latin America began to spend more on health and education (Huber et al. 2006, 2008; Kaufman and Segura-Ubiergo 2001; Segura-Ubiergo 2007).[4] And, as power dispersion increased and the left took power, the reform of the pension system became less likely (Brooks 2009; Castiglioni 2005; Huber 1996; Madrid 2003). However, the political processes behind the adoption and design of poverty relief programs (i.e., decisions about

---

[1] Scholarship defines clientelism in various ways. Some definitions emphasize that individual interests are promoted at the expense of collective interest (Putnam 1993; Sobrado Chavez 2000; Wantchekon 2003). Other definitions focus on the cost imposed on the client: "Political clientelism means the relations that are established between a patron who offers certain services and a client who in exchange for those services (or goods) permits the patron to govern and resolve collective issues without the client's participation" (Sobrado Chavez and Stoller 2002). Along the same lines, other scholars define clientelism as the concession of political rights on the part of the client in exchange for public favors, goods, or services (Fox 1994). Many define clientelism in terms of its consequences; for example, a weak democracy or a polity with little social capital would be considered clientelist. Finally, clientelism is also defined with respect to the procedural nature of the exchange (Kitschelt 2007); in these terms, exchanges that involve corrupt practices are bound to be clientelistic.

[2] For a discussion of the effects of clientelism see Fox 1994; Stokes 2005; Nichter 2008; Hicken 2011.

[3] In the case of the United States, it is well documented that the policies implemented by the government affect the quality of the democratic system (Campbell 2003).

[4] Scholars agree that democratization increased expenditures on health and education in Latin America, but they disagree about the effect of the regime transition on the lives of the poor. For example, Dion (2010) notes that following democratization, welfare for the growing numbers of unorganized poor people increased in Mexico. Weyland (1996), however, argues that organizational obstacles, such as clientelism, populism, and state fragmentation, have impeded redistribution toward the poor in many new democracies. Ross (2006) further argues that although democracies spend more on education and health than nondemocracies, higher expenditures do not translate into wealth improvements for the poor. He provides evidence that democracy has little effect on infant mortality rates.

program benefits, eligibility criteria, operational rules, etc.), remain elusive, perhaps because antipoverty programs are "late-comers to the social-policy mix" in most countries in Latin America (Haggard and Kaufman 2008, 3).[5]

The central contribution of this book is an explanation of the politics of conditional cash transfer programs (CCTs), one of the most prominent types of antipoverty programs in operation in Latin America and one of the most significant social policy innovations of recent decades. As described in detail in Chapter 2, this type of poverty relief program is built on the idea that targeted cash transfers to poor households, usually paid to the mother or primary caregiver, fight poverty more effectively than income transfers to the poor through subsidies for food, transportation, electricity, and the like. The size of the cash transfer varies, "ranging from 4 percent of household consumption in Honduras to about 20 percent in Mexico" (Adato and Hoddinott 2010, 11).[6] Yet the most innovative component of CCTs is that, to break the intergenerational transmission of poverty, cash transfers are contingent on investments by poor people themselves in their children's nutrition, health, and education. CCTs promote human capital accumulation by making cash transfers conditional on regular school attendance and visits to public health centers, in which children receive vaccinations and regular checkups, and mothers attend health and nutrition training workshops (Adato and Hoddinott 2010). Thus, a well-designed CCT allows a poor family to keep children in school rather than sending them to work, and reduces future poverty by making it likely that relatively more of the welfare gains accrue to children (Ravallion 2006a).

Right- and left-leaning governments alike have found reasons to adopt this social policy innovation. Indeed, CCTs are so attractive to politicians that even left-leaning presidents such as Luiz Inácio Lula Da Silva in Brazil and Alan García in Peru continued the operation of CCT programs inherited from right-leaning governments. As of early 2012, seventeen countries in Latin America had adopted a CCT.[7] Collectively, these programs reach 27 million of the poorest households in the region. On the basis of the success of CCTs in Latin

---

[5] Mesa-Lago's (1989) pioneering work on the welfare state in Latin America notes that social insurance programs have been in place in many countries in the region since the nineteenth century to protect civil servants and members of the armed forces, and since the beginning of the twentieth century to protect groups of workers in strategic sectors. Yet the development of social assistance programs has for the most part lagged behind.

[6] In many CCTs, cash transfers are determined by the number of children in the household, their age and gender. And, the size of the cash transfer per child is calculated by estimating the costs of sending the child to school, including the forgone income if the child attends school instead of working.

[7] All CCTs began as small-scale programs. For example, initially in Mexico *Progresa* covered 300,000 households and in Brazil small regional cash transfers were developed. Coverage has expanded in most countries, however, there is considerable variation. In terms of absolute coverage, CCTs range from 11 million families (Brazil), to 215,000 (Chile), to pilot programs with a few thousand families (Nicaragua). In terms of relative coverage, CCTs range from about 40 percent of the population (Ecuador), to approximately 20 percent (Brazil, Mexico) (Fiszbein and Schady 2009).

America, governments in Bangladesh, Burkina Faso, Cambodia, Indonesia, Kenya, Macedonia, Nigeria, Pakistan, Philippines, Turkey, and Yemen now use cash transfers as their main policy instrument for social assistance (Fiszbein and Schady 2009). International organizations such as the World Bank and the International Monetary Fund endorse and sponsor CCTs throughout the developing world.

CCTs appeal to governments on the right because they target resources to poor children, who are generally perceived as a particularly deserving group. CCTs are also cost-effective and market-compatible. Compared to pensions, which typically entail large budgetary costs, CCTs are relatively inexpensive, often costing less than 1 percent of GDP.[8] Compared to generalized subsidies, in-kind food subsidies, and price controls, CCTs limit the capture of resources by the nonpoor, generate minimal market distortions, and avoid long-term welfare dependence by restricting program eligibility to poor households with school-age children.

From the perspective of left-leaning governments, CCTs are appealing because they are instruments of redistribution and social inclusion. In contrast to in-kind food subsidies, which are difficult to deliver to rural areas with extensive population dispersion, mountainous terrain, and poor roads, cash transfers have no expiration dates and entail no storage costs. Moreover, CCTs express solidarity with vulnerable families, and they respect poor families' decisions on how to spend the additional income they offer. Thus, CCTs transform a social assistance program into a program that allows poor households to decide how to overcome their condition.

Beyond ideologically driven reasons, CCTs are appealing because they provide a direct link to poor citizens. Such a link is of value both to politicians who are interested in improving the lot of poor people and to those who are interested in using the targeted resources to amass political support (Weyland 1999). Thus, compared to other welfare state policies, which are ideologically charged, CCTs appeal to larger group of politicians. Moreover, in contrast to the expansion of welfare programs in Latin America from 1950 to 1980, which generally took the form of entitlement legislations (Haggard and Kaufman 2008), CCTs do not have the status of entitlements.[9] This means that CCTs' coverage and level of benefits depend on a yearly approved budget, and not the other way around, as is the case for entitlements (Romer 1996). Therefore, CCTs are relatively easier to modify compared to other welfare state policies.

---

[8] CCTs are cost-effective despite the high initial fixed costs associated with their design. See Caldés, Coady, and Maluccio (2010) for a cost-benefit analysis that takes into account the costs of transferring the money to beneficiaries, as well as the costs of activities associated with other program design attributes, such as targeting and monitoring of conditionalities
[9] The few exceptions are Ecuador's *Bono de Desarrollo Humano*, and the short-lived *Proyecto 300* in Uruguay.

The proliferation of cash transfer programs in Latin America has coincided with a period during which poverty and inequality have decreased, for the first time in decades. From 1992 to 2009, the fraction of the total population in Latin America living on less than US$2.50 a day decreased from 28 to 16 percent. Over the same period, the fraction of the population living on less than US$4 a day decreased from 44 to 30 percent.[10] Between 2000 and 2007, inequality in Latin America declined as well: in 12 countries in the region, the Gini coefficient decreased an average of 1.1 percent a year (Lopez-Calva and Lustig 2010).[11] These trends fuel enthusiasm for CCTs as instruments to tackle poverty. However, most CCTs have been politically controversial at one time or another, and many have been accused of fostering clientelism.

Despite the apparent policy convergence, CCTs vary in ways that matter both for their welfare consequences and for our theoretical understanding of them. Chief among the attributes that vary across CCTs in Latin America is program design – specifically, the degree to which operational rules limit politicians' ability to manipulate program resources for political gain. At one extreme is the pioneering Mexican cash transfer program, *Oportunidades* (initially called *Progresa*), which uses a combination of geographical targeting and proxy means testing to identify eligible households. Program operations are standardized, and a centralized bureaucracy is in charge of administering the program, but the disbursement of the cash transfers is outsourced to banks. To ensure that an incumbent party cannot use the program to boost its electoral support, expansion of the program is prohibited during the six months before a presidential election. One of the most scrutinized social policies in the country, the program is subject to independent evaluation. The International Food Policy Research Institute evaluated *Oportunidades* during the early years of its operation and found that transfers were well targeted to poor households, beneficiaries were meeting conditions of school attendance and visits to health centers, and the program was having a positive effect on the lives of poor people.

At the other extreme is the Bolivian cash transfer program, *Bono Juancito Pinto*, which began operations in 2006. This program initially offered a cash transfer to students enrolled in first to fifth grades in public primary schools. The operational rules of the program limit to some degree the ability of the executive to interfere directly in the operations of the transfer. For example, to circumvent the politicized bureaucracies that are in charge of other social programs, the program requires that the armed forces deliver the cash transfer. However, the executive retains substantial discretion over the program. The

---

[10] Socio-Economic Database of Latin America and the Caribbean, CEDLAS and The World Bank 2005.
[11] Gini coefficient or Gini index is an economic measure of inequality in income distribution that ranges between 0 and 1. A value of zero would indicate perfect equality in income distribution. As inequality increases, the Gini coefficient also increases. Between 2000 and 2007, inequality decreased most in Brazil, Ecuador, and Paraguay and increased in Costa Rica, Honduras, Nicaragua, and Uruguay (Lopez-Calva and Lustig 2010).

operational rules of *Bono Juancito Pinto* do not include mechanisms to monitor or evaluate program operations in a systematic way (Morales 2010), and there are no limitations on when program expansion and benefits increases can occur. In 2008, when President Evo Morales proposed and won a recall referendum, the coverage of the program expanded by almost 40 percent – the largest expansion the program has seen.

The emergence of CCTs and the variation in the programs' design present an opportunity to revisit important questions: when do politicians govern for the benefit of the poor and when do they not? And when do politicians tie their own hands in crafting social policies?

THE STUDY OF CCT PROGRAMS

Existing theories of the welfare state do not account for the development of CCT – and, of course, they were not intended to do so. Take, for example, the power resource theory, which argues that differences in welfare regimes can be traced back to the balance of power between labor and capital. The stronger unions are, the argument goes, the more powerful are social democratic and labor parties. In turn, left-leaning governments spend more in the public sector and pursue policies that benefit the working class (Esping-Andersen 1985; Korpi and Shalev 1979; Skocpol and Amenta 1986). Although the power of labor and the ideological orientation of governments explain the expansions of old-age and disability pensions in Latin America (Dion 2010; Huber 1996; Huber et al. 2008; Segura-Ubiergo 2007),[12] they do not by themselves account for CCT proliferation, because both right- and left-leaning governments have implemented this type of poverty relief program.

The context of CCTs is different from the context in which Latin American governments first developed their social protection schemes, or from the contexts of Western Europe and the United States that motivated the power resource theory. When CCTs emerged, governments were dealing with the aftermath of the debt crisis of the 1980s and their economies had begun a process of deindustrialization, which consisted on a contraction in manufacturing and agricultural employment (Carnes and Mares 2010). Fiscal constraints obstructed the expansion of the welfare state, even among left-leaning governments (Huber et al. 2008). And deindustrialization split labor between workers in the formal sector of the economy who have access to the welfare state and workers in the informal sector with little access to health and education services (Edwards 1995). Welfare state insiders and outsiders differ in their

---

[12] By the time CCTs were adopted, most countries had old-age and disability pensions, but only a few had universal coverage. Huber (1996) explains that the development of social insurance in Latin America closely mirrored the balance of power in society. In most countries, social insurance covered first the military, civil servants, and the judiciary. Coverage was next extended to strategic sectors of the middle and upper working classes, and only then was coverage extended to selected other sectors of the working class.

preferences about public spending (Rueda 2005). Thus, the relation between left-leaning governments and pro-poor policies in contemporary Latin America is not straightforward.

Iversen and Cusak (2000) argue that deindustrialization led to an unambiguous increase in the demand for public spending among countries in the Organisation for Economic Co-operation and Development (OECD), and thus an increase in the size of the welfare state. In their account, left-wing governments were particularly prone to increase public spending when electoral turnout was high. However, Huber, Mustillo, and Stephens (2008) show that partisanship "does not matter for the overall amount of social expenditures" (431) in Latin America from 1970 to 2000.

If it was not ideology, what motivated some governments and not others to adopt a CCT? Why did some governments design programs with more exacting operational guidelines than others? A common argument in Latin America postulates that state bureaucrats – technocrats, to be more precise – determine the origin, characteristics, and evolution of public policies. State-centered explanations assume that bureaucrats can, and often do, act independently of underlying socioeconomic forces (Geddes 1994). The notion of bureaucratic supremacy has a long tradition. For example, Guillermo O'Donnell's (1973) classic work on bureaucratic authoritarianism attributed the democratic collapse in the region to coalitions between civilians and military bureaucrats that successfully circumvented politicians. Cleaves (1974) also argued that bureaucrats blocked policy reforms proposed by both leftist and right-wing governments. More generally, bureaucrats often appear to implement policies without the support of dominant interest groups.[13] That a bureaucracy is powerful, however, does not necessarily mean that it is insulated from political interests.[14]

At first glance, CCT programs seem to be the result of bureaucratic supremacy for three reasons. First, CCTs confer benefits on poor people, who have rarely demanded policy concessions from the state in a successful way. Second, economists have dominated the study of CCTs[15]; thus we know more about the effects of CCTs on economic and human capital outcomes than about their politics. Finally, most of the few insightful studies of CCTs' politics focus on a single country (Díaz-Cayeros et al. 2007; Hunter and Borges 2011; Maldonado Trujillo 2012; Zucco 2013). Among these studies, the pioneering

[13] Geddes (1994) points out: "In Latin America most governments began to implement industrialization policies that systematically disadvantaged the producers of primary product exports at a time when agriculture and mining remained economically dominant. The more recent history of the region offers numerous additional examples of policy changes that have injured powerful economic groups. No one believes that these groups are weak or without influence, but those who propose a focus on the state point out that they have not proven to be insurmountable obstacles to governments bent on pursuing policies that disadvantage them" (3).
[14] See, for example, Snyder (2001) for an account of how political rather than technocratic interests were determinants of policy outcomes after the transition toward neo-liberalism in Mexico.
[15] For a thorough review of this literature, see Fiszbein and Schady (2009).

Mexican and Brazilian CCTs have deservedly garnered most of the attention. Yet, as I show in this book, the Mexico and Brazil CCTs have operational systems that presuppose a certain degree of bureaucratic expertise, but other CCTs in the region lack such demanding operational systems. Therefore, the extent to which bureaucrats implement CCTs in a professional and insulated way is an outcome to be explained.

Another possible answer to why some governments adopted CCTs and some chose programs with more exacting rules than others relates to state capacity. Díaz-Cayeros and Magaloni (2009) show that countries with greater bureaucratic capacities (as measured by the rate of immunization against measles) are more likely to adopt a CCT program. They argue that "the more capable a state is, the more likely it should be to create a program involving the kinds of administrative burdens that cash transfers require" (12). This insight provides an important building block for understanding the conditions under which CCTs are adopted. However, bureaucratic capacity is endogenous to the political process (Geddes 1991). Thus capacity, like bureaucratic insulation, is an outcome to be explained.

Finally, policy diffusion could explain the proliferation of CCTs. Because later CCT adopters had the experience from earlier adopters, governments in the region could learn from or emulate each other.[16] Furthermore, the World Bank, the Inter-American Development Bank, and other international agencies have actively promoted CCTs,[17] contributing to their broad diffusion.

On the other hand, policy diffusion does not fully account for previous waves of social policy reform. As Weyland (2006) explains in his study of the spread of the pension privatization model: "Even in the era of globalization, national sovereignty persists and gives countries – including weak underdeveloped countries – significant room for maneuver. Due to to this autonomy, nations retain a considerable margin of choice in deciding whether to adopt a foreign model or not" (4). Furthermore, Brooks (2007) argues that the adoption of policies that are easily enacted and reversible is not governed by policy diffusion processes. Because CCTs are inexpensive – at least, compared to pensions – and are not constitutionally granted entitlements, cross-national peer effects may not apply. I will show that policy diffusion is relevant, but it is not the most important determinant of governments' decisions about the adoption and design of CCTs.

Domestic politics shape policies even in sectors in which "technical complexity heightened the influence of financial markets and expertise" (Murillo 2009, 3). Therefore, to understand the politics of CCTs, we need to better understand the domestic constraints under which state officials operated.

---

[16] For a description of the mechanisms of policy diffusion, see Shipan and Volden (2008).
[17] In fact, in response to the food and financial crises of the late 2000s, the World Bank lent $2.4 billion to finance the initiation or expansion of CCT programs around the world (World Bank 2009).

THE ARGUMENT IN BRIEF

The argument I develop in this book is that a combination of economic crises and domestic political considerations explains why some governments chose to implement a CCT with stringent operational rules and forgo their own discretion to tackle poverty, some chose to implement CCTs without such operational rules, and yet others chose not to implement a CCT at all. In addition, I show that the same factors that explain policy adoption had consequences for policy outcomes and the political lives of the poor.

The Causes of CCTs

An economic crisis may, through its welfare losses, persuade societies to enact major policy changes that would be unacceptable otherwise (Drazen and Grilli 1990; Hirschman 1985). Yet Latin American countries have experienced economic crises throughout their modern history. Why were the economic crises that preceded the emergence of CCTs different? There were three reasons.

First, the economic downturn was distinct in its severity and duration. During the 1980s, most countries in the region experienced economic stagnation, decline in real per capita income, and raging inflation. Economic crises were so severe that the decade became known as the "lost decade" (Grindle 1996). In a fiscal crisis resulting from high debt and the halting of credit from industrialized countries, governments implemented stringent macroeconomic reforms that embraced fiscal prudence and monetary restraint. Many also restructured their economies, opened their markets to trade and foreign investment, privatized state-owned firms, and deregulated important sectors of their economy (Fraga 2004; Stokes 2001). As a consequence, the living conditions of many Latin Americans deteriorated.[18] Guillermo O'Donnell noted the gravity of the situation:

> The social situation in Latin America is a scandal. In 1990, about 46 percent of Latin Americans lived in poverty. Close to half of these are indigents who lack the means to satisfy very basic human needs. Today there are more poor than in the early 1970s: a total, in 1990, of 195 million, 76 million more than in 1970. These appalling numbers include 93 million indigents, 28 million more than in 1970. The problem is not just poverty... The rich are richer, the poor and indigent have increased, and the middle sectors have split between those who have successfully navigated economic crises and stabilization plans and those who have fallen into poverty or are lingering close to the poverty line (1996, 1).

Second, during this period, the number of self-employed, seasonally employed, and underemployed people, as well as people working in the service

---

[18] According to the Human Development Report, per capita GDP declined from $1,965 (in 1987 U.S. dollars) in 1980 to $1,793 in 1990 (Garland 2000). In the early 1990s, more than 10 million children under the age of five were malnourished.

sector, increased considerably, while the number of people living as subsistence farmers in the rural areas declined. Thus, a substantial portion of the labor force in Latin America became part of the informal economy. Indeed, workers excluded from mainstream institutions of the welfare state became a majority in many countries.[19]

Third, most governments dealing with the aftermath of the lost decade were young democracies (Stokes 2001).[20] Keeler (1993) argues that large-scale public dissatisfaction stemming from an economic crisis creates a sense of urgency for action that particularly affects democratic governments. The expectation that the costs of inaction are high influences the position of both incumbent governments and their opposition regarding policy reform.

The importance of economic crises in shaping governments' policy responses to fight poverty in the 1990s has not gone unnoticed. There is a consensus that Latin American welfare states were insufficiently developed (Mesa-Lago 1997). Spending on health and education was regressive (Edwards 1995),[21] and the few social assistance programs in operation disproportionately benefited nonpoor people and residents of large and relatively wealthy cities (Tendler 2000).[22] Therefore, if democratic governments wanted to improve the lot of poor people, they had to innovate (Mesa-Lago 1997; Weyland 1999). In Mexico, as Díaz-Cayeros, Estévez, and Magaloni (2007) argue, an economic crisis weakened the ruling coalition and generated demands from within the incumbent party to limit presidential authority over the social sector.

I do not assume that all politicians want to help the poor. Rather, I argue that economic crises motivate governments to take action and impose a cost on politicians who propose a clientelist response to the crisis when other politicians reject such a response. Similarly, economic crises impose a cost on politicians who reject a nonclientelist response when other politicians propose it. These costs are grounded on changes triggered by economic crises in the society at large. As Carnes and Mares (2010) put it: "An increase in the economic insecurity of wage earners in the formal sector contributed to the formation of coalitions between this group and the poor" in favor of policies with a higher pro-poor bias (108). Once economic crises create the conditions for a new pro-poor social coalition, whether governments craft pro-poor policies with stringent operational guidelines depends on the resistance, and the costs

---

[19] The country with the highest rates of informality in the region was Bolivia, where more than 70 percent of the labor force was excluded from social security benefits, and the country with the lowest rate of informality was Uruguay, with close to 40 percent (Socio-Economic Database for Latin America and the Caribbean, CEDLAS and The World Bank, various years).

[20] Starting in the 1990s, democracy replaced previous systems of government in several countries in the region, and democratic regimes have persisted with few interruptions (Stokes 2001).

[21] Governments subsidized curative medicine more heavily than preventive care and higher education instead of primary education.

[22] See Social Funds and Poverty Reduction: Making Social Funds Work for Poor People, DESA, 2003.

Introduction

associated with it, they face in congress – that resistance can come from the president's own party or from the opposition.

The adoption of a policy and the design of that policy are intrinsically political matters (Moe 1989). CCTs are no exception. Agency structure and operational rules matter both for efficiency reasons and because they limit the extent to which politicians can manipulate program resources for political purposes. Thus, the decision to implement a CCT and the design of that CCT are inevitably caught up in a political struggle that goes beyond issues of efficiency in fighting poverty.

Democratic executive governments with a sense of urgency to respond to a crisis are better off adopting a CCT than relying on inadequate existing social policies to deal with the economic downturn. To do so, the government needs to select an agency to operate the CCT, delineate a set of activities that the agency will undertake, and get funding for the program. Although legislators cannot directly influence the decision to adopt a CCT or the design of the program, they can use their budgetary powers to be part of the policymaking process (McCarty 2004; Ting 2001). Scholars of Latin America have not reached a consensus about the role of legislators in policymaking. Some argue that despite the continued period of democracy, presidents have extraordinary legislative and policymaking powers (Alesina et al. 1999; Baldez and Carey 1999; Stein et al. 1999), and legislatures function as rubber stamps.[23] Others, however, argue that Latin America has transitioned from hyper-presidentialism to governments impaired by legislative gridlock (Mainwaring 1993; Valenzuela 2004). The argument in this book builds on the notion that legislators have become "blunt veto players" with budgetary powers to cut the appropriations desired by presidents (Jones et al. 2002, 675)[24] and that multiple veto players in the legislature influence the evolution of social assistance (Díaz-Cayeros et al. 2007; Dion 2010). This book shows, perhaps surprisingly, that Latin American legislators influence policy adoption and design even in countries where the legislature is not well supplied with money, perquisites, staffers, or other resources that are available to highly professional legislatures.[25]

---

[23] Throughout the second half of the twentieth century, legislatures seemed to play a minor role in policymaking. Schneider (1991), for example, shows how Brazilian presidents were able to use their vast appointment powers to pursue the industrialization of the country. Centeno (1999) shows that presidents in Mexico were successful in transforming and manipulating bureaucracies to further their policy objectives.

[24] Legislatures have unrestricted authority to amend budgets in Argentina, Bolivia, Costa Rica, Ecuador, Dominican Republic, El Salvador, Honduras, Mexico, Nicaragua, Panama, Paraguay, Peru, Uruguay, and Venezuela. In Brazil and Colombia, legislatures may increase expenditures only if they identify new revenue streams. In Chile, presidents set upper limits on total expenditures, within which assemblies may negotiate specific allocations (Shugart and Carey 1992).

[25] For a discussion of the differences between professional and unprofessional legislatures, see Berry et al. (2000); Fiorina (1994); Hibbings (1999); and Rosenthal (1996). Professionalization

When the interests of the president and the median legislator are not aligned, conflict arises.[26] One case of misalignment is when the president and the median legislator are from different political parties. A legislator from an opposition party knows that if she funds a CCT with a lax design, the president can claim the credit for the welfare gains associated with the policy reform. Moreover, as the incumbent, the president can take greater advantage of the opportunities that a lax CCT offers in terms of building and strengthening patronage bases. If the legislator does not fund a CCT with a lax design, she can blame the president for promoting a clientelist policy in times of crisis – a course of action that gives her a bonus of political capital. Thus, if the president proposes a CCT with a weak design, a legislator from the opposition has incentives to refuse to fund it.

On the other hand, if a legislator from the opposition funds a CCT with a design that suppresses political discretion, the president can still claim the credit for innovating to fight poverty, but the more stringent operational rules limit the incumbent's opportunities to use program resources in a clientelist fashion. If such a legislator does not fund a CCT with a stringent design, she incurs the cost of rejecting a poverty relief policy that is both more effective in dealing with poverty and less discretionary than the existing policies. Thus, if the president proposes a CCT with a design that limits political discretion, a legislator from the opposition has incentives to fund it, even if it produces a boost for the executive, as long as the CCT is superior to the status quo polices.

Anticipating the reaction of the median opposition legislator, the president is better off proposing a CCT with a stringent design. With this course of action, the president limits his own discretion over the policy, but he also limits other politicians' ability to use the program to build and strengthen patronage bases. He prefers to implement an insulated CCT than to face a scenario in which the legislature refuses to fund the program because the president cannot credibly commit not to manipulate the program in his favor. In such a scenario, the president not only would fail to respond to the economic crisis, but would

---

of legislators is conceptually different from the institutionalization of legislatures. Institutionalization refers to the presence of boundaries that insulate the legislature from its political, economic, and social environment. Professionalism of legislators relates to the resources available to legislators, such as staff, space, and time to legislate, as well as monetary compensation (Rosenthal 1996). Resources allow legislators to travel to their districts, devote time and energy to campaign activities, and consequently increase their capacity to legislate. In contrast, unprofessional legislators are poorly compensated, have fewer staff, and have shorter legislative careers (Fiorina 1994). Democratic endurance has brought with it a progression toward legislative institutionalization, but the degree of professionalism of legislators still varies widely in Latin America. In fact, professionalism is in part a product of institutional design. For example, Jones et al. (2002) argue that in Argentina legislators remain unprofessional because of electoral rules. Fiorina (1994) traced professionalism in U.S. state legislatures in part to institutional features such as term limits.

[26] The median legislator is the pivotal member of congress. Her position reflects the preferences of the majority in the legislature, as such she is the most decisive legislator. Focusing on her allows me to make a more parsimonious argument. I elaborate on this decision in Chapter 3.

pay the political costs of promoting a clientelist policy when there is discontent associated with the crisis. The worse the crisis, the higher the costs of promoting a clientelist response or of rejecting an insulated policy, all other things being equal.

Conflict also arises when the president and median legislator are from different factions in the same party. If the president's faction controls the party's machine, then the political game plays out much as when the legislator is part of the opposition. If the legislator's faction controls the party machine, then the president is better off opting for a CCT with stringent operational rules because such an insulated program is more effective at fighting poverty and limits the extent to which his rival faction can use program resources for patronage.

When the interests of the president and the median legislator are perfectly aligned, then the president can adopt a CCT without tying his own hands with stringent operational rules. Such a policy appeals to the president and legislators because, as long as the CCT is better at dealing with the crisis than previous policies, the president can claim credit for improving the lot of the poor, and the policy design leaves open the opportunity to use program resources for building and strengthening patronage bases.

Needless to say, if either the economic crisis is not pressing or the CCT does not have an advantage over the existing policies, then the conditions that nudge governments to tie their own hands unravel.

This argument is related to the vast literature on the political economy of delegation.[27] A core prediction in this literature is that politicians are more likely to delegate policymaking to bureaucrats when their preferences are similar. The more politicians' and bureaucrats' preferences diverge, the less likely delegation becomes. Empirical studies of delegation patterns in the United States have generally found support for this prediction (Epstein and O'Halloran 1999; Volden 2002; Wood and Bohte 2004). It is unclear, however, whether delegation decisions follow similar principles in Latin America, where legislators are less professional and bureaucracies have less administrative capacity (Huber and McCarty 2001). To better capture the Latin American context, the argument in this book departs from previous work in three ways. First, most existing work conceptualizes politicians as members of congress and bureaucrats as representatives of the interests of the president; I follow more recent work that distinguishes between the president and the bureaucracy (McCarty 2004; Ting 2001). Second, in theories of delegation, congress determines how much discretion the president has over policymaking, and the president decides in turn how much effort he will put into moving a proposed policy closer to his preferred point. I reverse the sequence of actions, to reflect that in Latin America the president initiates the process of policymaking and has the upper hand in policy negotiations. Yet legislators are relevant because they have

---

[27] See, for example, McCubbins et al. (1987); Epstein and O'Halloran (1994); and, more recently, de Figueiredo (2002) and Huber and McCarty (2004).

budgetary powers that they can, and do, use to move policy closer to their preferences (McCarty 2004; Morgenstern and Nacif 2002). Third, previous work takes bureaucratic capacity as given (Huber and McCarty 2004); in this book, bureaucratic capacity is endogenous along the lines of Geddes's (1991) model of the level of professionalism of the bureaucracy.

The implications of my argument contrast with two influential theories in political economy. One posits that incumbent governments adopt policies that suppress their own discretion when they expect to lose power (de Figueiredo 2002; Grzymala-Busse 2007; Moe 1989). By insulating policies from political manipulation, the incumbent aims to tie the hands of the next government. The implication of this theory is that presidents who anticipated losing the next election (or anticipated that their parties were bound to lose, in the case of term-limited presidents), should be more likely to adopt CCTs with stringent operational rules. Such intertemporal calculations, however, do not account for CCT adoption and design because CCTs are not entitlements; therefore, the incumbent cannot effectively tie the hands of the next administration. If the incumbent's motivation was to tie the hands of the next administration, then we should see presidents trying to grant CCTs entitlement status. Yet, this is not in the Latin American experience.

Another theory posits that veto players create policy paralysis (Tsebelis 2002), instead of policy insulation. In fact, the welfare state literature has documented numerous cases where veto players prevent welfare state expansion and welfare retrenchment (Brooks 2002; 2009; Castiglioni 2005; Huber 1996; Madrid 2003). These studies, however, focus predominantly on pension systems, which are not the same policy domain as social assistance, as I discuss in detail in Chapter 2. This book argues that a president without legislative support will, in fact, face greater difficulty in introducing a CCT than a president who controls the legislature. As in other policy domains, conflicting preferences provide the president and legislators with incentives to counteract each other's actions. But, in the particular case of CCTs, which are relatively inexpensive and do not affect organized labor's interests, the economic crisis and its associated costs motivate politicians to surpass the policy gridlock.

The Consequences of CCTs

Politicians are not interested in influencing operational rules; they are interested in shaping policy outcomes. The president implements a policy that closely mirrors its design because legislators can revise the policy's budget on a yearly basis. Thus, repeated interactions between a president and legislators lead to systematic differences in policy outcomes between presidents who face resistance from legislators and presidents who do not.

The argument has several implications for policy outcomes. First, as we have seen, when the president and legislators are aligned, they can design and implement a CCT that is vulnerable to political manipulation. Such policies tend to offer more opportunities for corruption (Huber 1996) and rent-seeking and to benefit only a portion of the intended beneficiaries, in turn depriving many poor people of government resources (Geddes 1991; Stokes et al. 2012). A CCT without such operational rules as fixed eligibility criteria, monitoring systems, and independent program evaluations has a less robust implementation. The expectation, then, is that although there may be some discrepancies between policy design and implementation, the same factors that lead to a stricter policy design also lead to more robust implementation.

A second implication relates to the expansion of CCTs. Media speculations abound about presidents increasing program enrollment close to elections to boost their support. Yet there are no studies that provide systematic evidence of a link between political-economic cycles and the expansion of CCTs. I show that when the president and legislators are not aligned, CCT enrollments are less vulnerable to political business cycles.

Third, the argument has an implication for CCT survival. A CCT with a design that limits political discretion is more effective at fighting poverty and is less vulnerable to political manipulation. Thus it gives a president more arguments to defend the policy and gives people more reasons to approve of it. Such broader public support could be directly linked to the program's survival rate. A politicized CCT, on the other hand, could be supported by a smaller coalition and would thus be more likely to be dismantled.

A fourth implication of the argument relates to the strength of patron-client relations. In Latin America, where the manipulation of government spending for electoral purposes has been the rule rather than the exception, it is tempting to conclude that all CCTs foster clientelism. However, adopting a CCT with more elaborate rules and more robust operations (a "neutral" CCT), which is more effective in fighting poverty and is more insulated from politics, erodes patron-client relations. The vote of a wealthier CCT recipient is more expensive for political party brokers. Moreover, the implementation of a CCT with strict operational rules demonstrates to recipients that party brokers have less discretion to administer program resources. This informative effect also makes vote-buying more difficult. The income and informative effects together empower recipients to resist clientelism. In addition, stringent rules reduce the discretion of party brokers to operate the CCT program according to a system of rewards and punishments. For example, if the selection of program recipients is based on a poverty score, and cash transfers are systematically reaching recipients, party brokers have fewer opportunities to strategically manipulate program resources. This makes vote-buying more difficult because brokers can neither bestow program benefits nor punish recipients by discontinuing the stream of program benefits. Thus a neutral CCT helps poor people resist clientelism and also erodes patron-client relations by suppressing broker discretion.

Finally, the fact that CCTs with strong designs are increasingly popular among Latin American governments raises a fundamental question about the electoral returns of government spending in general, and of targeted benefits in particular. When a traditionally clientelistic party shifts away from discretionary spending to programmatic politics, can it retain the support of targeted voters? Speculations in the media about CCTs' electoral returns are widespread. During the 2006 presidential election in Brazil, *Bolsa Familia* was often mentioned as one of the factors explaining Lula's popularity among the electorate, particularly in the Northeast region of Brazil where a large number of program beneficiaries lived. Throughout the 2000 and 2006 presidential campaigns in Mexico, predictions abounded that households enrolled in *Oportunidades* would favor the incumbent party. In Colombia, the media speculated that the expansion of *Familias en Acción* was part of Uribe's strategy to improve his chances of being reelected for a second term in 2006. The most recent speculations concerned the Guatemalan CCT program, *Mi Familia Progresa*, headed by Sandra Torres, the country's former first lady and one of the most controversial candidates in the 2011 presidential election. In the period leading up to the elections, the media speculated that although Torres was unpopular in the capital, she had strong support from voters in rural areas where the CCT was most active (*The Economist*, March 15, 2011).[28]

Most of the scholarly evidence confirms that CCTs produce an electoral bonus for the incumbent (Cornelius 2004; De La O 2013; Díaz-Cayeros et al. 2007; Díaz-Cayeros and Magaloni 2009; Green 2006; Zucco 2013). However, scholars have made contradictory claims about why CCTs have such an effect. Some argue that CCTs persuade recipients to change their vote choice for programmatic reasons, such as retrospective voting (Díaz-Cayeros and Magaloni 2009). Others posit that beneficiaries of CCTs may be persuaded to vote against their preferences in response to threats of program discontinuation (Cornelius 2004; Schedler 2000). This book shows that when a CCT has operational guidelines that limit discretion, program benefits foster proincumbent support by mobilizing recipients, not by persuading them. The longer the duration of the program, the greater recipients' exposure to program benefits, and the more opportunities the incumbent has to take credit for positive program results.[29] Claiming credit, however, is closer to programmatic politics than clientelism.[30]

TESTING THE ARGUMENT

In few places are the politics of CCTs more salient than in Latin America, where these innovative poverty relief programs originated. Because of the variations in program adoption, design, and implementation, Latin America provides an

---

[28] The Constitutional Court of Guatemala ultimately confirmed the constitutional ban on relatives of the president running for office, so the incumbent party had no presidential candidate in 2011.
[29] On credit claiming, see the seminal work by Mayhew (1974).
[30] See Campbell (2003) for an account of how social policies in the United States shape political participation.

ideal setting to examine the factors that shape policy decisions, as well as to uncover the political consequences of such choices.

The empirical approach of this book provides a comprehensive answer to the questions of why some governments tie their own hands to fight poverty, and what the policy and political consequences of this decision are. I combine multiple qualitative research methods – archival work, interviews, participatory observation – with quantitative research, including the creation and analysis of a data set that follows over time the adoption, design, and operation of cash transfers in Latin America; a regression discontinuity design; the downstream analysis of a field experiment; and a subgroup analysis of a list experiment in Mexico.

The book presents case studies of the origins and evolution of cash transfer programs in Mexico, Colombia, Guatemala, Peru, and Argentina to illustrate the logic and plausibility of the argument. These cases vary in the most relevant independent variable of the argument: presidents' alignment or misalignment with legislators. One manifestation of misalignment is a divided government, but the more general concept includes cases in which checks on the president come both from legislators of his own political party (for example, when they belong to rival factions) and from legislators of opposition parties.

Mexico's *Progresa* and Colombia's *Familias en Acción* originated in contexts in which presidents faced resistance both from their own political party and from opposition parties. In Mexico, when President Zedillo's government designed the CCT, around 1996, his political party (the Institutional Revolutionary Party, or PRI) controlled Congress, as it had for decades. However, the president was not part of the PRI's old guard. In the legislative elections of 1997, the PRI lost control of the lower house of Congress for the first time. In Colombia, because of disagreements with their own parties, President Pastrana (who launched the CCT) and President Uribe (who rolled it out) competed as independent candidates in their respective elections. Guatemala's *Mi Familia Progresa* and Peru's *Juntos* illustrate contexts in which presidents faced resistance from opposition parties. President Colom in Guatemala and President Toledo in Peru governed with legislatures controlled by the opposition. Finally, Argentina's *Plan Familias*, launched by President Kirchner, originated when his party controlled Congress, and *Asignación Universal por Hijo* originated when President Fernández de Kirchner's party no longer controlled Congress. Thus, the case studies in the book offer rich cross-national variation, and some of them also offer valuable within-country variation in the independent variable of interest.

To further test the predictions of my theory on a larger set of cases, I include statistical analysis based on a data set I constructed that includes all countries in Latin America during the period 1990 to 2011. The unit of analysis in this data set is the country-year. The data set includes both countries that had implemented a CCT by 2011 and countries that had not. For country-years with a CCT program in operation, the data set includes details on program design and operations.

Finally, to systematically test the arguments of the book about the political consequences of CCTs, I turn in Chapters 6 and 7 to the Mexican case. The research questions in these chapters make a focus on one country more appropriate, because the institutional and political factors remain constant. Moreover, my argument predicts that, within a country, recipients of a strict CCT behave differently than do nonrecipients. Although Mexico's CCT is among the programs with more stringent guidelines, it is far from being an outlier. To illustrate that the argument is not exclusive to Mexico, I include qualitative evidence from Colombia, Guatemala, Peru, and Argentina.

Even though the context of this book is Latin America, I believe that the research addresses a broad theoretical question that is relevant to other regions in the world and is relevant to the study of other poverty relief policies. After all, the phenomenon of CCTs is broader than Latin America, and the phenomenon of executive governments limiting their own discretion to pursue policy reform is broader than CCTs. Of course, there are limits to how much one can generalize findings based on a region or policy domain. In particular, the countries in this study are multiparty presidential systems in which there was effective political competition during the period of study for this book. Still, the basic elements of my argument could apply in other settings. For example, in the Philippines, President Macapagal Arroyo launched a CCT program, the *Pantawid Pamilyang Pilipino Program* (4Ps), during the food price crisis in 2008. A year before, the country held legislative elections, in which the president's National Union of Christian Democrats (or Lakas-Christian Muslim Democrats) won 89 of the 240 seats of the House of Representatives. President Arroyo's administration was marred by corruption and election fraud charges.[31] Still, like other presidents facing resistance from Congress, she adopted a CCT with a strict design, which includes fixed eligibility criteria, health and school attendance conditions, and monitoring systems. The World Bank conducted a randomized trial to evaluate program impacts and found that, after 2.5 years of implementation, the program increased school enrollment among younger children, increased school attendance, improved children's nutrition, and reduced severe stunting (World Bank 2013).

Another example: In Turkey – a parliamentary democracy – Prime Minister Ecevit launched the Social Risk Mitigation Project (SRMP) in 2001, when he faced considerable resistance from Parliament. In the 1999 elections, the prime minister's Democratic Left Party (DSP) won 136 of the 550 seats of the Grand National Assembly. Unable to form a single-party government, the prime

---

[31] Opposition members attempted to impeach President Arroyo in July 2005 and in June 2006. Both attempts concerning allegations of fraud and vote rigging in the 2004 presidential elections were subsequently dismissed (Inter-Parliamentary Union, 2007 report). In 2012, President Arroyo was arrested on corruption charges.

minister formed a coalition with the Nationalist Action Party and the motherland party (ANAP). However, the DSP-led coalition unraveled and elections were held almost 18 months ahead of schedule (Inter-Parliamentary Union, 1999 report).[32] Prime Minister Ecevit faced an adversarial president, two earthquakes that killed about 200,000 people, and a stock market crash, in which 40 billion dollars (or about 20 percent of the Turkish gross national product) was lost overnight (Kalaycioglu 2010). Consistent with my argument, Turkey's CCT has a strict design and robust implementation. The program uses a proxy-means test to select recipients and coverage is highest for the poorest decile, benefits are distributed through banks and the postal service, health and school attendance conditions are established and verified monthly, and the International Food Policy Research Institute (IFPRI) evaluated the program (Fiszbein and Schady 2009). IFPRI's evaluation detected problems with the management information system in early years of the program. Still, SRMP increased enrollment rates in secondary school among girls and increased vaccination coverage significantly (Ahmed et al. 2007). Thus, even in these contexts, checks on executive power matter for CCT design and outcomes.

Finally, my argument can be extended to study other antipoverty policies. For example, African governments are increasingly adopting Unconditional Cash Transfers (UCT), which do not make transfers contingent on children's attendance at school and health centers. Certainly, in Africa, governments face serious fiscal and human capital constraints and international organizations play a more prominent role. Still, domestic politics may matter. Consider the case of Malawi – a country where 61 percent of people live below the US$1.25 a day poverty line.[33] The government implements the Social Cash Transfer scheme, which has no school or health requirements; however, it has fixed eligibility requirements, program processes are monitored by the District Council and the District Social Welfare Office, and UNICEF-Malawi collaborated in a randomized control trial to evaluate program impacts. President Mutharika launched the program two years after the 2004 election, in which his party, the United Democratic Front, won 49 of the 193 seats of the National Assembly. Then, the country had been afflicted with three successive years of drought, a devastating human immunodeficiency virus (HIV) epidemic, and a shortage of foreign aid precipitated by concerns about governmental corruption and poor economic management.[34] Short of a legislative majority and faced with a serious economic and social crisis, President Mutharika opted for a UCT with operational rules that include fixed eligibility criteria, monitoring systems, and independent program evaluations – all processes that limit politicians' ability to manipulate programs for political gain.

---

[32] In July 2002, key ministerial allies of the prime minister and legislators from the ruling coalition, including the DSP, left the government coalition (Inter-Parliamentary Union, 1999 report).
[33] World Bank's Poverty and Inequality Database.
[34] Inter-Parliamentary Union, report 2004.

As I demonstrate in this book, some presidents in Latin America tied their own hands in crafting antipoverty programs, in part because it is costly for politicians to promote clientelist policies in times of economic crisis.[35] However, the argument in this book also explains why some presidents choose not to reform their poverty relief programs, whereas others adopt CCTs with weak designs. In addition, this book explains why politicians are often tempted to relax programs' operational guidelines. Without continuing checks on presidential authority, programs are vulnerable to manipulation, which in turn can deprive many poor people of the benefits of CCTs. The unequal allocation of resources can increase inequality rather than reduce it (Bardan and Mookherjee 2011) and ultimately can make the enterprise of lifting people out of poverty less effective (Magaloni et al. 2007). Thus, the arguments and evidence presented in this book have implications for our understanding of the heterogeneous effects of CCTs on education and health outcomes across Latin America. Ultimately, the effectiveness of poverty relief efforts can be traced back to the political dynamics explored in this book.

PLAN OF THE BOOK

Social spending has been the object of great scrutiny in scholarly work. Yet central questions about how, when, and why governments use social spending to improve the lives of the poor remain unanswered. Chapter 2 argues that social assistance disbursements are analytically distinct from the more general concept of social expenditure. Therefore, to better understand the political conditions that lead governments in Latin America to redirect resources toward the poor, it is useful to focus on social assistance programs, their design, and their implementation. The chapter then provides a detailed account of CCT programs. The last section of the chapter presents two indexes that I constructed to capture the variation in the design and implementation of cash transfer programs operated in Latin America between 1990 and 2011, including their targeting rules, conditionalities, recertification processes, transparency and monitoring systems, and independent evaluations. The indexes are based on programs' operational rules and on more than 100 documents produced by national and international agencies. The chapter reveals previously unexplored variation both within and across countries in the degree to which program rules and regulations limit politicians' discretion. Figure 1.1 presents a snapshot of this variation.

Chapter 3 presents the argument in greater detail, working up to the empirical implications that are evaluated in Chapters 4 through 7. Chapter 4 presents evidence using my panel data set on the adoption, design, and implementation of CCTs. Drawing from regression evidence, I show that presidents facing a

---

[35] See Stokes et al. (2012) for an account of the costs of clientelism, which include rent-seeking and inefficient targeting by brokers.

Introduction

FIGURE 1.1 Average strictness in program design. *Note:* The darker the color, the stricter the program design.

congress controlled by the opposition or higher legislative checks adopt CCTs with stricter designs. I compare my explanation to other prominent theories and find only limited support for them. To increase confidence in my conclusions, I also employ a regression discontinuity design, which takes advantage of the arbitrariness of the rule that determines when a president's party controls a majority of seats in congress. Such arbitrary rules provide "as-if randomized" variation in one of the key variables of my argument (Angrist and Pischke 2009). I then examine the origins and the evolution of CCT programs in Mexico, Colombia, Peru, Guatemala, and Argentina, where presidents faced various degrees of resistance from the legislatures. The material for these five case studies comes from congressional archives and media coverage, as well as interviews with key stakeholders in Mexico. The quantitative analysis, together with the qualitative insights gained through the case studies, strongly supports the book's argument.

In Chapter 5, I first examine the implementation of policies to determine whether the same factors that lead to strict operational rules also lead to robust implementation. Second, I test the assertion that the political factors that lead to strong policy design also lead to the elimination of political-economic cycles that result from the expansion of CCT programs during election years. The last test in this chapter aims to prove that programs with weaker designs and more flawed implementation are more likely to be dismantled than programs with stronger designs and more exacting implementation. The evidence in this chapter confirms that the dynamics among presidents and legislators influence important policy outcomes that relate directly to the programs' effectiveness in eradicating poverty.

CCTs influence the quality of democracy. In Chapter 6, I argue that a CCT program that ties the hands of the executive affects clientelism. Drawing on in-depth interviews with program recipients, participatory observations of program meetings in Mexico, and data from a nationally representative survey among Mexican households, I show that, compared with other survey participants, recipients enrolled in a CCT program with a strong design are well informed about the funding sources of the program, are less likely to report participating in vote-buying exchanges, and feel more free to cast a ballot according to their preferences. These results are borne out by measuring vote-buying through such nonintrusive instruments as a list experiment. Through interviews with political brokers from both the incumbent and opposition parties in Mexico, I demonstrate that local authorities and political brokers resented the implementation of the CCT program because it decreased their margin of discretion. Finally, I also document that CCT recipients are well informed in Guatemala, Peru, and Colombia and that local authorities and brokers in these countries also reacted negatively to the introduction of CCT programs.

In Chapter 7, I document the proincumbent effects of the Mexican CCT program with the downstream analysis of a unique randomized field experiment conducted in the early stages of the program. I also show that the mechanism through which the Mexican CCT raises support for the incumbent is closer to programmatic politics than clientelism. The chapter then suggests that when CCT programs are operated in a programmatic way, they are compatible with healthy democratic habits, such as participating in elections, and have the attractive feature of fostering proincumbent support.

Introduction

Overall, this book demonstrates that governments' strategies to tackle poverty are influenced by the relationship between the president and legislators, and in turn, the policies implemented affect the prospects of eradicating poverty and the quality of democracy. To conclude the book, I summarize the central findings and discuss some unsettled questions about the future of CCTs. I conclude that given the incentives of politicians to manipulate programs for political gain, both presidents and legislators should continue to invest in improved program monitoring methods that allow them to ensure that politicians – whether in the executive, legislative, or local branches of government – will not manipulate antipoverty programs in a way that undermines the efforts to fight poverty.

2

The Universe of Cash Transfer Programs

Social spending has been the object of great scrutiny in scholarly work. Yet central questions about how, when, and why governments use social spending to improve the lives of the poor remain unanswered. The first part of this chapter argues that to better understand the political conditions that lead governments in Latin America to redirect resources toward the poor, it is important to place social assistance disbursements into a separate category of social expenditure and to focus on program design and implementation, in addition to aggregate public expenditure. The chapter then introduces conditional cash transfer programs as social assistance policies deserving of scholarly attention. The last section of the chapter presents two indexes that capture the variation in the design and implementation of cash transfer programs across countries and over time in Latin America.

ON THE RELEVANCE OF THE DESIGN OF ANTIPOVERTY PROGRAMS

Aggregate statistical measures such as social expenditure per capita paint a picture of stability across middle-income countries in Latin America. However, this characterization masks the myriad of social policy reforms that have taken place across the region in recent decades. Aggregate measures do not reveal, for example, the profound transformation in pension systems from public risk-pooling systems to individual market-based designs in many countries in Latin America (Brooks 2009),[1] nor do they capture the more recent surge of non-contributory pensions targeted to poor households (Carnes and Mares 2009).

---

[1] Between 1992 and 2002, Peru, Argentina, Colombia, Uruguay, Mexico, Bolivia, El Salvador, Costa Rica, Nicaragua, and the Dominican Republic partially or fully privatized their public pension systems (Madrid 2003).

In addition to masking social policy reforms, expenditure per capita and other widely used aggregate measures conflate broad spending concepts that are not all directly related to social policy. For example, many definitions of aggregate social spending include expenditures on social protection, social assistance, health, and education, but also include expenditures on infrastructure, rule of law, and defense. Therefore, although aggregate social spending may reveal the size of a state, it does not offer much insight into the amount of resources that a country allocates to directly address poverty or the extent of redistribution that takes place. The question as to which of the disbursements labeled as social spending have immediate consequences for the welfare of the poor, and which qualify as redistribution, is difficult to answer. For example, expenditures on health and education are linked in more direct ways with pro-poor investments than other components of social spending, but in practice even these disbursements could fail to reach the poor. The construction of a hospital, for example, benefits impoverished communities only if the hospital is accessible to them. Similarly, spending on education benefits poor families only if their children can attend school and learn.

Aggregate measures also conflate social insurance and social assistance policies. The former provide shelter to those suffering a temporary adverse shock in their earnings or needs (Mookherjee 2006, 233). The latter often involve a strategy to encourage long-term investments in assets and capabilities by those deprived of such. Whereas social insurance aims to buffer temporary shocks, social assistance policies seek to counteract the debilitating effects of poverty, a condition that is hardly temporary (Mookherjee 2006, 233).[2] Thus, the relationship between aggregate social spending and the welfare of the poor is far from a straightforward one.

Because aggregate social spending figures fail to shed light on policy goals, in many cases these expenditure figures also fail to provide insight into governments' political agendas. Esping-Andersen, in his classic work on the welfare state, explains: "Expenditures are epiphenomenal to the theoretical substance of the welfare state... it is difficult to imagine that anyone struggled for spending per se... What matters for workers are the actual conditions of their social policy coverage – the level and duration of social policy benefits, the stringency of eligibility criteria, and so on" (1990, 625). Mares (2005) further explains that "expenditures-based measures do not capture questions of policy design that are politically salient and distributionally divisive" (19–21). Thus,

---

[2] Social insurance schemes certainly have consequences for poverty, because some schemes may redistribute the costs and risks of protection against loss of income. Research on social insurance in Latin America reveals important distributional consequences of the individualization of risk. Brooks (2009) explains that low-skilled, low-wage workers and women were most affected by the individualization of risk because their labor is often interrupted, poorly compensated, or not remunerated at all. However, the conceptual difference between insurance and assistance is that the former tends to be temporary, whereas the latter does not.

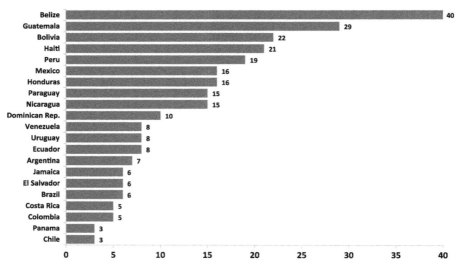

FIGURE 2.1 Child labor in Latin America. *Source:* UNICEF, Special Edition on Children's Rights, 2010.

to understand the politics behind social programs, our focus should shift from levels of expenditure to the details of policy design.

Within the universe of social assistance program, this book studies conditional cash transfer programs, a type of antipoverty program implemented since the 1990s in Latin America. These programs aim to break the intergeneration transmission of poverty by improving the capabilities of children of impoverished families, one of the most vulnerable populations in any context. The International Labor Organization estimates that globally around 210 million children between the ages of 5 and 14 were working in 2000, with approximately half of them working full-time (Udry 2006). This statistic is consistent with UNESCO's estimates that one in every five primary school-aged children was not enrolled in school in 2000. In Latin America, child labor is a pressing problem in many countries. According to estimates by UNICEF, in Belize 40 percent of children between the ages of 5 and 14 are working. In Guatemala, the estimate is 30 percent, in Peru 20 percent, in Mexico 16 percent, and in Colombia, one of the countries with the lowest rates of child labor in the region, 5 percent of children work (see Figure 2.1).[3]

The extent of child labor in Latin America, which maps to the extent of poverty, underscores the importance of understanding the politics behind

---

[3] The statistics on child labor correspond to the following years: Belize, 2001; Guatemala 2006; Peru, 2007; Mexico, 2007; and Colombia, 2007 (United Nations Children's Fund, 2010).

CCTs, which serve to counteract child labor and other suboptimal parental decisions, such as underinvestments in children's nutrition and health, and can ultimately contribute to long-term poverty reduction.[4]

CCTs have become the most salient antipoverty programs currently operating in the region. Three out of ten poor families in Latin America are enrolled in such a program. Conditional cash transfer programs are not salient only for recipients, they are often, if not always, the flagship programs of governments, as well. Administrations implementing cash transfers are unapologetic about reaching out to welfare state outsiders. Great effort goes into branding these programs as innovative instruments to improve the well-being of poor families and children, with slogans like "*Bono Juancito Pinto* is for universal children's education," "*Programa Familias* for social inclusion," and "*Bono* for Human Development." As a consequence, in many countries in Latin America CCTs have garnered broad support. Given the importance of CCTs for recipients and governments alike, studying this type of antipoverty program sheds light into the broader question of how and why governments use social spending to improve the lives of the poor.

Between 1990 and 2011, there were thirty-three programs in Latin America that disbursed cash transfers aimed at improving investments in children's human capital. In 1990, Chile was the only country with a policy that focused on improving poor children's education and health – the *Subsidio Único Familiar* program. By 2011, seventeen countries in the region were systematically delivering cash transfers to poor families with the hope that children would stay in school and receive regular checkups by doctors (see Table 2.1).

The Mexican program, *Oportunidades*, is perhaps the archetype of a conditional cash transfer. The program delivers cash transfers to the female heads of poor households in rural communities with the objective of breaking the intergenerational transmission of poverty by promoting investments in children's education, health, and nutrition. Unlike previous Mexican programs, which funneled resources through the education and health sectors, Progresa aims to increase the demand for these services by transferring cash directly to households.[5]

The program consists of three complementary components. The first is a cash transfer, primarily intended to subsidize food expenditure, which comes

---

[4] It is well documented that poverty and child labor are mutually reinforcing. When parents are poor, children may be sent to work and therefore remain out of school. As a consequence, these children grow up to be poor adults, and the cycle of poverty continues (Udry 2006). Moreover, children bear the risk that comes with parents' decisions to underinvest in their human capital. Consider a parent's decision to send a child to school. Education enhances a child's future welfare, yet the household as a whole may benefit in the short term from avoiding the costs of schooling.

[5] From September of 1997 to 2000, Progresa operated only in rural areas. After the right-wing party's (PAN) presidential victory in 2000, the program continued to operate in rural areas and was expanded to semiurban areas using parallel criteria to select recipients. In 2003, the program was extended to urban areas.

TABLE 2.1 *Conditional Cash Transfers in Latin America*

Country	Program	Year
Argentina	Plan Familias por la Inclusión Social	2004
	Asignación Universal por Hijo (AUH)	2009
Bolivia	Bono Juancito Pinto	2006
Brazil	Bolsa Família	2003
Chile	Subsidio Único Familiar (SUF)	1981
	Chile Solidario	2004
Colombia	Familias en Acción. Fase I	2001
	Familias en Acción. Fase II	2007
Costa Rica	Avancemos	2006
Dominican Republic	Tarjeta de Asistencia Escolar (TAE)	2001
	ILAE	2005
	Solidaridad	2005
Ecuador	Bono Solidario	1998
	Bono de Desarrollo Humano	2003
El Salvador	Red Solidaria	2005
	Comunidades Solidarias	2009
Guatemala	Mi Familia Progresa (MIFAPRO)	2008
Honduras	Programa Asignación Familiar (PRAF) I	1991
	Programa Asignación Familiar (PRAF) II	1998
	Programa Asignación Familiar (PRAF) III	2006
Jamaica	Program of Advancement Through Health and Education (PATH)	2002
Mexico	Progresa	1997
	Oportunidades	2003
Nicaragua	Red de Protección Social	2000
	Sistema de Atención a Crisis	2005
Panama	Red de Oportunidades	2005
Paraguay	Tekopora	2005
	Propais II	2005
Peru	Juntos	2005
Uruguay	Proyecto 300	2000
	Plan de Atención Nacional a la Emergencia Social (PANES)	2005
	Asignaciones Familiares in Plan de Equidad	2008

with a nutritional supplement targeted to children between the ages of four months and two years, as well as pregnant and lactating women. In addition to the cash transfer, children of program beneficiaries receive scholarships intended to compensate parents for the opportunity cost of sending children to school and enable children to stay in school. Finally, basic health care is provided for all members of the household, with particular emphasis on preventive health care.[6] On average, households receive a transfer of approximately thirty-five U.S. dollars per month, which represents around 25 percent of the average income for poor, rural households before program benefits. Of the total amount of the transfer, education scholarships represent 50 percent; the nutritional component comprises 36 percent; in-kind food supplements represent approximately 4 percent; and medicines and other services provided by the health clinics account for 10 percent. Thus, more than 85 percent of the benefits of the program are in the form of cash. Transfers are paid every two months (Levy 2006).[7]

As children advance through school, the scholarship amount that households receive increases to offset the growing opportunity costs of schooling as children mature and are more likely to engage in household production or market work (Todd and Wolpin 2006). In addition, the education transfer is slightly higher for girls, who have lower secondary school enrollment rates than boys. In its original design, *Progresa* grants were provided to children from the third grade through secondary school. In 2001, grants were extended to cover students at the high school level. Therefore, the total amount of the grant depends on the number of children in the household, as well as the gender and age of each child, though the transfer is capped at a preestablished upper amount.

The program is one of the largest efforts in Mexico to invest in poor children's education through the demand side. In 1997, *Progresa* covered 300,000 families, with a budget of US$60 million. By 2000, the program covered more than 5 million families, with a budget of US$3 billion (Adato and Hoddinott 2010; Levy 2006).

Compared to previous programs based on general subsidy schemes, *Progresa* is more redistributive. In 1994, the highest and lowest income decile benefited from the main food subsidy at almost the same rate, 6 and 7 percent, respectively. In contrast, the highest income decile does not benefit from *Progresa*'s food component, whereas the lowest decile received 35 percent of it (Scott 2001).

Other conditional cash transfer programs in the region have less elaborate operational rules compared to *Oportunidades*. In Bolivia, for example, the administration of Evo Morales launched a transfer scheme called *Bono Juancito Pinto* in 2006. This program was originally funded by resources made available through nationalization of the oil industry and transferred 200 soles (approximately US$26) to students in first and up to fifth grade enrolled in a public school. Currently, the program reaches all students in public primary schools.

---

[6] Poder Ejecutivo Federal, 1997.
[7] Interventions in the health service package include basic sanitation; family planning 35 services; prenatal, childbirth and puerperal care; vaccinations; prevention and treatment of diarrhea, parasites, respiratory infections, tuberculosis, high blood pressure and diabetes mellitus; and first aid for injuries (Parker and Teruel 2005).

The peculiarity of this program is that the army is in charge of implementing the program and distributing the cash to students. What makes *Juancito Pinto* a candidate for inclusion in the universe of conditional cash transfer programs is that money is delivered directly to children, and the operational rules of the program, though not strongly enforced, specify that children need to meet school attendance requirements to receive the money.

EXAMINING VARIATION IN PROGRAM DESIGN AND IMPLEMENTATION

The Mexican and Bolivian examples illustrate that cash transfer programs in the region vary widely in terms of their design and implementation. To further examine this variation, I compiled information on the operational rules and implementation of all cash transfer programs operating between 1990 and 2011 in Latin America that were aimed at increasing low-income households' access to education and health care, with special attention paid to those programs specifically designed to reach children in poor families.

Based on information available in the programs' operational rules and more than 100 official documents and reports created by national and international research centers, I construct two indexes. The first measures the extent to which program design regulates the actions undertaken by program agencies, from the selection of recipients to the evaluation of program impacts, and the second measures the degree to which program implementation complies with the design.[8] I score the operational rules of programs along the following dimensions: targeting of beneficiaries, conditions to receive program benefits such as behavioral requirements on the part of households, mechanisms to verify eligibility status, monitoring and transparency systems, and evaluation mechanisms. To capture variation in program design over time, the unit of observation is not the program but each set of programs' operational rules. All programs in the study have more than one set of operational rules, adding to a total of sixty operational rules. In the next section, I outline my criteria to score operational rules on their design and implementation along each of the following dimensions.[9]

Targeting

Targeting is widely used to identify and select the beneficiaries of cash transfer programs. The most common targeting mechanism in Latin America is narrow

---

[8] As will become clear in the next section, the implementation index measures minimum compliance with design. As such, this index is a conservative measure of the extent of variation in program implementation.
[9] To validate the author's scores, two research assistants, who were not familiar with the hypotheses, scored operational rules independently using the coding rules described in this chapter.

The Universe of Cash Transfer Programs

targeting based on geographic indicators or proxy-means tests. The adoption of geographic and proxy-means targeting has been shown to be the most effective way to ensure programs reach their intended targets and achieve the goal of redistribution (Coady et al. 2004; Ravallion 2006b; Van de Walle 1998). Because this type of targeting suppresses much of the discretion of program agencies over the selection of beneficiaries, I code programs as narrowly targeted if their operational rules include provisions to conduct geographic or proxy-means targeting. I do not code programs as such if either they employ less demanding forms of targeting such as self-targeting or broad indicator targeting, or they have no rules to guide the selection of recipients.

To assess whether programs adhere to their targeting systems in practice, I use evidence from program documentation and reports produced by international and national research centers. If program operators report errors of program inclusion or exclusion, which indicates that they keep track of the number of eligible families not enrolled in the program and the number of noneligible families enrolled in the program, I code these programs as complying with targeting criteria, since documenting errors in enrollment is a signal of program operators' efforts to target program resources effectively.

Design 1. A transfer scheme is narrowly targeted if the operational rules include a geographic or proxy-means targeting mechanism.

Implementation 1. Errors of inclusion and exclusion are reported in program documentation.

Based on these coding rules, for example, *Oportunidades* in Mexico is coded as a narrowly targeted program in the design index because eligibility is based on a measure of poverty constructed from both census data and household income surveys. The formula used to allocate program resources is clear and fixed, and it is described in detail in the federal budget, which is proposed by the president but approved in the Chamber of Deputies. The program in Colombia is also coded as narrowly targeted in the design index. The first stage of *Familias en Acción* used a proxy-means testing system called SISBEN, which included household-level characteristics such as the construction material of the dwelling, access to a sewage system, average education of family members older than 12 years old, and years of schooling of the head of household, as well as his or her eligibility to receive other federal benefits. This targeting system also took into account household income, the number of children under six years old, and the number of family members older than 12 who were working. Eventually this system was replaced by a targeting scheme that excluded variables from the poverty score that are easy to manipulate, such as self-reported years of schooling and self-reported income. The new system incorporates characteristics that individual households cannot misreport, such as the size of the village and aggregate socioeconomic indicators, as well as observable household characteristics such as the construction material of the floor, number of toilets, whether there is a telephone land line, and the type of cooking fuel used by the household.[10]

The few programs that do not use proxy-means or geographical targeting systems are not coded as narrowly targeted in the indexes. In Ecuador, for example, President Jamil Mahuad launched the self-targeted *Bono Solidario* in 1998 with the aim of compensating poor households for the elimination of generalized subsidies on cooking gas, gasoline, diesel fuel, and electricity. Payments to households were disbursed through the National Banking Network. To enroll in *Bono Solidario*, people who considered themselves eligible for the program filled out a sworn declaration at Catholic and Evangelical churches containing their personal and socioeconomic data (without the requirement that they be members of these churches). The data were then transferred to the National Banking Network.[11] This program is not coded as narrow targeted in the design score because it was self-targeted, and it is not coded as targeted in the implementation index because there is no information about errors of inclusion or exclusion in the program documentation.

After Jamil Mahuad was forced out of office in 2000, the interim administration of Gustavo Noboa, who was appointed by Congress, audited *Bono Solidario* and found that the self-targeting system was functioning poorly. Neither the churches where people submitted their sworn income declarations nor the National Banking System monitored the quality of the data provided. As a consequence, the information in the program database contained numerous inconsistencies, and enrollment in the program did not prioritize poor families.[12]

Bono Solidario was ultimately replaced by *Bono de Desarrollo Humano*, a new conditional cash transfer program that uses a proxy-means test based on information obtained through a national survey to select program recipients.[13] The target population includes families in the first and second quintile of the income distribution.[14] In the new program, payments are still the responsibility of the National Banking System. However, special attention is given to verifying the accuracy of information. The database used by banks is cross-referenced with data from the social security administration, the electric companies, and the transportation administration to ensure that people with stable jobs, an energy consumption above the established cutoff for eligibility, people with loans, or people who own a vehicle are excluded from receiving program benefits.[15] Thus, for the purpose of the indexes *Bono de Desarrollo Humano* is narrowly targeted both in its design and in its implementation.

[10] CONPES Social 055, 2001.
[11] ESS pp. 6, Inform no. 2, Special audit of *Bono Solidario*, 2001.
[12] OIT, ESS p. 6, Inform no. 2, Special audit to *Bono Solidario*, 2001.
[13] Sistema de Identificación y Selección de Beneficiarios de Programa Sociales
[14] Registro Oficial, May 7, 2003.
[15] ESS p. 6.

The Universe of Cash Transfer Programs

Finally, the only program that uses broad targeting is the *Bono Juancito Pinto* program in Bolivia. Because the program targets all students attending a public primary school, the program is coded as not being narrowly targeted, in design or in implementation.

Conditionalities

Design 2. A cash transfer scheme is conditional on education if a minimum threshold of school attendance is required and there are established protocols for verifying conditionalities.

Implementation 2. There is documentation of verification happening, and there is evidence in program documentation that households that do not comply are penalized.

Design 3. A cash transfer scheme is conditional on health if a minimum threshold of health checkups is required and there are established protocols for verifying conditionalities.

Implementation 3. There is documentation of verification happening, and there is evidence in program documentation that households that do not comply are penalized.

Progresa is a conditional cash transfer program because benefits are contingent on children's school attendance (only three absences per month are allowed), regular medical checkups and consultations at health care centers for children, and parents' attendance at informational meetings where physicians, nurses, and program officials discuss health, hygiene, and nutrition. The requirements are verified through school and health clinic records. Most countries that make transfers conditional on school attendance and regular health care checkups use protocols similar to those of the Mexican program. This is the case with *Mi Familia Progresa* in Guatemala, *Juntos* in Peru, and *Familias en Acción* in Colombia. Other programs in the region make cash transfers contingent solely on school attendance, like *Bono Juancito Pinto* in Bolivia, or have no protocols to verify conditionalities attached to program benefits, like the *Bono Solidario* program in Ecuador, which in practice provides unconditional cash transfers for mothers with children younger than seventeen years old.[16]

Verifying that conditionalities are met is a complex process that involves staff at the program's headquarters, participation from schools and health centers, and a municipal liaison, who is typically the representative for the program in the local government. Reports on the early stages of operation of *Familias en Acción* in Colombia illustrate the challenges presented by this process. In

---

[16] CEPAL www.risalc.org/portal/proyectos.

2005, only 14 percent of municipal liaisons mentioned that they verified the health conditionality according to the processes authorized by the program's central administration. Similarly, only 18 percent of municipal liaisons reported following the correct procedures for verifying the school attendance requirement. Furthermore, 52 percent of schools reported not knowing the number of students enrolled in the program, and 27 percent of personnel at the health centers reported having no record of how many families in the program visited the center.[17]

Given the complexity of the process, I code programs as having the characteristic of conditionality if there is evidence from program records that program operators are penalizing families that do not comply with conditions. For example, the first phase of the Colombian program is coded as not complying with the conditionalities. However, when the second phase of *Familias en Acción* was initiated in 2008, program administrators designed a new system for tracking compliance with program conditionalities, which involved improving the flow of information between the municipal liaisons and the program's headquarters, the introduction of a membership card for mothers enrolled in the program, and, in urban areas, the introduction of a smart card for program beneficiaries.[18] The mechanisms substantially improved the verification process for program requirements. By the end of 2008, the program was able to verify compliance with health and schooling requirements for 91 and 92 percent of families, respectively, as well as to temporarily suspend transfers to families that were not meeting the conditions.[19] Thus, the second phase of the Colombian program is coded as complying with the conditions.

Progress toward verification of conditionalities has not always followed the trajectory of the Colombian program. There are some programs that have produced yearly reports of program activities since their inception, which are publicly available and include the number of families enrolled in the program whose payments are temporarily suspended because they did not comply with education or health requirements. This is the case for MIFAPRO in Guatemala.[20] However, there are also programs that have made very little progress with respect to ensuring verification of conditionalities, such as the *Bono de Desarrollo Humano* program in Ecuador. Although it is a conditional cash transfer program according to its operational rules,[21] the Ministry of Social Development has reported that operational challenges and high turnover among the program's technical staff prevent the verification of compliance with conditionalities (2007). Similarly, the evaluation reports of *Bono de Desarrollo Humano*

---

[17] Informe a la Banca, 4o Trimestre, 2005.
[18] Guía de verificación de cumplimento de compromisos de salud y educación en el SIRC 2008.
[19] Informe a la banca, 2008.
[20] In its first year of operation, 87 percent of enrolled families complied with the school attendance requirement, and 91 percent complied with the requirement of taking children to health checkups (Consejo de Cohesión Social 2009).
[21] Registro Oficial, May 7, 2003.

conclude that conditionalities are not effectively verified (Martínez Dobronsy and Rosero Moncayo 2007, Schady and Araujo 2006).

Recertification

Design 4. The operational rules include a recertification process or an exit strategy.

Implementation 4. There is evidence that a recertification process takes place periodically (such as income surveys among recipients) and that families graduate from the program.

The distinctive feature of cash transfer programs in the region is the focus on improving children's human capital. The challenge of this as a poverty relief strategy is that eligibility of households shifts over time. To maintain a focus on investments in children, programs should include processes that ensure that families whose children have grown up transition out of the program. Typically, operational rules that take this temporal dimension into account include provisions to periodically evaluate the eligibility of enrolled households through surveys and include provisions ensuring that families that lose their eligibility status for reasons related to their composition (i.e., families no longer have school-age children) exit the program. Operational rules that incorporate periodic surveys and explicit exit strategies are coded as having a recertification process in their design.[22] To assess programs' compliance with recertification guidelines, I looked for evidence on the collection of periodic surveys to assess eligibility of program participants, and reports on the graduation rate of households from the program due to changes in household composition.

Transparency and Monitoring Systems

The next dimension of the indexes is meant to capture whether the design of the program demonstrates an effort to make program operations transparent and to identify program malpractices caused by either political reasons (i.e., local bureaucrats using program to proselytize) or lack of capacity, or insufficient information.

Design 5. The operational rules include processes to monitor program operations and that guarantee transparency in program operations.

Implementation 5. There is evidence that a system of monitoring is in place, such as an audit system, and program operators regularly publish program expenses, schedules of transfers, and enrollment updates.

---

[22] Protocols for the temporary suspension of benefits due to changes related to behavioral reasons (i.e., not complying with conditionality) are not included in the coding of recertification, because they are captured elsewhere.

Program management and operations ultimately rests in the hands of bureaucracies. Local bureaucrats have in practice the ability to distort programs in both intentional and unintentional ways. This is true for programs that are centralized, like the Mexican *Oportunidades*, which is administered by an agency created for the purpose of operating the program, but it is also true for programs with a more decentralized structure, like the Argentinean and Brazilian programs. Because cash transfer programs' operations involve regional offices, as well as municipal staff, teachers, and health center personnel, there are multiple ways in which a program's implementation can depart from the intended design. For example, an audit of the *Bono Solidario* program in Ecuador, conducted between August 2000 and July 2001 by the interim government of Gustavo Noboa, revealed late payments to program beneficiaries, a substantial surplus of cash intended to reach poor families still in the bank, and the collection of cash transfers by deceased people. Most of these irregularities could be traced to lack of accurate or updated information.[23] However, the audit also revealed that program benefits were concentrated in urban areas, and that poor people in rural areas were excluded from the program because they lacked official documentation and had limited access to banks.[24]

MIFAPRO in Guatemala illustrates a different set of policy distortions orchestrated by local bureaucracies. Whereas in Ecuador distortions seem to be related to information deficits, in Guatemala teachers in some municipalities have refused to keep records necessary for the school attendance conditionality. Similarly, health providers are distressed by the increase in demand for health services. Perhaps of even greater concern is that there are cases where community leaders have illegally charged for services related to the program that are beyond their jurisdiction.[25]

Program administrators are aware of these possibilities, and several programs in the region include provisions to make program operations transparent and to monitor compliance with rules. I coded programs as having a transparency and monitoring system if the design of the program includes processes to produce and make available information about the program such as audits, or an alternative form of periodical quality control of program operations. To code compliance, I distinguished programs for which there is evidence that regular monitoring takes place and the program agency periodically publishes program expenses, schedules of transfers, and enrollment updates.

In Colombia, for example, since 2003 the central office of the *Familias en Acción* program has selected a random sample of recipient households (using probabilistic sampling techniques) to survey each year. Whereas surveys from the first two years aimed to monitor specific program operations, since 2005 the survey has aimed to provide a global understanding of the program

---

[23] Informe no. 2, Auditoria Especial al pago del *Bono Solidario*, 2001.
[24] OIT and ESS.
[25] Consejo de Cohesion Social 2009.

operations. In addition, the program routinely audits participating schools and health centers and collects performance indicators. Similarly, the operational rules of *Bono de Desarrollo Humano* in Ecuador include provisions for the Ministry of Social Wellbeing to collect program documentation from a sample of recipients and contrast it with schools' official records to ensure that the verification process for conditionalities, which is led by local staff, operates according to regulations.[26]

Operational rules that indicate that civil society is in charge of quality control but do not specify the resources available to citizens to monitor program operations are not taken as effective transparency and monitoring mechanisms, because in order for civil society to effectively monitor the operation of these programs, they need access to information about recipients, schedules of transfers, and a counterpart in the program bureaucracy to expose program misuse. Therefore, if the rules do not specify an explicit procedure or provide civil society with the input necessary to monitor the program, programs are coded as lacking monitoring systems. This is the case for the *Bono Juancito Pinto* program in Bolivia, whose operational rules specify that social organizations are in charge of monitoring program operations, but do not specify any procedure through which organizations can effectively comply with this mandate.[27]

Evaluation

Design 6. The operational rules include provisions that allow for the independent evaluation of program impacts.

Implementation 6. An international or domestic agency has produced a report based on an evaluation of the program.

Progresa was the first social program in Mexico to be evaluated through a randomized control trial. The design and implementation of the evaluation was in the hands of program officials in collaboration with the International Food Policy Research Institute (IFPRI). The evidence was extremely positive. In terms of program operations, the evaluation shows that the eligibility criteria described in the rules of operation predict actual enrollment in the program (Skoufias, Davis and de la Vega 2001).

Regarding the program's effects on children's well-being, the evaluation found that "after only three years, poor Mexican children living in the rural areas where *Progresa* operates have increased their school enrollment, have more balanced diets and are receiving more medical attention" (Skoufias and McClafferty 2001, 3). More specifically, children 1 to 5 years old participating in *Progresa* had a 12 percent lower incidence of illness (Gertler 2000, 2004) and an 18 percent lower incidence of anemia (Gertler and Boyce 2001) than

[26] Decreto Ejecutivo 512, August 7, 2003.
[27] Gaceta Oficial de Boliva, October 26, 2006.

nonparticipating children. In addition, the program had positive effects on children's growth rates. The impact of *Progresa* was equivalent to an increase of 16 percent in mean growth rate per year (corresponding to one centimeter) for children ages 1 to 3 enrolled in the program (Behrman and Hoddinott 2000). The effects of the program are stronger among vulnerable subgroups. For example, *Progresa* children between the ages of 8 and 10 whose mothers had no education grew an additional 1.5 centimeters (Fernald et al. 2009). Beyond physical health indicators, enrollment in the program was also associated with a decrease in children's behavioral problems (Fernald et al. 2009).

Although the program was designed to target children, adults in *Progresa* households were also found to be healthier than adults in non-*Progresa* households (Gertler 2000). Adults in *Progresa* households demonstrated a significant reduction in the number of days they experienced difficulty with daily activities and in the number of days they spent in bed because they were sick (Gertler and Boyce 2001). Finally, *Progresa* was found to have an effect on household expenditure patterns. Households in the program spent 13 percent more income on food than households not participating in the program. Moreover, the additional food expenditure increased the acquisition of fruits, vegetables, meat, and dairy. Thus, dietary quality increased (Hoddinott et al. 2000).

With respect to *Progresa*'s effect on education, enrollment rates in primary school were high before the program began, but enrollment rates in secondary school were lagging, especially for girls. Not surprisingly, *Progresa*'s largest impact was reported for children who entered secondary school. For girls, the increase in enrollment rates was 20 percent, and for boys it was 10 percent (Parker and Teruel 2005). The years of childhood education gained translates into an 8 percent increase in income when these children become adults (Schultz 2001). Furthermore, the increase in enrollment as a result of *Progresa* was higher than the increase that would have been produced by the construction of additional secondary schools, which is estimated to be 0.46 percentage points for girls and 0.34 for boys (Coady 2000).

Mexico is not the only country that has enabled the systematic evaluation of its cash transfer program. The second cash transfer program to operate in Ecuador, *Bono de Desarrollo Humano*, included an evaluation component that was designed by program administrators in conjunction with the World Bank. The evaluation combined a panel survey with a regression discontinuity design, where people just below and just above the threshold that divided the first and second income quintile, as well as people just below and just above the threshold that divided the second and third quartile, were surveyed. The rationale for this design is that people around the threshold are very similar to one another. Therefore, although program benefits were not allocated randomly, as in the Mexican evaluation, researchers were still able to evaluate program impacts in a rigorous way. The baseline survey was implemented between June and August 2003, and the follow-up survey was conducted between January and March 2005. The survey was carried out by the Pontifical Catholic University

The Universe of Cash Transfer Programs

of Ecuador, an independent institution with no affiliation to the cash transfer program. In principle, the evaluation was designed to assess the relative gains in education and health, and the child labor outcomes, of people in the first quintile (who received fifteen dollars), people in the second quintile (who received eleven dollars), and people just above the threshold in the third quintile, who were not eligible to receive program benefits (Martínez Dobronsy and Rosero Moncayo 2007).

In practice, the evaluation of *Bono de Desarrollo Humano* was compromised by the government's decision to transfer the same amount of money (fifteen dollars) to people in the first and second quintile. At the time this decision was made, the baseline survey had already been completed. For purposes of the evaluation, the group of people just below and just above the threshold that divided the first and second quintile was consolidated into one group. Half of this group was then randomly selected to receive fifteen dollars contingent on children's school attendance, whereas the other half was excluded from program benefits for the duration of the evaluation. Although the random assignment was successful, only 78 percent of households assigned to the treatment group received the cash transfer. Of greater concern, however, was that 42 percent of households that were assigned to the control group received the cash transfer because the information on households' assignment was not received by operational staff on time (Schady and Araujo 2006). With these caveats, the evaluation suggests that the program decreased child labor and increased school enrollment, although the evaluation also suggests that the program did not have an effect on test scores (Ponce 2006) or on children's cognitive abilities (Ponce and Bedi 2010).

The Guatemalan program, *Mi Familia Progresa*, has undergone two rounds of evaluations since its creation in 2008. The first evaluation was conducted by two local institutions[28] and was a qualitative study about communities' and service providers' perceptions of the program.[29] The second evaluation, which began in 2009, was an impact evaluation designed and implemented by the Inter-American Development Bank and Mexico's National Institute for Public Health. This evaluation used propensity score matching and a regression discontinuity design to measure program impact. Other agencies have also assessed the workings of the program, such as Transparency International in 2009 and *Acción Ciudadana* in 2009 and 2010.

In Colombia, *Familias en Acción* was the first social program in the country to be evaluated while the program was still running as opposed to the ex-post evaluations commonly carried out.[30] The evaluation of *Familias en Acción* was designed and implemented between 2002 and 2005 by a consortium made up of the Institute for Fiscal Studies, Econometria, and Specialized

---

[28] Universidad Rafael Landivar and Instituto de Investiagaciones Economicas y Sociales.
[29] Universidad Rafael Landivar and IDIES 2009.
[30] Informe Evalución Impacto 2006.

Systems of Information. Unlike the evaluation of Mexico's *Progresa*, the evaluation of *Familias en Acción* did not involve random assignment of households to receive program benefits. Rather, the evaluation consisted of a three-wave panel study carried out in 122 municipalities in 2002, 2003, and 2006. Results from the evaluation suggest that in rural areas, the program was successful in promoting school attendance and regular visits to health centers and led to a decrease in diarrhea and an increase in food consumption. In urban areas, however, the program led to increased school attendance only among children in secondary school, and the magnitude of the effect was considerably lower than in rural areas. In addition to the panel study, program implementers in Colombia have piloted various logistical procedures and have also evaluated the effects of expanding program benefits to include displaced households.[31]

For purposes of coding the index, programs with operational rules that allow for the evaluation of program impacts by an independent agency were coded as 1, whereas all programs without such provisions were coded as 0. To capture compliance with evaluations, I looked for reports produced by independent agencies and coded programs as 1 if such documentation exists, and 0 otherwise. I code programs that have been evaluated only by governmental agencies as 0, because they have not undergone through an evaluation by an independent agency.

Based on these dimensions of cash transfer program design and implementation, I create the two indexes by adding the scores for each component. Figure 2.2 displays the dispersion of programs for both the design and implementation indexes. Because the two indexes vary both across and within programs, I present averages per program in the figure. Overall, programs have an average design score of 4.8 with a standard deviation of 1.4, and an average implementation score of 3.7 with a standard deviation of 1.9. Thus, governments in the region adopt program designs that are highly varied.

The second trend displayed in Figure 2.2 suggests that there is a positive relationship between design and implementation. Although implementation tends to lag behind program design, the two are never more than three points apart. If we plotted the points of programs alongside a hypothetical 45-degree line (indicating a perfect relationship between design and implementation), we would see that although most programs fall below the hypothetical line, the programs with less strict operational rules are the ones with the most flawed implementation. In other words, governments are not promising much more than they are delivering. In most cases, program rules and implementation change marginally over time. However, there are cases where we see programs disappear and new programs replace them.

---

[31] Informe final, Evaluación del Programa Familias para Población Desplazada, 2008.

The Universe of Cash Transfer Programs

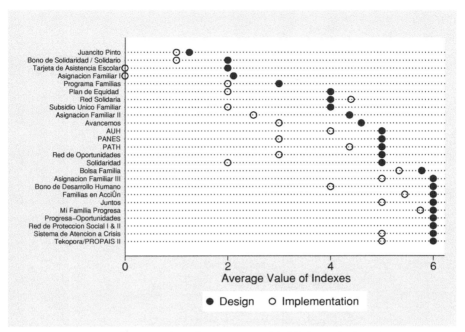

FIGURE 2.2 Average design and implementation of CCTs in Latin America.

In sum, Latin American governments are increasingly including programs that aim to transfer resources directly to poor families in their policy repertoires. Currently, seventeen countries in the region have launched a cash transfer program aimed at investing in children's human capital. The rapid diffusion of cash transfer programs has led to two misconceptions. First, many characterize the evolution of social assistance in Latin America as a retrenchment of the state and a progression toward residualistic welfare states. Yet the proliferation of cash transfer programs does not necessarily entail a retreat of the state. If we only considered the budget allocated to cash transfer programs, it may look like the state is not expanding to implement these programs. However, overall spending is a deceptive measure of the reach of the state. Although budgets for CCT programs are small compared to other public disbursements, these programs reach millions of poor households that were formerly outside the reach of federal governments.

In many countries, the operation of these programs has prompted governments to expand their presence throughout their territories. In addition, the informational requirements of these programs have spurred governments' efforts to collect demographic data that are essential not only for the purpose of social assistance, but also for more general governance issues. For example, in Argentina the recent launch of the *Asignación Universal por Hijo* program involved the creation of a data set that allows the government to identify

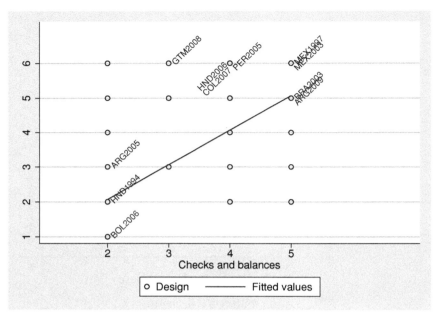

(a) Design score versus checks and balances

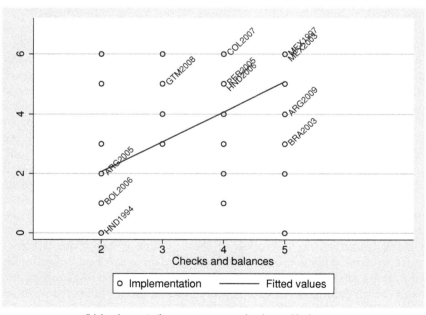

(b) Implementation score versus checks and balances

FIGURE 2.3 CCTs' design, implementation, and checks to presidential power.

and keep track of recipients of multiple governmental programs. Furthermore, the Argentinean government, like other governments in the region, now has a direct channel of communication with families traditionally left out of the welfare state.[32]

Second, the most common characterization of this evolution both in scholarly work and among practitioners is one where international agencies, in particular the World Bank and the Inter-American Development Bank, have precipitated the diffusion of a homogenous type of social assistance. Yet, as shown in this chapter, the design and implementation of cash transfer programs vary widely throughout the region. The rest of this book shows that this variation is not haphazard. Program design and implementation respond to domestic political dynamics. Figure 2.3 provides a first cut at my panel data. I graphed each program-year's design and implementation index against the extent of checks and balances between presidents and legislators in the corresponding year.[33] As the figure shows, even with the raw data, the higher the checks and balances, the more highly the programs score on both indexes. The graph also locates the position of some illustrative cases. For example, contrast Bolivia's CCT in 2006 with Brazil's in 2003. Whereas the former CCT scored low in the design and implementation indexes and was operated by a government facing low checks from congress, the latter scored high on both indexes and was operated by a government facing higher checks. Argentina and Honduras are also illustrative cases. In both countries, their programs scored low in both indexes when governments faced few checks. Yet, programs' design and implementation improve substantially once governments face higher checks.

---

[32] In Argentina, for example, the press reported that the federal government had access to the cell phone numbers of all program recipients, which allows the government to communicate directly with this population via text messages (*Nota de prensa*, Argentina, 2011).
[33] I describe how I measure checks and balances in detail in the next chapter.

3

Politics of Fighting Poverty

Some governments in Latin America adopted conditional cash transfer programs with operational rules that include strict eligibility criteria, well-defined operation rules, and rigorous implementation strategies; other governments adopted less robust CCTs; and yet other governments did not adopt a CCT at all. Why did some governments and not others pursue poverty relief programs insulated from politics? This chapter explains the political processes that led some governments to tie their own hands in crafting and adopting CCT programs.

The chapter is organized as follows: The next section introduces the players in the political game. Then, I describe in detail the actions available to each player and outline their preferences. Then, I discuss optimal policy choices. The chapter concludes with a discussion of the implications of the argument for policy outcomes.

Players

The executive government, president hereafter, is directly responsible for the design, adoption, and implementation of CCTs. Yet the president cannot act unilaterally, because CCTs are not entitlements. Program funds are reviewed and approved on a yearly basis by legislators, who are in charge of approving the federal budget. Thus, although legislators have less fiscal responsibility and are not directly responsible for decisions related to public policies (Murillo 2009), they can use their budgetary powers to influence public policies (Ting 2001).[1]

---

[1] See Amorim Neto (2006) for a study of why presidents decide to use executive prerogatives versus statutes that require legislative approval.

In principle, most political constitutions in Latin America grant powers of initiative to the president in budgetary matters, but grant legislators the power to approve or reject the president's budget. In practice, legislators throughout the region use their budgetary powers routinely, even in countries where restrictions on amendments exist,[2] and even in those cases when appropriations are approved through presidential decree powers (Shugart and Carey 1992).[3] The institutional budgetary arrangement is an avenue through which executive and legislative powers "keep each from exceeding its legitimate authority" (McCarty 2004, 413).

Elections produce a president (P) and one of three types of median legislators. The first type is a median legislator who is part of the president's political party and is part of the president's faction in the same party (L_c). Second, elections can produce a median legislator who is part of the president's political party but is not part of his within-party faction (L_{nc}). The final type is a median legislator who is a member of an opposition political party (L_o). The median legislator represents the preferences of the pivotal legislator in congress. These three types of legislators capture the fact that that the president and the median legislator may have conflicting preferences, even if they are from the same political party.

A fourth type of median legislator could, in principle, be legislators from the opposition who are part of the president's coalition. The literature on policymaking in Latin America has suggested that one way in which presidents form coalitions in congress is through the concession of appropriations that legislators can use for pork barrel projects in their constituencies (Stein and Tommasi 2008). In the case of pro-poor policies, however, the strategy of trading pork barrel resources for legislative support is insufficient because legislators know that it is difficult to counteract the political effects of a manipulated poverty relief program in favor of the president's party. Thus, legislators from the opposition would be unwilling to sell their support for a CCT program.

I will assume that players are interested in maximizing their political capital, which can be used, among other things, to win elections, advance political careers, and promote policies.

Players: President: P, Median Legislator: L_c, L_{nc}, or L_o

Actions

Nature dictates the extent of economic crisis. Given the economic and political context, the president can take one of three courses of action. First, he can do

---

[2] In Chile, for example, legislators can only shift the allocation of appropriated funds within a fixed budget.
[3] Shugart and Carey (1992) argue that "students of presidential systems have regularly mistaken delegated authority for the usurpation of [legislative] political power by presidents... but... the conditions under which delegation takes place can greatly constrain presidents from defying Congressional will" (131). Thus, even in cases where it may appear that legislatures have abdicated powers through delegation, authority can be revoked when needed.

nothing, in which case the policies in place in the status quo (SQ) continue to operate as the main policy instruments to deal with poverty. Second, he can design and propose a CCT with operational rules that do not limit his own discretion over policy implementation (PCCT). Third, he can design and propose a CCT with operational rules that that limit the government's ability to manipulate the program for political gain, such as fixed eligibility criteria, monitoring systems, and independent program evaluations (NCCT). To keep things simple for exposition, I assume that the president chooses one of the three discrete choices available to him. An alternative exposition could allow the president to chose the extent to which he will limit his own discretion, if he decides to move away from the status quo. Discrete and continuous actions, however, lead to the same political game and results.[4] Therefore, I keep the former for simplicity. In the following section, I describe in detail what each of the three actions available to the president entail.

Status Quo

Three factors characterize the status quo in the region: First, the stringent macroeconomic reforms of the Washington Consensus coupled with recurrent economic crises resulted in deterioration of the living conditions of many Latin Americans. Second, many countries throughout Latin America had begun a process of deindustrialization (Carnes and Mares 2010). Third, the policy repertoires to tackle the increased poverty were inadequate. In addition to their inability to reach the poor, social programs in the region were commonly characterized as vehicles for patronage because incumbent governments could distribute these resources in a discretionary manner (Tendler 2000). Thus, overall social assistance policies implemented in the region were ineffective in reducing poverty and vulnerable to being used for clientelist purposes.[5]

The combination of increased poverty rates, a formal welfare state that excludes a large portion of the labor force, and policy instruments that are inadequate to tackle poverty and are vulnerable to being manipulated for political purposes generates social discontent. Social unrest in many countries in the region took the form of protests and strikes in urban areas (Garland 2000),[6] and armed rebellion in rural areas.[7] The severity of the economic and social

---

[4] Because all CCT programs begin as small-scale interventions, I abstract here from the question of initial program size. In Chapter 5, I come back to the question of when do president scale up their programs.
[5] See: Social Funds and Poverty Reduction: Making Social Funds Work for Poor People, DESA, 2003.
[6] Although the debt crisis, and the turn to economic neoliberalism, eroded the influence of organized labor in many countries in the region, public sector unions were able to delay or block comprehensive reforms to welfare institutions (Dion 2010; Kaufman and Nelson 2004).
[7] Perhaps the most well-known and visible of rural movements was that of the *Zapatista* Army of National Liberation, which rose up in Chiapas, Mexico in 1994. Yet groups with similar

Politics of Fighting Poverty 47

crisis and the inadequacy of the status quo policies are an important element in the political game that follows.

A CCT without Operational Rules That Tie the Hands of the President

A second action available to the president is to design and propose a CCT without operational guidelines that limit his own discretion. A CCT is an appealing social policy because it is relative inexpensive (compared to pensions, for example) and effective at improving the life of the poor.

Considering the large share of the workforce in the informal sector and the restricted coverage of formal welfare protection (Barrientos 2004), other policy responses, such as a thorough reform to the welfare state or the incorporation of welfare state outsiders into existing institutions of social protection, were politically more controversial and unfeasible in terms of fiscal resources. Moreover, granting welfare state outsiders full access to the existing benefits of the welfare state would have been insufficient because few countries at that time had unemployment insurance schemes or social assistance programs to counteract the economic contraction. With a CCT, a president can target resources directly to the poor without disrupting organized interests and the middle class.[8]

With the decision to adopt a CCT come decisions about policy design and agency structure. The president knows that bureaucrats have incentives of their own (Bawn 1997, Epstein and O'Halloran 1999, McCubbins et al. 1987). Bureaucrats do not face elections directly and could be more invested in their own careers than in the success of the policies or the careers of politicians.[9] Aside from legitimate concerns about career prospects, bureaucrats may also be interested in rent extraction opportunities. Therefore, the CCT may be distorted in the bureaucratic chain of command. To control the agency, the president keeps the power of appointment and removal of government officials in charge of the program. The president's appointment power in this policy arena is by no means an exemption, as the composition of the cabinet is legally

---

demands operated during the 1990s in Chile (*Frente Patriótico Manuel Rodriguez*), in Colombia (the *Ejército de Liberación Nacional*), in El Salvador (the *Frente Farabundo Marti de Liberación Nacional* and *Fuerzas Armadas de Resistencia Nacional*), in Guatemala (*Fuerzas Armadas Rebeldes* and the *Ejército Guerrillero de los Pobres*), in Peru (*Movimiento Revolucionario Tupac Amaru*), among others. Many of these groups, including the *Zapatistas*, remain active today.

[8] O'Donnell cautioned at the time that governments in the region: "must take into account that pro-poor policies will mobilize concerns not only among the privileged but also among important segments of the middle class who, after their own sufferings through economic crises and adjustments, feel that it is they who deserve preferential treatment. These concerns... may coagulate in a veto coalition that threatens not only the policy goals of those governments, but also whatever economic stability or growth has been achieved" (1996, 6).

[9] For example, bureaucrats are concerned with maximizing their agency's budget – because resources come with perks, prestige, and greater career prospects.

a prerogative of the executive in all Latin American countries (Amorim Neto 2006).[10] Appointment powers, however, nudge the agency to act on behalf of the president (Bendor et al. 2001) but do not eliminate bureaucratic discretion.

A CCT without operational guidelines to control and monitor the implementing agency offers opportunities for corruption and for the building of patronage bases (Huber 1996). Because the agency is biased in favor of the president, it is likely that such opportunities benefit his patronage bases. Yet it is also possible that other politicians try to use the program to fuel their own political machines. The more politicians distort the policy for patronage purposes, the less effective the policy is at improving the living conditions of the poor.

A CCT with Operational Rules That Tie the Hands of the President
Finally, the president can opt for a CCT with operational guidelines that reduce bureaucratic discretion. As one example, operational guidelines can include a clear description of the processes that the agency must follow to select recipients, transfer resources, verify conditionalities, and so forth, as well as systems to monitor the agency and make program operations transparent. Rules can be included to regularly detect errors of inclusion and exclusion to the program, to detect when conditionalities are not verified, and to evaluate program impacts. Such provisions reduce bureaucratic discretion by establishing ex-ante rules that dictate what policy the agency must implement, and ex-post strategies of control (at the implementation stage) that enable the president and legislators to detect whether the program is manipulated for political aims.

A CCT with strict guidelines minimizes opportunities for corruption and for building patronage bases. With this course of action, the president ties his own hands. Yet he also minimizes other politicians' opportunities to manipulate the program to build or fuel patronage machines without being detected. A more neutral CCT is more effective in alleviating poverty.

Fund or Not Fund Policy
Because congress is unable to directly influence policy implementation, legislators must make use of budgetary mechanisms. If the president decides to move away from the status quo and propose a CCT, then the median legislator has two possible actions: fund or deny funding to the policy.

The Political Game

The series of actions of the president and the median legislator are depicted in Figure 3.1. The president proposes to stay in the status quo or proposes a PCCT

[10] In all countries in Latin America, presidents hold bureaucratic control of the CCT program's headquarters. The only exception was the Brazilian program until President Lula's reform in 2003.

Politics of Fighting Poverty   49

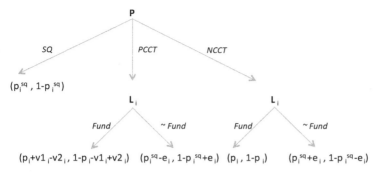

FIGURE 3.1 The political game. *Notes:* The players are: P, the president and L_i, the median legislator. Subscript i denotes the type of median (c, nc, or o). P can choose to stay in the status quo, propose a $NCCT$, or propose a $PCCT$. If P moves away from SQ, then L_i can either fund or not fund P's program. p_i^{sq} is the value of keeping only the status quo policies in place, p_i is the value of implementing a CCT, and e_i is the payoff from supporting a non-clientelist poverty relief program when the other player does not (or the payoff from rejecting clientelism). $v1_i$ and $v2_i$ are the value of clientelism for P and L_i, respectively.

or NCCT. If the president proposes either PCCT or NCCT, then the median legislator decides whether to fund or not fund the proposed policy. Thus there are five possible outcomes. I assume that each player has a strict preference ordering over the five. And, as is common in the literature of delegation, I assume that each player knows what game they are playing, and each knows the other knows (Bendor et al. 2001). Players choose optimal actions based on previous actions and expectations about future actions. I examine three theoretically relevant scenarios, including a president facing a median legislator from the opposition (L_o), from his political party but not from his faction within the party (L_{nc}), and from his party and his faction (L_c). Anticipating one of the central results, when a president faces L_c, he finds fewer reasons to tie his own hands when crafting the CCT than when he faces L_{nc} or L_o. Thus, perhaps surprisingly, even though L_{nc} and L_o have different preferences over policy outcomes, when the president faces either type of legislator he forgoes his own discretion over the CCT.

To innovate in terms of fighting poverty, power holders need to think that implementing a new poverty relief program is more convenient for them than continuing in the status quo. p_i^{sq} and $1 - p_i^{sq}$ represent the president's and median legislator's payoff from the policies in the status quo, respectively. The extent to which the status quo poses a threat of social unrest is critical to determine politicians' preferences. If the status quo's structural forces pose no threat, the president has little incentive to innovate in the social sector (Drazen and Grilli 1990, Hirschman 1985, Keeler 1993). On the other hand, when structural forces produce social unrest and the policies in the status quo are not effective to deal with the crisis, then the president has incentives to move away from the status quo and implement a social policy that improves the living conditions of the poor and quells social discontent in a more effective way compared to the status quo policies. The worst the status quo, the more likely the president is to consider designing and implementing either a PCCT or an NCCT program.

In a situation of economic crisis, politicians become interested in reforming social policies because the need for effective antipoverty policies is high. Politicians' incentives can come from selfish reasons such as career concerns, or can come from altruistic reasons such as other-regarding preferences. Regardless of what motivates politicians, as long as there is need for an effective poverty relief program, supporting a non-clientelist program can provide politicians with political benefits. Building on Geddes's (1991) model, e_i represents the payoff from supporting a non-clientelist poverty relief program, or rejecting a clientelist program, when the other player does not. The worst the economic crisis, the higher e_i is.[11]

p_i is the payoff the president gets from implementing a CCT, which transfers cash directly to people. $1 - p_i$ is the payoff the median legislator gets from the implementation of a CCT. Because the president is directly responsible for the policy's design and implementation, he is more likely to claim the credit for it. Thus, $p_i > 1 - p_i$.

A PCCT offers opportunities for using the program for clientelist purposes, whereas an NCCT eliminates them. $v1_i$ is the value of clientelism for the president, and $v2_i$ is the value of clientelism for the median legislator. $v1_i$ and $v2_i$ can be positive or negative.[12]

Case 1: President Faces Median Legislator from Opposition

Hereafter, I will drop subscript i because I will be describing a particular type of legislator. In this case, the median legislator is from the opposition.

If the president proposes a NCCT, then L_o has a choice between funding the program and getting $1 - p$ or not funding the program and getting $1 - p^{sq} - e$. NCCT suppresses bureaucratic discretion and limits opportunities for the incumbent party to build patronage bases. Yet, if an economic crisis exists, NCCT produces higher payoffs for the incumbent than do the status quo policies because the president can claim the credit for the policy innovation. This could give the opposition legislator reasons not to fund NCCT. However, L_o must also consider that status quo's policies are already biased in favor

---

[11] For simplicity, I assume that the costs from proposing a clientelist policy when the other player rejects it and those from rejecting a non-clientelist policy when the other player proposes it are symmetrical.

[12] The value of clientelism in this game is similar to the value of patronage on Geddes's (1991) model. However, in Geddes's (1991) model, the game is played by a legislator from the minority party and a legislator from the majority party.

Politics of Fighting Poverty

of the president's party and that there is a cost e of rejecting a non-clientelist poverty relief program. The higher e is, the more L_o prefers to fund NCCT than not to fund it.

If the president proposes PCCT, then L_o has a choice between funding the program and getting $1 - p - v_1 + v_2$ and not funding the program and getting $1 - p^{sq} + e$. Because the median legislator is in this case part of the opposition, $v_1 - v_2 > 0$. That is, the president values clientelism more than L_o because he is the incumbent. Thus, he has more control over the clientelist machine than does the opposition party. L_o is concerned that the policies in the status quo are biased in favor of the president's party, but the president cannot make a credible promise to L_o that he will not abuse his power and manipulate a PCCT for political aims. Furthermore, L_o has an incentive to deny funding to a PCCT because that way she gets the bonus that comes from rejecting a clientelist policy when the president proposes it. So, L_o prefers not to fund PCCT rather than to fund it.

Given L_o's decisions, and that the status quo is undesirable, the president decides between proposing NCCT and getting funding for it, in which case he gets the payoff p, or proposing PCCT and not getting funding for it, in which case he gets $p^{sq} - e$. For a president who faces economic turmoil, implementing a CCT is better than keeping only the policies in the status quo ($p > p^{sq}$) because a CCT is more effective at tackling poverty. This gives the president reasons to choose NCCT over a PCCT. Moreover, because e is positive, if the president opts for PCCT, which will get no funding, then not only is he left with the status quo inefficient policies but he also pays the costs of being blamed by L_o for proposing a clientelist policy in times of crisis. Therefore, when confronted with a median legislator from the opposition, the president is better off opting for NCCT. Thus, in this case, the president proposes NCCT and L_o funds it. The payoffs for each player are $(p, 1 - p)$.

Case 2: President Faces Median Legislator from His Party but from a Different Within-Party Faction

In the previous case, the president, being the incumbent, values clientelism more than the legislator from the opposition. Now, when the median legislator is from the president's party but not from his faction, it becomes relevant which faction controls the party's patronage machine, if one exists. First, consider the case in which $v_1 - v_2 < 0$, that is L_{nc} has more control over the party machine than the president.

If the president proposes NCCT, then L_{nc} has a choice between funding the program and getting $1 - p$ or not funding the program and getting $1 - p^{sq} - e$. The worse the economic crisis, the more likely it is that L_{nc} would prefer to fund NCCT than not to fund it because, as in the previous case, rejecting a nonpoliticized pro-poor policy when the president proposes it has a cost e, which increases with the extent of the crisis.

If the president proposes PCCT, then L_{nc} also has incentives to fund the policy. If L_{nc} funds the program, she gets $1 - p - v_1 + v_2$, and if she does not fund it, she gets $1 - p^{sq} + e$. Because $v_1 - v_2 < 0$, then when the president proposes PCCT, L_{nc} funds it because she gets the clientelist bonus.

Given L_{nc}'s dominant strategy of funding the president's policy, P decides between opting for NCCT and getting funding for it, in which case he gets the payoff p, or opting for PCCT and getting funding for it, in which case he gets $p + v_1 - v_2$. For a president who faces economic turmoil and is not in control of his party's political machine, $p > p + v_1 - v_2$. Therefore, the president is better off opting for NCCT and getting funding for it. With NCCT the president ties his own hands, but he also minimizes opportunities for his rival faction to manipulate the program. The payoffs for each player in this case are $(p, 1 - p)$.

Now consider the case in which $v_1 - v_2 > 0$, that is, the president's faction controls the party's machine. In such a case, L_{nc} prefers to fund neutral CCT because she values clientelist opportunities less than the president. She may be concerned that the president will design and implement a policy that increases the president's political capital at the expense of her own. This scenario produces the same results as in case 1 when the president faces a median legislator from the opposition. The president cannot credibly commit not to manipulate PCCT to his political benefit and hurt L_{nc}'s faction within the party. In such a case, L_{nc} prefers funding NCCT over not funding it, and prefers not funding PCCT over funding it. Then, as in case 1, the president opts for NCCT, which secures funding.

Case 3: President Faces a Median Legislator from His Party and from His Own Within-Party Coalition

A president who faces a median legislator from his within-party faction knows that he is dealing with an ally.

If the president proposes NCCT, then the median legislator has a choice between funding the program and getting $1 - p$ or not funding the program and getting $1 - p^{sq} - e$. The higher e is, the more likely it is that L_c would prefer to fund NCCT than not.

In this case, because the median legislator is an ally, the clientelist bonus is not a zero sum game. Each player gets a payoff V when a clientelist policy is implemented. Because they are allies, the president and L_c can trust that the policy implemented is aligned with their interest. So if the president proposes PCCT, then L_c has a choice between funding the program and getting $1 - p + V$ and not funding the program and getting $1 - p^{sq} + e$. L_c prefers to fund PCCT and get the clientelist bonus.

Given L_c decisions, the president decides between proposing NCCT and getting funding for it, in which case he gets the payoff p, or proposing PCCT and getting funding for it, in which case he gets $p + V$. For a president who faces

Politics of Fighting Poverty 53

economic turmoil and controls of his party's clientelist machine, $p < p + V$. Therefore, the president is better off opting for PCCT and getting funding for it. The payoffs in this case are $(p + V, 1 - p + V)$.

In sum, when the president faces a median legislator who is not from his own within-party faction or who is from the opposition, he forgoes discretion in program operations, but he also minimizes opportunities for politicians in general to manipulate the program without being detected. In other words, NCCT is adopted when the president and the median legislator are not aligned, because each side does not want the opposite side to reap the clientelist bonus of a manipulable CCT, all else equal.

The policy outcomes that result from the interactions between the president and the median legislator are:

Hypothesis 1: If there is no economic crisis, the result is the SQ

If there is an economic crisis, then:

Hypothesis 2: If P faces L_c, the result is PCCT

Hypothesis 3: If P faces L_{nc}, the result is NCCT

Hypothesis 4: If P faces L_o, the result is NCCT

IMPLICATIONS

When the president faces L_{nc} or L_o, he designs a neutral conditional cash transfer with more intricate operational rules. Yet the president keeps the power of appointment and removal of government officials in charge of the program. Thus, in principle, the president could implement the policy in any way he wants, regardless of the compromises he makes in the design. However, it is not in his interest to deviate from the policy design to implement a politicized policy, because he will face legislators repeatedly. As mentioned earlier in the chapter, CCTs are not entitlements; legislators can review their budgets on a yearly basis. If legislators feel that a president has moved the policy too far away from its design, then they may choose to revise the program's budget, which in an extreme case could lead to the discontinuation of a policy. For this reason, we can expect that a president who faces L_{nc} or L_o will have a particular interest in keeping program implementation in line with program design as much as possible, even if this means monitoring their own bureaucracies and making continuous investments in curbing his own discretion. Repeated interactions with congress allow legislators to threaten the president with cutting the policy's funding, which in turn motivates the president to keep the program insulated from political interests.

When the president negotiates with L_c, he designs a PCCT and delegates the implementation of the program to the agency without imposing mechanisms of control. A CCT without mechanisms to curb bureaucratic discretion offers more opportunities for corruption (Huber 1996). A conditional cash transfer with no operational rules such as fixed eligibility criteria, monitoring systems, and independent program evaluations has a less robust implementation. The expectation then is that, although there may be some discrepancies between policy design and implementation, the same factors that lead to a stricter policy design also lead to a more robust implementation.

Hypothesis 5: When a president faces L_{nc} or L_o, the CCT has a more robust implementation than when a president faces L_c.

From the various aspects of implementation, the expansion of programs, especially during election years, has constituted an important issue on which legislators across Latin America consistently agitate. Speculations about presidents using conditional cash transfer programs to boost their electoral support abound in the media. Yet there are no studies that provide systematic evidence for the presence of political-economic cycles in the operation of cash transfer programs. Thus, the question that remains is whether presidents manipulate program enrollment to improve their electoral fortunes.

A second implication of the argument is that when a president faces L_{nc} or L_o, the policy's design includes stringent operational guidelines that limit the bureaucracy's ability to manipulate the program for political gain without being detected. For example, a program with a design that includes processes to guarantee transparency in program operations (regular publication of program expenses, schedules of transfers, and enrollment updates) gives a president less room to manipulate enrollments according to the schedule of elections without legislators learning about it. Moreover, program guidelines may explicitly restrict enrollment of people close to election times, as in the Mexican case. The president knows that L_{nc} or L_o are willing to cut the funding of a politicized program. Thus, presidents who opt for CCT programs with more neutral designs are also less prone to use programs to fuel political business cycles. On the other hand, when a president faces L_c, he can expand a program following electoral cycles because the median legislator poses no threat to the policy's funding.

Hypothesis 6: Political factors that lead to strong policy design and robust implementation also lead to the elimination of political-economic cycles that result from the expansion of conditional cash transfer programs during election years.

The argument also has an implication for policies' survival. A CCT that limits political discretion is more effective at fighting poverty and is less vulnerable to political manipulation. Thus, a neutral design and a more robust implementation give programs two types of legitimacy: output and procedural legitimacy. The former justifies a policy based on its superior performance compared to other policies, the latter based on the process of implementation being better and more transparent than for other policies (Thatcher and Stone Sweet 2002).

A president has more arguments to defend a poverty relief program that effectively reaches its intended beneficiaries and improves their welfare. Similarly, when the president has evidence based on impact evaluations about the effectiveness of the program, he can better justify program continuation. On the other hand, defending an ineffective policy, especially in an antagonistic congress, is a more daunting task. Beyond legislators' responses to the policy, people are more likely to see an effective policy as legitimate than an ineffective policy. Thus, neutral CCTs are more likely to count with output legitimacy than politicized programs.

The basis of procedural legitimacy of poverty relief programs ultimately depends on people's understanding of the root causes of poverty. In Latin America, people rank characteristics of the political system highly among possible determinants of poverty. Corruption and inefficient bureaucracies are common explanations for poverty, as are explanations based on unfairness of the distribution of income and of the distribution of opportunities (Brooks 2009). Because many voters in Latin America believe that injustices found in political systems and ineffective institutions play a role in poverty, it is likely that policies that tie the hands of the president would garner more support from broad sectors of the population than those policies with less effective controls on presidential discretion.[13] Recent accounts of distributive politics in Latin America show that middle-class voters may support well-administered social programs (Zucco 2011), reject clientelism on moral grounds, and disapprove of policies that signal low quality of government, such as politicized policies (Weitz-Shapiro 2012a, 2012b). People are thus more likely to see a poverty relief program as legitimate if it is insulated from politics.

Output and procedural legitimacy help presidents form a coalition in support of policy continuation. Therefore, a neutral CCT garners broad support among the public, which could be directly linked to programs' survival rate. A politicized CCT, on the other hand, could have a smaller coalition supporting it.

Hypothesis 7: Programs with weaker designs – and more flawed implementations – are more likely to be dismantled than programs with stronger designs and more exacting implementations.

A final implication of the argument relates to the strength of patron-client relations.

When a president faces L_{nc} or L_o, CCTs have more elaborate rules and more robust operations and are therefore more likely to be insulated from politics and effective in fighting poverty. Where this is the case, CCTs erode patron-client

---

[13] The Latin American understanding of the cause of poverty contrasts sharply with that of the United States, where the causes of poverty are more likely to be perceived as related to personal choices, such as lack of effort (Alesina et al. 2001).

relations. On the other hand, when a president faces L_c, CCTs could cement clientelistic ties.

A neutral CCT fosters the demise of clientelism through three mechanisms. First, when programs include provisions to avoid mismanagement, they are more effective at increasing households' welfare. A wealthier household can, in turn, afford to distance themselves from local patrons, which makes vote buying more expensive for political parties' brokers.

Second, a program with strict operational rules has an informative effect on recipients. The more institutionalized a program is, the more information recipients have that program benefits do not depend on party brokers. This informative effect also makes vote buying more difficult, because voters learn that party brokers have less discretion to administer program resources. The income and informative effects together empower recipients to resist clientelism.

Third, conditional cash transfer programs that operate in a systematic way are more likely to be institutionalized, which reduces the discretion of party brokers to operate a program based on a system of rewards and punishments. For example, if the selection of program recipients is based on a poverty score, and cash transfers are systematically reaching recipients, party brokers have fewer opportunities to strategically manipulate program resources. This makes vote buying more difficult because brokers cannot bestow program benefits, nor can they punish recipients by discontinuing the stream of program benefits. Thus, a neutral CCT helps poor people to resist clientelism and also erodes patron-client relations by suppressing brokers' discretion.

Hypothesis 8: CCTs with more neutral designs and robust implementations foster the demise of clientelism.

The following chapters test these hypotheses with a mix of quantitative and qualitative evidence. Overall, the analysis that follows shows that the dynamics among presidents and legislators influences conditional cash transfers' design and has important policy outcomes that directly relate to the effectiveness of programs to eradicate poverty.

4

Explaining Policy Adoption and Design

The political processes behind decisions to adopt CCT programs shows that presidents in Latin America, during the period under study in this book, pursued their antipoverty agendas taking into account the reactions of legislators. This chapter presents an empirical analysis of the role of executive-legislative relations in the adoption and design of CCTs. The chapter begins with a quantitative analysis of the determinants of the adoption of CCTs with stringent operational guidelines and the adoption of CCTs with lax operational rules.

Then, to further test the plausibility of the argument, the chapter explores the emergence of CCT programs in five countries in Latin America. I first review the origins of Mexico's *Progresa* program, followed by a discussion of the Colombian CCT program, *Familias en Acción*. In both countries, the president faced antagonistic legislatures controlled by legislators of their own party but from different within-party factions. I then review the origins of Guatemala's *Mi Familia Progresa* and Peru's *Juntos* program, where presidents faced legislatures controlled by the opposition. Finally, I examine Argentina's CCT program, *Plan Familias*, implemented first when the president's party controlled congress, and I examine *Asignación Universal por Hijo*, implemented when the president no longer controlled congress. The quantitative evidence and qualitative insights support the argument that when the president faces an antagonistic legislature, he opts for designing and adopting programs with operational rules that suppress their own, and other politicians', discretion.

THE ADOPTION AND DESIGN OF LATIN AMERICAN CCTs, 1990–2011

Presidents' decisions about the adoption, or not, of a CCT with stringent or lenient design is a function of the alignment of the president's interests with those of legislators. A president whose interests are in line with those of legislators designs and adopts a policy with fewer rules that would limit his own control over the policy's implementation. In contrast, a president who faces resistance in congress designs and adopts a policy with more operational rules that suppress discretion.

To test the argument, in the statistical analysis that follows I use the data set I constructed that includes all countries in Latin America during the period from 1990 to 2011. The unit of analysis in the data set is the country-year. For country-years with a CCT in operation, the data set includes details on program design and operations.

Program design varies widely in Latin America, from programs with very few provisions such as Bolivia's *Juancito Pinto* to programs with detailed operational rules such as Colombia's *Familias en Acción*. Based on the design index I constructed for the programs (described fully in Chapter 2), the average program in the region had a design score of 4.8. Most programs have multiple operational guidelines throughout their life span. Although there are countries whose programs are below-average design throughout the period under study, as is the case in Bolivia, there are also countries whose programs have improved over time, like those in Ecuador and Honduras. Finally, there are countries whose programs have remained above-average in terms of their design, as in Mexico.

Because CCTs are not entitlements, each year governments need to decide whether they want to operate a CCT and its guidelines. To measure various aspects of this yearly decision, I define three dependent variables. First, I create a binary outcome that captures whether or not a country adopts a program with a stringent design. *CCT above mean* is a dummy variable that takes the value of 1 each year a country adopts a CCT with an above-average design (a value of 4.8 or higher in the design index) and 0 otherwise.[1] Second, it may be that the decision to adopt a stringent CCT is not symmetrical to the decision to adopt a lenient CCT. In other words, the determinants of one type of program need not be the determinants of the other. Therefore, the second dependent variable, *CCT below mean*, is a dummy variable that takes the value of 1 each year a country adopts a CCT with a below-average design and 0 otherwise. For both variables, their values remain unchanged until a new set of operational rules (either of the same or a different CCT) is adopted in the country, in which case their value changes according to the design score of the new set of operational rules. In the case in which a country's CCT expires and it is not replaced by a new program, *CCT above mean* and *CCT below mean* take the value of 0.

Certainly there are other ways to define a stringent and lenient CCT. For example, instead of using the overall mean design as reference value, it is possible to use the median design. For practical purposes, however, the mean

---

[1] To be clear, the category of 0 includes country-years where no CCT is adopted and country-years where a CCT with a below average design is adopted.

Explaining Policy Adoption and Design

and median of the design index are close to each other; therefore, using either statistic to define the threshold to distinguish stringent and lenient programs produces very similar results. Finally, the outcome of interest may be defined in a continuous way. Then, the third dependent variable, *Design score*, takes values of 0 when no program is adopted, and takes the value of the design index – from 1 up to 6 when a program's operational rules regulate targeting, conditionalities, certification, evaluation, and transparency of program operations.

To operationalize the alignment of interests between presidents and legislators, I first follow the literature on delegation, which commonly uses a measure of divided government to capture this concept. A measure of divided government, however, fails to account for instances where the president faces resistance from legislators of his own party. Thus, an analysis based solely on divided government is likely to underestimate the effect that resistance to the president's policy has on CCTs' adoption and design. To deal with this, in addition to divided government, I use a more comprehensive measure of the checks on presidential powers.

The two main independent variables capture the degree of political opposition and the level of checks on presidential powers stemming from congress. The first variable, *Divided*, measures whether the president controls the lower and upper houses in congress. *Divided* takes a value of 1 if the party of the president does not have a majority of the seats in congress, and otherwise takes a value of 0. For half of the country-years in my data set, which dates back to 1990, *Divided* has the value of 1. Chile experienced a divided government for 62 percent of the country-years in this study, making it the country with the longest exposure to this political phenomenon. Other countries in the study have had substantial experience with divided governments, as well. In Mexico and Peru, for example, the president's party controlled the majority of seats in congress 52 percent of the country-years. Some countries have less experience with divided governments. In Argentina, for example, the president's party has controlled congress for 62 percent of the country-years in the study.

The second variable, *Checks*, developed by Keefer (2002), combines the existence of divided control of two chambers in a bicameral system and the number of veto players. *Checks* is coded on a scale of 1 to 7 and takes higher values if the chief executive is competitively elected, if the opposition controls the legislature, if the president does not control a chamber in the legislature, and as the number of parties presumed to be allied with the president's party but which have an ideological orientation closer to that of the main opposition party increases. With the exception of Cuba, all countries in the study have experienced various levels of *Checks* since 1990. For example, *Checks* takes the value of 2 in Mexico from 1990 to 1996, and in 1997 it increases to 5. A country's trajectory with respect to checks on executive power is not always progressive or linear. In Peru, for example, *Checks* takes the value of 4 in 1990 and 1991, decreases to 3 in 1992, further decreases to 2 from 1996 to 2000, and then increases again to 4 in 2001. The two variables, *Divided* and *Checks*, are available in the database of political institutions (Beck et al. 2001, Keefer 2010, Keefer and Stasavage 2003). The advantage of using these variables is that they are based on objective criteria.

Estimating the effects of *Divided* and *Checks* on the adoption and design of CCTs using country-level data presents several challenges. Chief among them is that comparisons across countries may confound the effects of observable and unobservable characteristics, leading to erroneous conclusions about the relationship between measured variables. To mitigate this problem, at least to some extent, I begin by estimating regression models that include country-fixed effects. The inclusion of country-fixed effects is meant to control for characteristics at the country level that are fixed in the period under study. For each dependent variable, I first estimate a model controlling for country-fixed effects only, and then a model also including as control variables factors that my argument and previous work have considered relevant to the explanation of the origins and expansion of welfare programs. The objective of proceeding in this way is to show that the effects of *Divided* and *Checks* do not depend on the inclusion or exclusion of control variables.

Before describing in detail the set of control variables, a note on the regression models I use in this section is in order. *CCT above mean* and *CCT below mean* are dummy variables. Nonlinear models, such as probit or logit, are widely used to model dichotomous outcome variables. Yet, nonlinear models are cumbersome when specifications include fixed effects or when using panel data. One of the challenges is that nonlinear models drop from the analysis country-year observations with no within country variation in the dependent variable. As an alternative, linear probability models (LPM) work well with fixed effects and panel data. LPM present some challenges, too: their estimates are not constrained to the unit interval, and their standard errors may be heteroskedastic. However, both concerns can be easily dealt with. First, given that the main purpose of the analysis is to estimate the effect of *Divided* and *Checks* on the outcomes, and not to make predictions, the possibility that some predicted values are outside the unit interval is not relevant (Wooldridge 2002). Second, it is straightforward to estimate heteroskedasticity-consistent robust standard errors (Angrist and Pischke 2009). Given that both nonlinear models and LPM present advantages and disadvantages, in the main text I include LPM models because they work best with fixed effects, which in turn mitigate concerns about spurious correlations between the independent variables of main interest and dependent variables. Then, in the appendix, I include probit models to show that the results are robust to nonlinear specifications.

The concern that remains is that the effect of *Divided* and *Checks* may still be confounded with unobserved and time-varying factors that are not accounted for in the controls or the country-fixed effects. To provide additional evidence that *Divided* and *Checks* do in fact shape the outcomes, I employ a regression discontinuity design, which I describe after presenting the estimates of the regression models.

The controls in the regression models capture factors that my argument and previous scholarship have postulated as important determinants of the adoption and scaling up of social policies and welfare spending. First, in addition to the role of legislators, my argument postulates that economic crises nudge presidents to move away from the status quo. Furthermore, the worse the economic crisis, the more costly it is for the president to propose a manipulable CCT when legislators reject it, and the more costly it is for legislators to reject a nonpoliticized CCT when the president proposes it. To account for this, I include yearly inflation as a control variable in the models. I also include the extent of child labor in the country, which captures the negative effects of economic crises on poor households and measures the need for policies, such as CCTs, that directly benefit impoverished children.

Second, following previous work, I include the ideological orientation of the president as a control variable. There is a vast scholarship that shows that, among OECD countries, a left-wing government is more likely to increase social spending than is a right-wing government. In contemporary Latin America, ideology does not matter in the extent of social expenditures (Huber et al. 2008). Yet, even though right- and left-leaning governments have adopted CCTs, there could be a channel through which the president's ideology matters for a CCT's design and adoption.

Third, I include GDP per capita in the models because scholarship has suggested that richer countries can afford to spend more on welfare. This argument has its roots in Adolph Wagner's hypothesis that as countries develop economically, the size of the public sector increases. Empirical studies of the relation between GDP and the welfare state have produced mixed results (Carnes and Mares 2010).

Fourth, I control for the extent of deindustrialization in the country. Deindustrialization is "characterized by high rates of unemployment, high levels of atypical and part-time employment, and growing family instability" (Carnes and Mares 2010), as well high levels of welfare state outsiders. The motivation of this control variable is that, given the coverage of the welfare state in Latin America, the fewer people working in agriculture and manufacture, the greater the pressure on governments to reform social protection. Specifically, Carnes and Mares (2010) argue that deindustrialization leads to the introduction of noncontributory health and old-age insurance policies. Fifth, the effect of economic globalization on social spending has been the subject of substantial research (Cameron 1978, Rodrik 1997). I include a measure of trade openness that is meant to capture the vulnerability of the country to external factors. Finally, I also include in the models population size because policy reform may be more challenging in populous countries. As a reminder, because I estimate fixed-effect regression models, I am also controlling for factors that are time-invariant at the country level during the period of analysis.

These control variables, with the exception of the ideology of the executive, are available from the World Development Indicators and Global Development Finance data published by the World Bank (2010). The ideology of the executive comes from the database of political institutions (Beck et al. 2001, Keefer 2010).

Table 4.1 displays the results from the analysis when using *Divided* as the main independent variable. *Divided* has a statistically significant positive effect on the probability of a country of adopting a CCT with an above-average score, a statistically significant negative effect on the probability of adopting a CCT below the mean, and a positive and statistically significant effect on the design index. The effect of *Divided* is substantial: Presidents with a divided government are approximately 22 percentage points more likely to adopt a CCT with above-average design; they are 12 percentage points less likely to adopt a program with a below-average design; and, finally, their programs are almost one unit better in terms of design compared to presidents who control congress.

To better illustrate the magnitude of the effects, consider the estimates in Table 4.1, columns 1 and 3. In average, countries where the president controls congress, that is *Divided* equals zero, have a baseline probability of 6 percent of adopting a CCT with an above-mean design and a baseline probability of 7 percent of adopting a CCT with a below-mean design. With these baseline probabilities as a reference, a change in *Divided* from 0 to 1 implies almost a fourfold increase in the probability of adopting an above-average CCT (0.22/0.06), and almost a twofold decrease in the probability of adopting a below-average CCT (−0.12/0.07). In terms of the design score, a change in *Divided* from 0 to 1 is equivalent to transforming a program like *Asignación Familiar II* in Honduras circa 2001 into a program like *Bolsa Familia* in 2003. Therefore, a president facing a divided government is substantially more likely to adopt a CCT with stringent operational rules compared to a president with a unified government.

In addition to the role of executive-legislative relations, other factors play an important role in the process of designing and adopting a CCT. As described in Chapter 3, the extent to which an economic crisis poses a real threat of social unrest is critical to determining the president's preferences and the policy outcome. Given the economic and political context of the region in the late 1990s and 2000, the worse an economic crisis is, the more likely it is that a president will move away from the status quo and adopt any type of CCT. Table 4.1 shows that an increase in (log) inflation rates is positively associated with a higher probability that a president will adopt a CCT of any type and with a higher program design score. Economic crisis, therefore, sets the stage for social policy reform.

Unlike inflation, which nudges presidents toward a CCT without differentiating program designs, other economic and demographic factors tilt the balance toward a more stringent CCT. How appealing it is to adopt a stringent CCT rather than a more lenient CCT depends on the extent of poverty and

TABLE 4.1 *Effects of Divided Government on the Adoption of an Above-Average CCT, a Below-Average CCT, and Design Score*

	CCT Above Mean		CCT Below Mean		Design Score	
	(1)	(2)	(3)	(4)	(5)	(6)
Divided	0.224***	0.188***	−0.125***	−0.153***	0.899***	0.624**
	(0.042)	(0.046)	(0.032)	(0.039)	(0.252)	(0.262)
Left		−0.059		0.208***		0.198
		(0.048)		(0.045)		(0.251)
GDP		0.039		0.075***		0.435***
		(0.025)		(0.026)		(0.155)
Openness		−0.002		0.001		−0.000
		(0.001)		(0.001)		(0.007)
Inflation (log)		0.025*		0.027*		0.165**
		(0.014)		(0.015)		(0.073)
Population (log)		1.690***		−0.007		9.241***
		(0.253)		(0.188)		(1.410)
Deindustrialization		0.015**		0.004		0.093***
		(0.006)		(0.006)		(0.034)
Child labor		0.032***		−0.006		0.137***
		(0.007)		(0.009)		(0.041)
Constant	0.046**	−5.586***	0.125***	−0.438	0.615***	−31.889***
	(0.023)	(0.599)	(0.020)	(0.506)	(0.143)	(3.208)
Observations	580	326	580	326	580	326
R-squared	0.285	0.560	0.266	0.397	0.273	0.569
Country-fixed effects	yes	yes	yes	yes	yes	yes

Robust standard errors in parentheses.
***p < 0.01, **p < 0.05, *p < 0.1

the access poor people have to existing welfare institutions. Table 4.1 shows that child labor – a symptom and a cause of poverty – is positively related to the probability that a country adopts a CCT with a design above the mean, and it is positively related to a program's design score. These results are statistically significant at the 1 percent level. Child labor is not associated with the probability of adopting a CCT with a design below the mean. Deindustrialization is related to CCTs' adoption and design much as child labor is. The higher deindustrialization is, the more likely it is that a president will adopt a CCT with an above-mean design and the higher the program's design score, but deindustrialization does not increase the likelihood of adoption of a CCT with a below-average design. Finally, the larger the population, the bigger the challenge when it comes to fighting poverty and doing so in a cost-effective way. Therefore, like child labor and deindustrialization, a country's population is positively related to the adoption of a more stringent CCT, an increase in the design score, but not an increase in the probability of adopting a lenient CCT. In sum, child labor, population, and the extent of deindustrialization help explain why some presidents but not others tie their own hands when designing and adopting poverty alleviation policies.

On the other hand, other economic and political factors tilt the balance toward more lenient CCTs. To begin with, although GDP per capita is positively associated with design score, a country's economic wealth is only positively correlated with the probability of adopting a CCT with below-average design and is not associated with the adoption of a CCT with an above-average design. This result is compatible with the argument in Chapter 3 that presidents who do not consider the status quo as challenging may find no reason to tie their own hands with a stringent CCT. Surprisingly, all else being equal, the ideological orientation of the president has no significant effect on the probability of adopting a CCT with an above-average design or on the design score; however, it does have a positive effect on the probability of adopting a CCT with a below-average design. Finally, the openness of the economy has no effect in the adoption or design of CCTs. Two final notes about Table 4.1: First, the effects of *Divided* are robust to the inclusion of all control variables in the models. Second, even-number columns show that the effect of *Divided* is one of the most substantively important (and statistically significant) correlates of a CCT adoption and design.

Now, I turn to the analysis that uses *Checks* to measure the degree of political opposition and the level of checks on presidential powers stemming from congress. As a reminder, *Divided* and *Checks* measure related concepts. Because they are highly correlated to one another, including both in a regression model produces problems associated with multicollinearity, such as misleading standard errors accompanying the estimate of main interest. To test the argument of the book with an alternative measurement of the independent variable of interest, I estimate models similar to the ones presented in Table 4.1, but I

Explaining Policy Adoption and Design

exclude *Divided* and include only *Checks*. Table 4.2 presents the results from this analysis.

Consistent with previous results, an increase in *Checks* is positively associated with the probability of adopting a CCT with above-average design, is negatively associated with the probability of adopting a CCT with below-average design, and is positively associated with the design score. In terms of the magnitude of the effects, an increase in *Checks* from 2 to 5 (on a scale of 1 to 6), is associated with a 2.6-fold increase in the probability of adopting a CCT above mean, an 80 percent decrease in the probability of adopting a below-average CCT, and a 27 percent increase in the design score (off baseline averages of 0.08, 0.18, and 3.5, respectively). In other words, an increase in *Checks* from 2 to 5 translates into an improvement in the design score of a program equivalent to the difference between the program in the Dominican Republic and that of *Familias en Acción* in Colombia.[2,3]

The proliferation of CCTs in Latin America raises the question of whether some governments in the region learned from or emulated other governments. If so, does the diffusion of policy expertise in the region explain why some presidents, but not others, adopted programs with operational guidelines that limit governments' ability to manipulate the program for political gain? Indeed, the wave of CCT adoptions in a short period of time is indicative that some diffusion took place. Yet it is unclear to what extent such diffusion explains policy design choices. To test the role of diffusion systematically, I estimate models similar to those included in Tables 4.1 and 4.2, only this time I control for *Diffusion*, which measures for each country-year observation the average design score of CCTs in the previous year in all other countries (that is, the measure excludes previous design scores in the same country). *Diffusion*'s definition makes regression models drop from the analysis pioneering countries, for which there are no previous year's design scores. For this reason, I estimate the effect of *Diffusion* in separate models from those presented earlier in the chapter.

If diffusion explains why governments opt to tie their hands with stringent operational rules, then we should observe that the higher the average design score in the previous year in the region, the higher the design score is. The data, however, reveal a different pattern. Although *Diffusion* is positively and significantly associated with the design score when *Divided* is in the model, it is positive but statistically not significant when *Checks* are. Furthermore, *Diffusion* is positively and significantly related to the probability of adopting a CCT with a design below the mean (regardless of whether *Divided* or *Checks* are in

---

[2] These results are robust to the inclusion of *Checks* in a semiparametric way.
[3] Control variables in these specifications are associated with the dependent variables in a similar way as in models using *Divided*. The two exceptions are inflation and deindustrialization in the model explaining CCT above mean, which are still positive but estimated with less precision.

TABLE 4.2 *Effects of Checks on the Executive on the Adoption of an Above-Average CCT, a Below-Average CCT, and Design Score*

	CCT Above Mean		CCT Below Mean		Design Score	
	(1)	(2)	(3)	(4)	(5)	(6)
Checks	0.052***	0.069***	−0.044***	−0.048***	0.219**	0.320***
	(0.016)	(0.016)	(0.011)	(0.014)	(0.094)	(0.087)
Left		−0.045		0.186***		0.236
		(0.046)		(0.042)		(0.238)
GDP		0.034		0.064**		0.393***
		(0.023)		(0.027)		(0.139)
Openness		−0.002		0.001		−0.002
		(0.001)		(0.001)		(0.007)
Inflation (log)		0.019		0.034**		0.148**
		(0.014)		(0.015)		(0.072)
Population (log)		1.943***		−0.157		10.204***
		(0.255)		(0.177)		(1.438)
Deindustrialization		0.010		0.008		0.075**
		(0.006)		(0.006)		(0.034)
Child labor		0.035***		−0.008		0.151***
		(0.006)		(0.008)		(0.038)
Constant	−0.019	−5.906***	0.212***	−0.261	0.334	−33.261***
	(0.057)	(0.586)	(0.042)	(0.474)	(0.330)	(3.159)
Observations	572	326	572	326	572	326
R-squared	0.262	0.567	0.264	0.388	0.263	0.579
Country-fixed effects	yes	yes	yes	yes	yes	yes

Robust standard errors in parentheses.
*** $p < 0.01$, ** $p < 0.05$, * $p < 0.1$.

Explaining Policy Adoption and Design

the model), but it is not correlated with adopting a CCT with a design above the mean. Table 4.3 displays these results and also shows that the estimates of *Divided* and *Checks* are robust to including *Diffusion* in the specifications. Thus, although the idea of transferring cash to poor households to fight poverty certainly was diffused in the region, the decision of governments to adopt programs with operational rules that curb political discretion is mostly explained by domestic factors, such as divided government and checks on presidential power.

Divided governments and checks on presidential power stemming from congress are associated with the adoption of CCTs that curb political discretion. Yet, a question that remains is whether legislators' resistance to presidents is not only correlated but in fact leads to the adoption of CCTs with stringent operational rules. Previous estimates in Tables 4.1, 4.2, and 4.3 controlled for country-fixed effects and factors that scholarship has postulated as determinants of social spending. Yet, are governments with and without divided governments, or with and without checks on the president, different in ways that previous estimates did not take into account? For example, they could be different in ways that are unobserved and time-varying (say, perhaps clientelism eroded in one set of countries but not in the other)? If they are different, then a comparison between them confounds the effects of legislators' opposition with preexistence differences (continuing with the example, the effect of legislators' opposition may be confounded with differences in clientelism). I turn to a regression discontinuity design (RDD), which helps mitigate this concern.

RDD research design takes advantage of the arbitrariness that sometimes exists in rules determining independent variables of interest. Arbitrary rules provide good "as-if randomized" experiments (Angrist and Pischke 2009). One such arbitrary rule is that presidents whose political party controls fewer than 50 percent of seats in congress face a divided government. The arbitrary threshold of 50 percent is relevant for policymaking because in most countries in Latin America, federal budgets need the support of at least 50 percent of legislators to be approved. RDD compares policy outcomes when a president's party controls just above and just below 50 percent of legislators. Near the cutoff value, country-years where the president's party has majority in congress are a good counterfactual for country-years where the president does not have it.

A comparison between the economic and demographic characteristics, that is, baseline characteristics, of country-years below and above the 50 percent threshold validates the RDD empirical strategy. In the window of ±3 percent around the 50 percent cutoff, there are no statistically significant differences between the above and below country-years in terms of the ideological orientation of the president, GDP per capita, openness of the economy, inflation, deindustrialization, and child labor. The only exception is that country-years below the threshold are more populous than country-years above it. This

TABLE 4.3 *Robustness Check: Effects of Divided Government and Checks, Controlling for Diffusion*

	CCT Above Mean (1)	CCT Below Mean (2)	Design Score (3)	CCT Above Mean (4)	CCT Below Mean (5)	Design Score (6)
Divided	0.187***	−0.141***	0.648**			
	(0.047)	(0.040)	(0.264)			
Checks				0.069***	−0.044***	0.329***
				(0.016)	(0.013)	(0.088)
Left	−0.058	0.185***	0.166	−0.045	0.164***	0.197
	(0.049)	(0.041)	(0.258)	(0.047)	(0.039)	(0.245)
GDP	0.039	0.039	0.347**	0.035	0.028	0.302**
	(0.026)	(0.025)	(0.158)	(0.024)	(0.026)	(0.142)
Openness	−0.002	0.003***	0.003	−0.002	0.003***	0.002
	(0.001)	(0.001)	(0.008)	(0.002)	(0.001)	(0.008)
Inflation (log)	0.025*	0.034**	0.185**	0.018	0.040***	0.165**
	(0.014)	(0.015)	(0.072)	(0.014)	(0.014)	(0.072)
Population (log)	1.685***	−0.425	7.586***	1.964***	−0.531*	8.811***
	(0.394)	(0.313)	(2.153)	(0.386)	(0.297)	(2.107)
Deindustrialization	0.015**	0.002	0.089***	0.009	0.006	0.070**
	(0.006)	(0.006)	(0.034)	(0.006)	(0.006)	(0.034)
Child labor	0.032***	−0.006	0.138***	0.035***	−0.008	0.153***
	(0.007)	(0.008)	(0.041)	(0.006)	(0.007)	(0.037)
Diffusion	0.000	0.062***	0.198*	−0.001	0.060***	0.184
	(0.022)	(0.021)	(0.119)	(0.022)	(0.021)	(0.117)
Constant	−5.591***	0.443	−28.380***	−5.965***	0.521	−30.342***
	(0.904)	(0.690)	(4.791)	(0.876)	(0.648)	(4.649)
Observations	320	320	320	320	320	320
R-squared	0.558	0.374	0.575	0.565	0.361	0.585
Country-fixed effects	yes	yes	yes	yes	yes	yes

Robust standard errors in parentheses.
*** $p < 0.01$, ** $p < 0.05$, * $p < 0.1$.

Explaining Policy Adoption and Design

TABLE 4.4 *Regression Discontinuity Design*

	Descriptive Statistics (±3% Around Threshold)		
	(1)	(2)	(3)
	President's Share in Congress:		
	Below 50%	Above 50%	Difference
	Panel A: Baseline characteristics		
Left	0.36	0.42	−0.06
			(0.10)
GDP per capita	3.27	3.45	−0.18
			(0.47)
Openness	76.03	78.73	−2.69
			(8.68)
Inflation (log)	2.42	2.44	−0.02
			(0.21)
Population (log)	2.59	1.86	0.72
			(0.27)***
Deindustrialization	69.03	69.24	−0.20
			(1.71)
Child labor	8.58	9.93	−1.34
			(1.19)
	Panel B: Outcomes		
CCT above mean	0.35	0.08	0.27
			(0.076)***
CCT below mean	0.026	0.11	−0.08
			(0.055)†
Design score	2.1	0.85	1.2
			(0.453)***

***$p < 0.01$, **$p < 0.05$, *$p < 0.1$, †$p < 0.05$ in one-sided test.

imbalance, however, could be due to chance. Panel A of Table 4.4 contains these descriptive statistics. Because baseline characteristics are balanced close to the 50 percent cutoff, then differences in policy outcomes between the group below and above the cutoff can be attributed to whether or not presidents control the majority of congress.

If RDD estimates recover the relationships from previous estimations, then the argument that opposition to presidential powers stemming from congress leads to presidents tying their hands with respect to fighting poverty is on solid ground. The simplest and most transparent way to analyze the RDD is to compute, using observations that are in a small window around the key threshold, the difference in outcomes between the group that is below and above the cutoff (Dunning 2012). In the bandwidth of ±3 percent around the 50 percent cutoff, presidents who had fewer than 50 percent of seats in congress were 27 percentage points more likely to adopt a CCT above mean (this difference is statistically significant at the 1 percent level), 8 percentage points less likely to adopt a CCT below mean (this difference is marginally statistically significant in a two-sided test, but it is statistically significant at the 5 percent level on a one-sided test), and their programs had a design score 1.2 points higher than those of presidents who had more than 50 percent of seats (statistically significant at the 1 percent level). These simple differences in means show that legislative resistance to the president leads to programs with more stringent policy designs.

The advantage of difference-in-means analysis is its transparency. Yet, to assess the robustness of the findings, I now estimate two regression models for each dependent variable using the same observations in the ±3 percent window around the 50 percent cutoff. In the first model, I include country-fixed effects. In the second model, in addition to the country-fixed effects I add a control for population, which is unbalanced. Consistent with previous results, when the president's party controls 50 percent or more of seats in congress, CCTs with above-average design scores are less likely to be adopted, CCTs with below-average design scores are more likely to be adopted, and, overall, the design score of programs is lower (see Table 4.5). These results remain stable even when population is included in the models. Also, the estimates are statistically significant in five of the six models, which is remarkable given that the number of observations in the window of ±3 percent around the threshold decreases sharply.[4]

In sum, results from various statistical analysis are consistent with this book's argument. Whereas executives who face a friendly legislature adopt CCT programs with less strict operational rules, presidents who do not control the legislature and do face opposition in congress adopt more exhaustive operational rules that provide protections against political manipulation. The following case studies further show the plausibility of the argument.

CONDITIONAL CASH TRANSFERS IN PARLIAMENTARY DEBATES

When debating how to respond to the economic downturn, legislators throughout the region expressed concern about increasing total public expenditure, public debt ceilings, taxes, and reducing the benefits of organized interest groups. Ultimately, there were three common avenues to fund CCT programs. Several governments shifted resources from previous programs, especially generalized food subsidies, toward cash transfer programs. In addition, many countries eased the budgetary pressure of extending policy concessions to the

---

[4] An additional way to analyze RDD data is to estimate global polynomial regressions, which defines the quantity of interest as the limit of a regression function at the regression-discontinuity threshold. Global polynimial regressions include observations that are further away from the RDD threshold in the estimation. This makes groups on each side of the threshold less comparable to each other. Moreover, the accuracy of such analysis is highly dependent on the model (Green et al. 2009)

TABLE 4.5 *Effects of President's Party Legislative Majority on the Adoption of an Above-Average CCT, a Below-Average CCT, and Design Score*

	Regression Discontinuity Design (±3% Around Threshold)					
	CCT Above Mean		CCT Below Mean		Design Score	
	(1)	(2)	(3)	(4)	(5)	(6)
Above 50% (majority)	−0.358***	−0.375***	0.159	0.224***	−1.627***	−1.360***
	(0.089)	(0.099)	(0.106)	(0.083)	(0.440)	(0.429)
Population (log)		0.365		−0.370		1.994
		(0.655)		(0.388)		(3.231)
Constant	0.408***	−0.356	−0.017	0.718	2.332***	−2.139
	(0.063)	(1.423)	(0.069)	(0.840)	(0.340)	(6.953)
Observations	100	97	100	97	100	97
R-squared	0.622	0.644	0.365	0.440	0.717	0.722
Country-fixed effects	yes	yes	yes	yes	yes	yes

Robust standard errors in parentheses.
***p < 0.01, **p < 0.05, *p < 0.1.

informal sector by accepting loans from international agencies to finance part of the operations of cash transfer programs. Finally, in a few countries with profitable national oil industries, the funding of CCTs came from oil revenues. Thus, compared to pensions, CCT programs were a lighter fiscal burden.

In contrast to the expansion of welfare programs in Latin America from 1950 to 1980, which generally took the form of entitlement legislations (Haggard and Kaufman 2008), most countries denied cash transfers the status of entitlements.[5] Entitlements require a commitment from government to maintain a minimum number of beneficiaries and commit to providing benefits for a predetermined number of years (Romer 1996). Entitlements are complex policies because their budgets depend on program coverage, and coverage in any given year is uncertain because it depends on the demand for the program. Legislators tend to have less of the information and expertise required to assess the budgetary requirements of entitlements, which makes congress more hesitant to grant entitlement status to policies. Moreover, entitlements are hard to modify even if programs are under financial pressure.

Budgetary complexity is the likely reason cash transfers were not legislated as entitlements. Instead, cash transfer programs' coverage depends on federal budgets, and in all countries in Latin America, federal budgets are reviewed by legislators on a yearly basis. Thus, cash transfers' fiscal appeal together with their non-entitlement status lowered the stakes of the political negotiations in countries across the region.

Even programs that aim to compensate poor households for the elimination of generalized subsidies were not legislated as entitlements. For example, Mahuad's *Bono Solidario* was a transfer that aimed to reach the population that suffered most as a result of the austerity measures undertaken by the government. However, the decree that stipulates the creation of the program also establishes a ceiling for the program's budget and explicitly states that the number of program recipients will be determined by this ceiling.[6]

In addition to fiscal concerns, transcripts from parliamentary debates in the five countries under study show concerns about policy design, agency structure, and the effects of CCT programs on elections. Legislators from the incumbent party in these five countries were concerned with losing control over their programs, and legislators from the opposition throughout the five countries worried that CCTs were ultimately an electoral strategy.

Mexico

Reflecting on the administration of President Zedillo, during which *Progresa* was designed and first implemented, Luis Rubio, chairman of the Center

---

[5] The few exceptions to this trend are Ecuador's *Bono de Desarrollo Humano* and the short-lived *Proyecto* 300 in Uruguay.
[6] Decree 1186, art. 11, 1999.

of Research for Development, an independent Mexican research institution, writes: "From the outset of his term, Zedillo redefined the role of the presidency ... he relinquished extra-constitutional roles that had been adopted by all his predecessors, such as leadership of the [PRI] party and head of the national political class ... he called for a sweeping reform of the judiciary and the Supreme Court ... and he announced that he would maintain a "healthy distance" from the PRI and would refrain from intervening in the selection of his successor" (Rubio-Freidberg 1998, 14). With these decisions, President Zedillo furthered the democratic transition of the country. Yet PRI members, especially those from the old guard of the party, were President Zedillo's strongest critics (Rubio-Freidberg 1998, 18). President Zedillo's reforms, including the social sector reform, faced resistance from both his party, the PRI, and opposition parties.

In the following paragraphs, I explore the origins of the Mexican CCT, with special attention to the interactions of the executive and legislative branches of government. The changing balance of power among political parties in the Mexican congress, and its effect on policymaking, has not gone unnoticed. Díaz-Cayeros, Estévez, and Magaloni (2007) and Dion (2010), for example, highlight that the presence of multiple veto players in congress since 1997 has contributed to the expansion of social assistance. In this section, I further these insights and show that policymakers included provisions in the design of *Progresa* that limited the discretion of the executive and insulated the program from political pressures as a tactic to overcome multipartisan political resistance.

President Zedillo's administration began in December 1994 at the onset of a profound economic crisis. During 1995, the first year of the *Tequila crisis*, consumption fell approximately 10 percent in real terms, private investment contracted 30 percent, and inflation rose to 52 percent (World Bank 2001). More than 16 million people fell into poverty. Political instability and an indigenous rebellion, which began in the state of Chiapas in January 1994, aggravated the country's economic situation.

An innovative policy response was of paramount importance. Welfare programs at the time were indisputably inappropriate to deal with the crisis. In the mid-1990s, Mexico's federal government ran fifteen food subsidy programs: four were generalized and eleven were targeted at different urban and rural populations. These programs were operated by ten distinct ministries or agencies (Levy 2006). Despite the concentration of poverty in rural areas, 75 percent of the total budget for social assistance was funneled to urban areas. Santiago Levy, one of the architects of *Progresa* noted that "over half of the total budget was absorbed by the generalized bread and tortilla subsidies in the urban areas, where most of the income transfer was captured by non-poor households ... close to sixty percent of all poor rural families received no food support at all from government" (Levy 2006, 5–6). Moreover, the flagship community development program of the previous administration, PRONASOL, was deemed ineffective at reaching the extremely poor (Trejo and Jones 1998), and prone to inefficiencies associated with its political manipulation (Acedo Angulo and Ruiz Suárez 1995; Bruhn 1996; Dresser 1991; Kaufman and Trejo 1997; Molinar and Weldon 1994; Pérez Yarahuán 2005).

President Zedillo instructed the then general secretary of the National Population Council (CONAPO), José Gómez de León, to craft a policy to improve the education of poor children through direct transfers to their mothers. In parallel, Santiago Levy, then undersecretary of expenditure at the Ministry of Finance, headed the design of a cash transfer program, which was meant to target poor families, recipients of previous in-kind food subsidies, and to condition resources to attendance to health centers (Yaschine and Orozco 2010). Making receipt of transfers contingent on poor people's investments in their own nutrition and health was meant to distinguish this new program from previous paternalists policies (Levy 2006). José Gómez de León, an established scientist, and Santiago Levy, a recognized economist, had the unconditional support of President Zedillo. Moreover, Santiago Levy, from the Ministry of Finance, led the reallocation of resources from inefficient food subsidies, especially the tortilla subsidy, to *Progresa*. Still, from the onset, program designers expected resistance to the new program from within the PRI and the opposition. Thus, efforts were made to produce evidence to defend the program.[7]

The first pilot of the Mexican CCT program was carried out from August to October 1995 in the state of Campeche, located in the southeastern region of Mexico, quite far from Mexico City. According to Santiago Levy, program designers concealed the pilot as much as possible and elicited the discretion of Campeche's governor by offering funds for a new highway.[8] Santiago Levy explained that their intention with the pilot study was "to be ready with numbers when the time came to convince people."[9,10]

During the negotiations surrounding the federal budget of 1997, when the CCT was first discussed in congress, legislators from the governing party (PRI) were initially under the mistaken idea that the program, at the time called Program for Nutrition, Health, and Education (PASE for its acronym in Spanish), would consist of decentralized disbursements for scholarships and subsidies to the health sector. A PRI legislator summarized the budget discussion in these terms: "Fellow congressmen: the public budget for 1997 has been discussed at length in the committee. The most relevant aspect are...the budget has a social intention; fifty-six cents of each peso will be allocated to social

---

[7] Author's interview with Santiago Levy, Mexico City, August 2005.
[8] Author's interviews with Santiago Levy and Daniel Hernández, Mexico City, August 2005.
[9] Author's interview with Santiago Levy, Mexico City, August 2005.
[10] In contrast, PRONASOL's administrator, Carlos Rojas, noted that, although his program had multiple standardized processes to deliver program benefits, his unit did not document any of them. PRONASOL was operated at a time when the PRI controlled both the executive and legislative, and the president had support from his party in congress. Carlos Rojas, in hindsight, believes that proper documentation would have helped the program. (Author's interview with Carlos Rojas, Mexico City, August 2005.)

Explaining Policy Adoption and Design

development... Also, for the first time [the budget] presents programs that target subsidies to a specific population group. This is the case of PASE... this program promotes a more decentralized social policy oriented to the most vulnerable groups."[11]

Objections from PRI legislators increased when it became evident that the CCT was a centralized program aimed to invest in the demand for health and education, as opposed to the supply of such public services. PRI legislators wanted to know with greater certainty who was responsible for administering program funds. They demanded the decentralization of program resources, and, in a surprising turn of events, they demanded more transparency in the allocation of resources. One PRI legislator stated: "We are not satisfied with the process of decentralization of the budget; in particular we need to make the funneling of resources for basic education more transparent. We should build and consolidate a Social Comptroller. Likewise, a challenge we need to face, considering the sovereignty of the states, is the decentralization and effectiveness of public expenditures in the municipalities, which is the level of government closest to citizens."[12]

Opposition parties opposed the 1997 federal budget because, among other reasons, they believed that the resources of the antipoverty program were used in inefficient and clientelistic ways. They demanded the elimination of the president's discretion in the allocation of social policy resources. A PRD legislator explained his party's objections to the program by saying: "Minister [of Finance], we think that this program cannot be serious, is a new electoral program, is a substitute for PRONASOL to win votes in 1997, but it will not solve the problem of poverty."[13]

The right-wing PAN also objected to the 1997 federal budget and the CCT on the ground that the program was centralized. The right-wing legislative bloc proposed that federal money should be distributed to the states following a concrete formula, and that resources should be spent on the supply side of the education sector such as increasing the number of teachers in the most impoverished areas.[14] Despite criticism from all parties to the poverty relief program, the still PRI-controlled congress approved the 1997 federal budget.

In the 1997 legislative elections, the PRI lost control of the majority of the Lower House on Congress. Thus, President Zedillo presented the 1998 federal budget to the Lower House, which for the first time in decades was no longer under the control of the PRI. The atmosphere was polarized.

By this time, the CCT program had been renamed *Progresa*. Legislators from the PRI again demanded more information about the program and the president's plan for its evolution.[15]

---

[11] Parliamentary debates 41, 12/11/1996.
[12] Parliamentary debates 41 12/11/1996.
[13] Parliamentary debates 28, 11/15/1996.
[14] Parliamentary debates 41, 12/11/1996.
[15] Parliamentary debates 7, 9/11/1997.

The Minister of Finance explained in a congressional session:

> I will answer the specific question about *Progresa* [for the years of 1997 and 1998]. Because the program is comprehensive and it has procedures for the selection of the target population, we have planned to move forward in a prudent but steady way with this program. As I mentioned, this program initiated its first phase with an enrollment of 160 thousand families, and we are planning to reach 400 thousand families toward the end of the fiscal year. If we observe satisfactory results over the coming months regarding the processes to select recipients and the mechanisms to deliver the components of the program, we will propose to this Lower House of Congress that for next year, *Progresa* continues its enrollment in other states in the Republic to incorporate a larger number of families living in extreme poverty... I should highlight that in the successive phases of the program, we will continue to carry out the selection of states and localities based on objective indicators of the location of poverty. This selection is independent of political considerations or discretional choices. This program has been designed with mechanisms that allow us to identify and verify that recipient communities and families are in fact living in extreme poverty. If this program is successful, then our objective is to gradually replace various subsidies that are now directed in an isolated way to poor families.[16]

During the negotiations of the 1998 federal budget, PRI legislators tried to protect the funding for previous programs that benefited the party strongholds. One PRI legislator said in a congressional session: "The PRI legislative bloc considers that we must increase the budget allocated to the development of rural areas by at least twenty-one percent and we must prioritize resources allocated to [programs such as] alliance for the rural areas, credit without collateral, temporary employment, crop conversion, commercialization and development of agricultural infrastructure among others."[17] Soon after, the party endorsed the PROCAMPO program.[18]

Legislators from opposition parties continued to express their concern that *Progresa* was clientelistic during the discussions surrounding the 1998 federal budget. One PAN legislator explained that his party was against the federal budget proposal because the government "has fostered dependency in a paternalistic way;... in every corner of the country, social programs have been denounced for being used in clientelistic ways for electoral purposes in favor of the incumbent party."[19] A PRD legislator told the minister of finance that his parliamentary group was prepared to use their budgetary powers to block the *Progresa* program. He stated: "Minister, we want to honestly tell you that *Progresa* will not get the approval of this Chamber, it is very difficult what you propose. We advise you to revise this project before the executive sends it to this Lower House of Congress."[20]

---

[16] Parliamentary debates 7, 9/11/1997.
[17] Parliamentary debates 31, 11/19/1997.
[18] Parliamentary debates 39, 12/10/1997.
[19] Parliamentary debates 8, 09/12/1997.
[20] Parliamentary debates 8, 09/12/1997.

Explaining Policy Adoption and Design

A recurring objection to *Progresa* from all parties was its centralized structure. One PAN legislator remarked: "Programs come and programs go. Before it was PRONASOL, now it is *Progresa*, but the mistaken focus has not changed. The programs continue to be centralized because [the government] conceives federalism as the bestowal of resources, but not as the decentralization of decisions and prerogatives."[21] The PAN's proposal during the negotiations over the 1998 federal budget, which was supported by the PRD, was to decentralize all resources allocated to fight poverty, so that municipalities would be responsible for policymaking.[22]

In response to legislators' concerns about the program, the minister of finance explained in a congressional session the potential positive effects of the health component of *Progresa* in the short and medium term, as well as highlighting the fact that the program was targeted to women because they have the most influence in the nutrition of the family.[23] Moreover, the minister explained that in 1995 the government had initiated a process of decentralization of resources to municipalities and had incrementally increased resources to local governments. The minister also explained that unlike previous administrations, the government had established transparent criteria to allocate *Progresa* resources. With respect to this latter point, the minister explained to legislators: "What we need is to guarantee the transparency and equity in the allocation of social expenditures."[24]

The decentralization of a substantial amount of federal resources for Education, Health, and Social Infrastructure was critical to elicit the support of parties for the 1998 federal budget (Díaz-Cayeros et al. 2007). Yet legislators, in particular those from the right-wing party, demanded also that the executive further develop operational guidelines to limit the executive's discretion over the antipoverty program. Legislators from the PAN objected that previous social programs lacked clear objectives and mechanisms to evaluate the effectiveness of the policy. One PAN legislator argued that there was a "need to specify the target of program resources and the operational rules for operating such resources."

The minister of finance explained to congressmen that *Progresa* was not only efficient but would avoid clientelism. He reiterated that *Progresa* was different from previous efforts to fight poverty and stated that *Progresa* "is not a clientelistic program, it is not a program that transfers resources to organizations, or to groups that have been traditionally favored in a political way. This is a program that aims precisely to break with this notion because this is a program that can be audited... the way that resources are distributed,

---

[21] Parliamentary debates 8, 09/12/1997.
[22] More specifically, the PAN proposed to reallocate resources from Ramo 28 to Ramo 26, Parliamentary debates 8, 09/12/1997.
[23] Parliamentary debates 10, 9/18/1997.
[24] Parliamentary debates 8, 09/12/1997.

how things are being done, and the mechanisms to do things can all be audited."[25]

Legislators from the PRI and PAN eventually reached an agreement with the president. Left-wing legislators, however, remained opposed to the CCT program throughout the negotiations of the 1998 budget. PRI legislators approved the federal budget, though not without expressing their discontent. One legislator remarked that: "We will approve the budget decree. Yet, it has to be said that what we have accomplished is not enough"[26] PAN legislators agreed to fund a poverty relief program as long as resources were not funneled only to the strongholds of the incumbent party, and as long as the policy had strong evaluation mechanisms.[27] A PAN legislator who summarized the results of the negotiations stated: "For the first time in the party's legislative history, PAN approves the federal budget. We will insist that the government further strengthen the federal system, and that it further decrease the discretion of the executive, and improve transparency through informing Congress in sufficient and timely ways."[28]

Although the decentralization of other resources played a critical role in the negotiations over the 1998 budget, PAN's approval of the federal budget would have been unlikely had the government only offered to decentralize additional resources to the states. The president designed a policy that tied his hands, and decreased all politicians' discretion over the policy which ultimately helped convince right-wing legislators of the programmatic importance of *Progresa*.[29]

Looking back at the early stages of *Progresa*, three features set it apart from other poverty relief programs in Mexico. First, *Progresa*'s operational rules were from the start explicitly nonpartisan. The program has always had clear and fixed criteria for determining eligibility, so program benefits are not subject to political manipulation. These criteria have been based from the start of the program on a geographical measure of poverty constructed from census data and household income surveys. The program resources and the formula used to allocate them have been described in detail in the federal budget since the first years of program operations. The provisions in the federal budget decree have explicitly prohibited the use of the program by any political party. Since 1998, all documents, materials, and forms that program beneficiaries receive are required to include the following text:

We remind you that your participation in *Progresa* and receipt of benefits are in no way contingent upon affiliation with any specific political party or voting for any specific candidate running for public office. No candidate is authorized to grant or withhold

---

[25] Parliamentary debates 31, 11/19/1997.
[26] Parliamentary debates 42, 12/13/1997.
[27] Parliamentary debates 31, 11/19/1997.
[28] Parliamentary debates 42, 12/13/1997.
[29] See Chapter 6 in this book and Maldonado Trujillo (2012) for more details on how program rules limited the discretion of local politicians.

benefits under the program. Eligible beneficiary families will receive support if they show up for their doctor's visits and health education talks and if their children attend school regularly. Any person, organization, or public servant that makes undue use of program resources will be reported to the appropriate authority and prosecuted under applicable legislation. (Levy's translation 2006: 107)

Second, *Progresa* was insulated from the executive's temptation to disproportionately increase the list of beneficiaries close to election time. Although the program was ready to launch in January 1997, its operation was delayed until August, one month after the midterm elections of that year.[30] This practice was codified into law by including in the budget bills a prohibition to enroll new beneficiaries in the program in the six months before an election.

Third, an independent evaluation of *Progresa* was conducted in the early stages of the program. It was the first social policy in Mexico rigorously evaluated, and the evaluation was designed and implemented in collaboration with the International Food Policy Research Institute (IFPRI).

Regarding the agency in charge of the program, *Progresa* was first designed, and then assigned a place in the federal bureaucracy.[31] To administer *Progresa*, a new autonomous agency was created within the Ministry of Social Development. This agency is in charge of the implementation of the program all the way down to delivering cash transfers to beneficiaries. The program circumvents intermediaries, including traditional and powerful mechanisms of federal resource distribution, such as governors, and the state-level bureaucracy of the Ministry of Social Development.

Although the program had rules from its conception, President Zedillo maintained bureaucratic control over the agency. He was in charge of unilaterally appointing the director of the agency, and a committee to oversee the program was also set up comprising representatives from the ministries of Education, Health, and Social Development. All ministers are appointed directly by the president without ratification from congress. For the initial years of program operations, the president appointed a scientist as director of the agency. This contrasts with programs operated in previous administrations that were administered by prominent politicians.[32]

In sum, resistance by politicians from all parties to the president's antipoverty policy led the president to design a cash transfer program with rules that included ex-ante and ex-post controls on the bureaucracy. In addition to the program design, the incentives of the new bureaucracy were further shaped

---

[30] Author's interview with program designer's, Mexico City, August 2005.
[31] Author's interview with program designers, Mexico City, august 2005.
[32] The first coordinator of Progresa, Gómez de León, was trained as a demographer at the Catholic University of Leuven, Harvard University, and Princeton University. Before coordinating *Progresa*, he had been the Director of the Mexican Population Council (Conapo) and had coordinated the Department of Demography of the Center for Economic and Demographic Studies at the Colegio de Mexico.

by a decree establishing that using *Progresa* or any other social program for political reasons is a federal offense. Legislators from all parties were skeptical about the program, but ultimately decided not to block the program's budget. This outcome would have been unlikely had the program's design excluded provisions to limit the executive's discretion.

Colombia

In Colombia, SISBEN I, the first targeting mechanism used to select program recipients of various social assistance programs, was notorious for its political manipulation. The system was established under the administration of President Ernesto Samper, who served from 1994 to 1998 and faced fewer institutional checks from congress than any other president during the period under study in this book.[33] President Pastrana, who succeeded President Samper, faced a very different political and institutional configuration characterized by the presence of greater institutional checks on his power.[34] President Pastrana commissioned an independent evaluation of the targeting system, in part because he faced greater checks from legislators.

The evaluation confirmed that SISBEN I had been manipulated by staff in charge of conducting the census interviews to determine eligibility for various social programs. The evaluation also detected systematic underreporting of people's incomes by people themselves, and opportunistic manipulation by staff of the timing of the interviews.[35] The evaluators of SISBEN I concluded that the system needed reforms. They recommended pilot projects to test new targeting instruments and standardization of procedures, as well as a permanent process of monitoring of the new targeting system to ensure the quality and accuracy of the information and promote efficiency in identifying the poorest households in the population.[36]

In 2000, shortly after the evaluation results of SISBEN I were made available, President Pastrana launched the Colombian CCT program *Familias en Acción* as part of the peace-building program called *Plan Colombia*. In its early years of operations, the *Familias en Acción* program was fairly small. The program was first evaluated in 2002 by a team composed of representatives of national and international agencies including the International Monetary Fund, the World Bank, the Inter-American Development Bank, and the Institute for Fiscal Studies.

In 2003, Alvaro Uribe was elected president, and he continued program operations. President Uribe split from the Liberal Party when the party denied

---

[33] The World Bank data on political institutions records a value of 2 for this period. President Samper is probably best known for his involvement in a scandal surrounding the flow of drug cartel money to his presidential campaign.
[34] In the WB data checks increase from 2 in 1998 to 5 in 1999.
[35] CONPES Social 055, 2001.
[36] CONPES Social 055, 2001.

Explaining Policy Adoption and Design 81

him the presidential nomination and ran as an independent candidate in the 2003 elections. As a consequence, the president lacked support of most legislators, including those of the Liberal Party.[37] Among Colombian commentators, there was a great deal of speculation about the alignment of various parties and movements in the legislature. Neither the Liberal Party, with 32.5 percent of the seats, nor the Conservative Party with 12.7 percent of the seats, had a clear majority. In addition to legislators from these two traditional parties, congress was populated by legislators from numerous movements and political parties, as well as independents. The fractionalization of parties in congress was a direct result of a 2002 electoral law that allowed political parties to subscribe to multiple lists for a single seat, and allowed the registration of independent candidates for congress.[38] Thus, even if President Uribe had not run as an independent candidate, he would not have had a majority of support in congress.[39]

In 2003, congress legislated that the executive government was responsible for the design and elaboration of budget indicators that enabled legislators to evaluate and control the implementation of the CCT program.[40] The law specified that three members of the economic committees in each chamber of congress would be responsible for this evaluation.

President Uribe's administration was responsive to the congressional mandate. Government accountability, efficiency, and the development of the poorest areas of Colombia were a central part of Uribe's national development plan during his first term.[41] To make the targeting system of social assistance more transparent, the president replaced the old SISBEN I with a new targeting mechanism called SISBEN II. The new targeting system used a different questionnaire and a new scoring algorithm to select the households eligible for the *Familias en Acción* program. The algorithm has been kept secret to prevent the manipulation of the system (Camacho and Conover 2011). The government

---

[37] In fact, the World Bank data set codes checks during the period between 2002 and 2010 as missing value.
[38] For the 2002 elections, for example, 227 lists of candidates were registered to compete for 102 seats in the Senate, and a similar situation occurred with respect to the Lower House of Congress.
[39] Despite the fractionalization of parties and political movements represented in Congress, the 2002 legislature produced important political legislation. In 2003, congress reformed the electoral law to decrease the number of parties in congress. The reform increased the threshold for party registration to 2 percent of the vote, restricted parties from splitting lists, and prohibited independent candidates. Moreover, this legislature reformed the constitution to allow President Uribe to run for reelection. This reform led some commentators to characterize the legislature as Uribinista. Yet, this ex-post judgment ignores the negotiations that the president undertook to pursue his political and policy goals. Although it is hard to assess the support that President Uribe had during his two terms, institutional checks throughout his presidency remained relatively high. In the World Bank data, the checks to presidential powers variable is coded as 4 during Uribe's administrations.
[40] Law 812, approved on June 26, 2003.
[41] See: "*Hacia un Estado Comunitario*," Plan Nacional de Desarrollo, 2003–2006.

also set guidelines to limit conducting eligibility interviews or assigning social benefits in periods leading up to an election. Thus, the system of targeting in Colombia has limited opportunities for political manipulation.[42]

President Uribe expanded the coverage of *Familias en Acción* during his second term using the new and more transparent targeting mechanism. In preparation for the program expansion, the operational rules of the program included additional ex-post mechanisms of control of the agency in charge of program operations, such as random spot checks of various program operations. However, the president kept bureaucratic control over the agency because appointment decisions remained a prerogative of the executive. An evaluator of the program concluded that *Familias en Acción* produced overall positive effects on the health and education outcomes of beneficiaries; however, the evaluation suggested that the program needed to get some distance from the president.[43] Given the president's bureaucratic control over the program, the operational rules of the program, including the mechanisms to tie the president's hands, played a more political role than just controlling bureaucratic drift. The rules were there to appease the opposition.

Peru

In Peru, President Toledo underestimated the chances that a congress controlled by the opposition would refuse to finance his first policy choice with respect to a CCT program. The initial policy proposal, designed in 2005, involved cash disbursements to families living in extreme poverty with the condition that children attend school regularly and that children and pregnant women regularly access health services. This design of this initial proposal did not include provisions to reduce the executive's discretion. As a consequence, legislators refused to fund the original policy. The president revised the design of his policy, and ultimately congress approved the budget for the program. In the following paragraphs, I review this political process.

In February 2005, President Toledo announced his intentions to launch the *Plan Pro-Peru* after program details were leaked to the press by political opponents. Accusations that the president was preparing a vote-buying strategy for the upcoming 2006 presidential election tainted the perceptions of the program. Many politicians saw the launch of the program as a political maneuver by Toledo's party to regain popularity. Lourdes Flores and Alan García, presidential candidates in the 2006 election, claimed the program was being used as an electoral strategy. García's critique focused on the program's lack of a planning process, and Flores questioned whether the government was

---

[42] Camacho and Conover (2011) find that there is still room for improvement in terms of detection of cheaters and restricting the selection of households eligible to programs to non-electoral periods.

[43] *Camino Recorrido.*

Explaining Policy Adoption and Design

making sufficient effort to ensure that the program resources were reaching those most in need of social assistance.

One congressman succinctly expressed the position of legislators in Congress during the time leading up the elections:

We do not question the need to implement large-scale social programs like *Pro-Peru*, but we are concerned with the nature of the policy proposal and its technical viability. An improvised policy so close to the next electoral process means that thousands of millions of soles will be wasted... the poor cannot wait any longer and they need the State's assistance until the economy is able to guarantee them employment and an adequate income. But this does not mean that we will allow the government to use the poor as an excuse to return to clientelist practices. We all have the responsibility to ensure that this initiative works, but we need to oversee it permanently.[44]

In March 2005, congress solicited the presence of state-officials involved in the design of the program, including the Ministers of Economy, Health, and Women and Social Development, at a series of hearings to discuss program characteristics and its budget. During their presentations, the ministers were elusive about the program's design and the geographic areas that the program would cover. Indeed, ministers were hesitant even to defend the name of the program, *Pro-Peru*.

The president of the Council of Ministers explained in a press conference when pressed by reporters to talk about the program:

The program is not finished. Today we spent more than an hour studying the proposal [in the session of the council of ministers], and when completed the program will be announced in detail to the country... We are not crafting something new. It has been mentioned that programs exist in Brazil, Mexico, and other countries. Everything will be done in a transparent way, and the resources for the program, since they are additional expenditures, will have to go through Congress, and Congress will make the modifications that are considered appropriate. Here [in this administration] nothing will be imposed without the necessary information. We plan to implement it in May not in February. We are collecting information to make sure that the beneficiaries are the poorest because in Peru there are many poor, and most likely we will not reach all of the poor, but at least the poorest of the poor. So, that is where we are. The program is not finalized, is being discussed internally, and we greatly appreciate receiving suggestions of any kind. Today, in a survey that will hopefully be disseminated by journalists, fifty-eight percent of Peruvians supported the proposal of a social assistance program. Fifty-eight percent is high, considering those who did not express an opinion. Now, as you know, polls are not the absolute truth, but you have to use them when you like them and when you do not... So I think it is interesting to know the support [social assistance] already has. Almost sixty percent of the population say they are in favor of social aid to the needy.[45]

---

[44] http://www.congreso.gob.pe/congresista/2006/jperalta/Art-Opinion/0023.htm
[45] Press conference following the session of the Council of Ministers No.263, *Presidencia del Consejo de Ministros*, February 15, 2005.

On April 7th, 2005, the president signed a decree that created the National Program of Direct Assistance to the Poorest, or *Juntos*, Peru's first CCT program.[46] Legislators' objections, however, continued. Congressmen from the American Popular Revolutionary Alliance (APRA) publicly refused to approve the federal budget for the program. One congressman stated that "the government is improvising, and pulling an ace from its sleeve. The program has no structure, has clear electoral purposes, and is not sustainable."[47] A congresswoman explicitly demanded a "transparent social policy that guarantees that the program is treated as a pilot project ... and is further operated only after evaluating its results based on census data."[48]

The push-back from legislators was not in vain. As a first concession, the president changed the name of the program from *Plan Pro-Peru*, which was similar to the name of the president's party, to *Juntos*. To boost support for the newly named program, the president presented it as the government's flagship program to achieve the Millennium Goals. It was clear that the president and his staff were taking legislators' concerns into consideration. The President of the Council of Ministers explained that "in a democratic regime each [branch of government] plays a role ... This is called balance of powers. We, in a democracy, have to accept it, and it does not bother us. On the contrary, we have articulated our actions taking this into consideration. I have repeated numerous times that in the previous fifty years, each time the president lost the majority in Congress, there was a coup. This is the first time in fifty years that a democratic and legitimate government has been sustained with an opposing parliament. The first time ... What does this mean? That Peruvians have to get used to a parliament where the executive has no majority. We need to keep the system because that is the mandate of the people."[49]

The change in the program's name and the alignment of the program with the Millennium Goals were insufficient to take the program off the agenda in congress. Some of the concerns that legislators expressed in plenary sessions related to the program's budget. For example, a legislator from the opposition demanded that the federal budget include specific line items that allowed congress to identify the allocation of transfers, with particular attention to "*Pro-Peru* or *Juntos*, or however they call it now, which could show signs of corruption."[50] Meanwhile, a congressman from National Unity said that his party would not vote in favor of the budget because "it was irresponsible to

---

[46] Supreme Decree No. 032-2005-PCM.
[47] "*APRA no aprobará la partida de programa social Juntos.*" La República, June 06 2005. http://www.larepublica.pe/06-06-2005/apra-no-aprobara-la-partida-de-programa-social-juntos
[48] Anti-corruption Blog, July 27, 2005 (Transparecia julio2005.pdf).
[49] Press conference following the session of the Council of Ministers No. 263, *Presidencia del Consejo de Ministros*. February 15, 2005.
[50] Parliament debates, April 21, 2005.

Explaining Policy Adoption and Design

begin to give away money without having a well-defined program, a list of eligible households, the budget, and a definition of program objectives"[51]

Other concerns expressed by legislators related to the criteria to select program recipients. A legislator from APRA expressed a concern that without a census of the poor, it was likely that the allocation of resources through *Juntos* would benefit the undeserving.[52] A legislator from Popular Action (PAP) shared this concern and highlighted a study conducted by the University of the Pacific that suggested massive leakages of benefits to the non-poor in the operation of the subsidy for milk.[53]

To appease some of these concerns, the president of the Council of Ministers presented legislators with a more detailed account of the *Juntos* program, including a description of its targeting system and its scope, in May 2005. He also notified legislators that the executive intended to ask congress to approve a credit to finance part of the program's operations.[54] Nevertheless, legislators were hesitant to approve the budget and the additional funding.

A legislator representing a coalition of opposition parties explained his position to the president of the Council of Ministers by stating: "The relevant question is what will be done with 120 million new *soles* from now until the end of the year? There is no formal proposal, or pilot project, or implementation rules ... [the program] can be operated to win an electoral audience. This is why we propose not to block an efficient program like the ones implemented in so many other countries, rather we want a pilot project that cannot be politically manipulated. Therefore, we must limit the resources of the program. I say no to the 140 million that the government wants, but yes to 60 million from now until the end of the year."[55] Negotiations over the funding delayed the launch of the program.

Lack of resources was not the reason why legislators from opposition parties hesitated to approve the program's budget. As explicitly mentioned by a legislator of CP: "The problem with *Juntos* is not if there is money or not, it is of action. When surveyors go to Chuschi to set up the pilot they will enroll their families, or teachers will enroll their wives. This is the real problem."[56]

---

[51] "APRA no aprobará la partida de programa social Juntos." *La República*, June 06 2005. http://www.larepublica.pe/06-06-2005/apra-no-aprobara-la-partida-de-programa-social-juntos. A few congressmen presented alternative policies to improve the living conditions of the poor. For example, a congressman from *Concertación Parlamentaria* proposed to use the cash transfer money to provide potable water to the poor (*"Financiamiento de Juntos no sería aprobado, advierten." La República*, June 19, 2005. http://www.larepublica.pe/19-06-2005/financiamiento-de-juntos-no-seria-aprobado-advierten).
[52] Parliament debates, April 28, 2005.
[53] Parliamentary debates, June 23, 2005.
[54] Parliament debates, May 11, 2005.
[55] Parliamentary debates, June 23, 2005.
[56] Parliamentary debates, June 23, 2005.

Legislators from the opposition wanted guarantees that the president would not politicize the program. They proposed that the program should circumvent the agency in charge of previous social programs, which was known for its inefficiency and its politically motivated leakages of program resources. Legislators also proposed that the president take more time to prepare the details of program implementation, and that the scale-up of the program should be delayed until after the presidential elections.[57] A final proposal from legislators was the creation of a transparency committee to oversee the implementation of the program.[58]

The political turbulence over the program's budget motivated the president to strengthen the design of the program, as well as create the board of transparency, which incorporated representatives from various social sectors, including members of the church.[59] Legislators from the incumbent federal party sided with the president. One such legislator stated: "It hurts to be told that we work with electoral goals in mind. We are not like the governments of the past that financed assistance programs to do politics and, like some say, bring water to their well. We are a new party, with quality, decency, and we want to govern in conjunction with all other political parties."[60] Legislators from the president's party argued that the administration "does not intend to do politics with this program, and what has been proposed is that the transparency board oversees the implementation. Certainly, this congress also has to oversee the program so that the money is not used to fund proselytism. But to say that congress, having the money, will not help the poorest sectors is a mistake."[61]

Legislators from the president's party also argued that in addition to the transparency committee, the fact that the program was conditional on achievements in health and schooling would ensure that overseeing the program was not a problem.[62] After provisions had been incorporated into the program design, congress finally approved the budget to fund program operations.

During his presidential address to congress on July 28th 2005, President Toledo formally presented the program to legislators. He highlighted three features of *Juntos*. First, he stated that the program aimed to reach Peruvians living in extreme poverty and to provide them with basic health, nutrition, and

---

[57] Concerns with electoral business cycles were explicitly mentioned in congress. For example, one congressman stated: "Other countries have been successful because they set aside the bureaucracy that makes social programs inefficient and slow. We question the improvisation, and above all that they want to execute the program in their last year of government, when they are about to leave" (parliamentary debates, September 1, 2005).

[58] Congresswoman Anel Townsend from Political Party Democracy was active in this process. She suggested a national agreement to prevent the political use of the program.

[59] Parliamentary debates, June 23, August 25, and September 1.

[60] Parliamentary debates, June 23, 2005.

[61] Parliament debates, August 25, 2005

[62] Parliament debates, August 25, 2005.

education services through the provision of cash incentives. He also noted that the program was intended to help people in areas that had previously been affected by the violence of Shining Path to obtain identification cards, which he argued was a right in itself.[63] Second, the president restated the program budget requirements and the plan to scale up the coverage. Finally, the president reiterated the creation of the Transparency Committee and thanked Archbishop Luis Bambarén, a leader of the campaign against the program, for accepting the position of chair of the board. To further demonstrate his commitment to transparency, the president vowed to make the lists of program recipients available in churches, public schools, and medical centers.[64]

The program was inaugurated in the district of Chuschi (Ayacucho) in September of 2005. The ceremony was led by President Toledo and three cabinet ministers, as well as the director of the program and representatives from the United Nations Development Program. Chuschi was chosen because of its significance as the place where the Shining Path committed its first terrorist act in 1980. After the ceremony, Archbishop Bambarén announced that "the social assistance program, *Juntos*, will not be politicized... it is not just distributing money to the people; we are remembering the poor in Peru." He also suggested that opponents of the program become better informed, and urged beneficiaries to comply with the school and health requirements. Finally, he highlighted that the program had a rigorous selection process, which prioritized areas most affected by violence.[65] In the first phases of the program, enrollment took place in the seventy poorest rural districts in Peru in four different regions.[66]

Directly after the inauguration event, legislators from the president's party continued to defend the program against criticism from opponents of *Juntos*. In one plenary session, a legislator in favor of the program stated: "When it is about peasants and indigenous communities, there is never support for them [in congress], even if we always talk about the poor... We, legislators, need to worry about oversight, and ensuring that resources are reaching the poorest of the poor. It shouldn't be so easy to disqualify the program as politicized, unless you are against *Juntos*. We, the peasant communities, salute the program because our fellow peasants never get anything."[67]

Election day in 2006 came, and APRA's candidate, Alan García, won the presidency. In his first address to Congress, President García announced that austerity was going to distinguish his administration. To illustrate his plans he said: "Austerity will begin with my presidency. I have found more than 400

---

[63] For the effect of cash transfer programs on registration rates, see Hunter and Borges Sugiyama (2011).
[64] Parliamentary Debates, July 28, 2005. The transparency committees were included in the Supreme Decree 062-2005-PCM of August 8th, 2005.
[65] *"Bambarén dice que Juntos no es sólo para repartir dinero" Expreso*, September 8, 2005.
[66] Huancavelica, Ayacucho, Huanuco and Apurimac.
[67] Parliament debates, November 24, 2005.

employees, in addition to security personnel. I will reduce them by half. Fifteen million have been spent on furniture and rugs, but with that amount of money we could have financed assistance through *Juntos* to cover 14,000 families during a year. There has been no priority on social spending. Poverty relief programs need to be integrated to avoid duplication and inefficiencies. We will coordinate the existing 122 programs, and will improve the allocation of the milk subsidy. Similarly, we will improve the processes of the cash transfer in *Juntos*, and we will reduce operation and marketing costs."[68]

President García's administration, which was ideologically to the left of the previous administration, modified the language used to describe *Juntos* to emphasize the program's role in promoting children's development and social inclusion. Discussions between the president of the Council of Ministers and legislators throughout 2006 reflect this change. At one point in a parliamentary debate, the president of the council stated, "We want everyone's commitment to fight for our children against everything that hurts them... The *Juntos* program is adjusting its operation to achieve social inclusion and promote the development of human capacities."[69] Along with the focus on children, the new administration continued to emphasize the nonpartisan nature of the program. When the president of the council announced to legislators that the president planned to expand the program, he reminded congress that "It is our intention, and I emphasize this, that this program will be operated without political criteria. We appreciate the work done by the Transparency Committee, and by its chair Archbishop Luis Bambarén."[70]

Legislators from various parties expressed their support for continuing the funding of the program in 2007 and 2008. One legislator remarked that the *Juntos* program "prevents the State from operating it in a clientelistic way. It has been targeted rigorously, it cannot be manipulated... It is Peru's contribution to the Latin American experience; we want it to continue its success without being politically manipulated. The World Bank, and PNUD continue to believe in it, because it has been operated in a rigorous way."[71] Similarly, a legislator from GPN stated: "We need to guarantee the funding for social programs. We cannot lower the goal for *Juntos* and abandon children to undernourishment. What crime have children committed? The State is responsible for the future of children in Peru."[72]

Despite their continued support, legislators have kept a watchful eye over program operations. Discussions about cutting the program's budget reappear on a yearly basis. In 2005, legislators warned the minister of economy that they were aware that the government was not going to be able to spend the full

---

[68] Parliament Debates, July 28, 2006.
[69] Parliament debates, April 25, 2007.
[70] Parliament debates, August 24, 2006.
[71] Parliament debates, December 6, 2007.
[72] Parliament debates, November 25, 2008.

programmed budget before the end of the year. They also questioned the targeting of the program when they learned from a press report that some recipients saved part of the money. One legislator argued: "Why do we propose cutting *Juntos*'s budget? Because in today's newspaper we read that program recipients are saving the money. Why would a poor person save 100 new soles? Because he is not poor, because he has money... Our proposal is to suspend the program, and redistribute its resources."[73] Three years later, legislators continued to call for government transparency and accountability in the operation of *Juntos*. A legislator from the opposition remarked that *Juntos* "had to be well operated. [The government] say that they need more time for the program's evaluation. Now more than ever, it is our responsibility to demand the evaluation of social programs... We cannot give up our right to demand accountability from those responsible for social programs."[74]

In sum, after the president was willing to tie his hands, legislators agreed to fund the president's policy, but legislators have continued to make clear that they are willing to use their budgetary powers to ensure that the president does not politicize the program.

Guatemala

In Guatemala, the candidate for the National Unity of Hope (UNE) party, Alvaro Colom, won the 2007 presidential elections. The victory of President Colom marked the first time in 53 years that a left-leaning political party occupied the presidency in Guatemala. In the congressional elections, however, UNE won only 48 of 158 seats in congress, so the president did not have a majority of support among legislators.[75]

In 2008, President Colom launched the cash transfer program *Mi Familia Progresa* (MIFAPRO). Although the current design of the program in many ways resembles the design of the Mexican cash transfer program, the original design and operational rules of MIFAPRO included fewer provisions to tie the hands of the president. From its early years of operation, the program has used a targeting system that takes into account feedback from World Bank economists. In addition, the program operations have become more transparent, and the program has been evaluated by both national and international organizations. One of the most important factors in the improvements in program design and implementation is legislative pressure. To illustrate this point, I review a few developments in recent years in the program's operation that are related to agency structure, transparency in the recipient lists, and monitoring of the program.

---

[73] Parliament debates, November 24, 2005.
[74] Parliament debates, March 1, 2008.
[75] Guatemala went through a civil war throughout the 1980s, and a peace agreement was signed by the movement *Unidad Revolucionaria Guatemalteca* in 1996.

Similar to presidents in other countries in Latin America, President Colom maintained bureaucratic control over the agency responsible for operating the cash transfer program. However, the president's desire to exert influence over the cash transfer program was more apparent in Guatemala than in other countries because the president appointed his wife, Sandra Torres de Colom, to coordinate the Council for Social Cohesion, the agency in charge of various social programs, including MIFAPRO. The bureaucratic control of the president and his wife over MIFAPRO fueled criticisms from legislators and civil society alike.

Some legislators stated that the programs operated by the president's wife in the Council for Social Cohesion were a political windfall for the president and a part of an electoral strategy for the president to stay in power.[76] Other legislators questioned the cash transfer program on the grounds that it was not operated with transparency.[77] Further complaints about the program were related to the system used to target program beneficiaries. In particular, legislators complained that the census takers did not capture the poorest of the poor because they couldn't reach their communities or couldn't find them in their homes, or because the people themselves refused to report their demographic information.[78]

Concerned that the cash transfer program was simply a vote-buying strategy, legislators brought the issue of agency structure to the Supreme Court early in 2009. Legislators argued that the constitution does not allow the Office of the President to operate social programs directly, and therefore MIFAPRO should be reassigned to a different agency in the federal government. The Supreme Court ruled in favor of the legislators, and the cash transfer program, along with its operating budget, was transferred to the Ministry of Education in March 2009, where the president created the System of Social Assistance to oversee the program.[79]

Six months after the cash transfer program was reassigned to the Ministry of Education, the minister resigned, arguing that the ministry did not have sufficient funds to operate its programs, including the cash transfer program.[80] Congress summoned the newly appointed minister of education to congress to discuss the results of the cash transfer program, as well as the reasons why the ministry had designated information on the identity and addresses of recipients

---

[76] "Opositores Ven Botín Pol'itico." *Prensa Libre*, September 6, 2008. http://www.prensalibre.com/noticias/Opositores-ven-botin-politico_0_167983822.html

[77] "Sandra Torres: Hay que saber fiscalizar." *Prensa Libre*, October 28, 2008. http://www.prensalibre.com/noticias/Sandra-Torres-saber-fiscalizar_0_168584254.html

[78] "Quejas sobre Cohesión Social obligan nuevo censo." *Prensa Libre*, February 24, 2009. http://www.prensalibre.com/noticias/Quejas-Cohesion-Social-obligan-censo_0_7202445.html

[79] "Programa Mi Familia Progresa pasa a Educación." *Prensa Libre*, March 5, 2009. http://www.prensalibre.com/noticias/Programa-Familia-Progresa-pasa-Educacion_0_600017.html

[80] "Renuncia Ministra de Educación." *Prensa Libre*, September 2, 2009. http://www.prensalibre.com/noticias/Renuncia-Educacion-Ana-Ordonez-Molina_0_109190960.html

Explaining Policy Adoption and Design

confidential.[81] The practice of legislators summoning the minister of education, as well as other members of the federal government, to address legislators' concerns became so regular that President Colom stated: "We cannot continue with a Congress that takes away forty percent of the time of Ministers with their hearings."[82]

Perhaps the most controversial issue surrounding MIFAPRO was the list of program recipients. The Ministry of Education, most likely by presidential instruction, kept the list secret for as long as it could. Legislators, who wanted access to the list, consulted the Supreme Court. The Court's opinion was that the Ministry of Education had to make the list of recipients available to the comptroller's office, the entity in charge of overseeing the program.[83] A congresswoman from the *Encuentro por Guatemala* party pressured the Ministry of Education to release the list in February 2009. The president defended the position of the ministry, which was not to release the list, and argued that for security reasons it was a mistake to make the list of recipients public. Legislators perceived this argument as an excuse that the president was using to avoid making the program more transparent.[84]

In April of 2009, Congress approved a law to promote public access to information. With this law, the Ministry of Education had no choice but to publish the names of program recipients on its website, though they continued to refuse to publicize recipients' identification numbers or their addresses.[85] The Ministry of Education delivered the names of recipients to congress in January 2010. However, legislators were not appeased because it was impossible to assess the quality of the information without the identification numbers. In response to the incomplete release of recipients' data, the Court ordered the Ministry of Education to share the complete information with the general comptroller.[86] Shortly after this ruling, the Court also

---

[81] *"Ministro de Educación debe responder sobre Mi Familia Progresa."* Prensa Libre, February 7, 2010. http://www.prensalibre.com/noticias/Ministro-Educacion-responder-Familia-Progresa_0_203979631.html

[82] *"Colom arremete contra diputados."* Prensa Libre, April 25, 2010. http://www.prensalibre.com/noticias/Colom-arremete-diputados_0_250174995.html

[83] *"Corte de Constitucionalidad avala fiscalización de Cohesión Social."* Prensa Libre, January 22, 2009. http://www.prensalibre.com/noticias/CC-avala-fiscalizacion-Cohesion-Social_0_6601804.html

[84] *"Colom responsabiliza a diputados por problemas de los beneficiados de Mi Familia Progresa."* Prensa Libre, February 4, 2009. http://www.prensalibre.com/noticias/Colom-responsabiliza-beneficiados-Familia-Progresa_0_7199809.html

[85] *"Fideicomisos serán Públicos."* Prensa Libre, April 21, 2009. http://www.prensalibre.com/noticias/Fideicomisos-publicos_0_28797197.html

[86] *"Corte de Constitucionalidad ordena a Mifapro dar informe sobre beneficiarios."* Prensa Libre, December 4, 2009. http://www.prensalibre.com/noticias/CC-ordena-Mifapro-informe-beneficiarios_0_165586856.html. Also see: *"CSJ da tres días a ministro para entregar información sobre Mifapro."* January 6, 2010. http://www.prensalibre.com/noticias/CSJ-ministro-entregar-informacion-Mifapro_0_184781546.html

ruled that the Ministry of Education must share the information with legislators.[87]

The minister of education failed to comply with the Court's ruling, and again withheld information from congress. As a consequence of failing to obey the Court's order, the Court ordered the dismissal of the minister of education.[88] In March 2010, shortly after the minister's dismissal, the Ministry of Education finally shared the required information with congress. Since then, information about program enrollment, including the full list of program recipients, has been public.

The previous discussion demonstrates how legislators used the Court to shape the rules governing the cash transfer program, but also their own budgetary powers to influence the development of the program, especially with respect to the establishment of monitoring mechanisms. The president's wife, Sandra Torres de Colom, as head of the Council for Social Cohesion, regularly attended congressional sessions to negotiate increases to the budget allocated for social assistance programs with legislators. Congress was not always responsive to her petitions and on several occasions refused to approve additional funds for program expansions.[89] In exchange for additional resources, legislators requested the codes that identified the cash transfer program in the federal budget. The president shared those codes with congress, and as a result legislators are able to track program spending in the budget.[90] In addition, congress asked that each program recipient be assigned a unique identification number to make the monitoring of program enrollment more feasible.[91]

Finally, in addition to the monitoring and evaluation mechanisms already in place, in 2010 the president created a civil society monitoring system to oversee the execution of the program.[92] At the time this book was written, MIFAPRO was the most evaluated program in Guatemala. National agencies such as the National Institute of Statistics and the General Comptroller's Office, as well as international agencies such as the Mexican National Institute for Public Health

---

[87] "MIFAPRO deberá dar datos a Montenegro." *Prensa Libre*, January 23, 2010. http://www.prensalibre.com/noticias/Mifapro-debera-dar-datos-Montenegro_0_194980555.html
[88] "Bienvenido Argueta es destituido de Educación." *Prensa Libre*, February 26, 2010. http://www.prensalibre.com/noticias/Bienvenido-Argueta-destituido-Educacion_0_215378475.html
[89] "Congreso no logra quórum necesario para aprobar seis préstamos de urgencia nacional." *Prensa Libre*, January 28, 2009. http://www.prensalibre.com/noticias/Congreso-necesario-prestamos-urgencia-nacional_0_6602527.html
[90] "Consejo de Cohesión Social presenta su sitio de Internet." *Prensa Libre*, November 4, 2008. http://www.prensalibre.com/noticias/Consejo-Cohesion-Social-presenta-Internet_0_169183663.html
[91] "Habrá registro único de beneficiarios de programas sociales." *Prensa Libre*, August 28, 2011. http://www.prensalibre.com/noticias/politica/registro-unico-beneficiarios-programas-sociales_0_542945948.html
[92] "Álvaro Colom instala observatorio ciudadano en medio de críticas." *Prensa Libre*, February 5, 2010. http://www.prensalibre.com/noticias/Alvaro-Colom-observatorio-ciudadano-criticas_0_202779791.html

(INSP), USAID, and the Inter-American Development Bank, have evaluated the program.

Congress eventually approved additional resources for the program, though in preparation for the 2011 presidential elections, they took measures to ensure that the program could not be used to influence the election. Legislators' concerns were fueled by the decision of UNE to name Sandra Torres as their presidential candidate. UNE's candidate choice became a political scandal because Guatemala's constitution forbids relatives of the president to run for office. The presidential couple divorced in an attempt to circumvent this constitutional restriction, but the Supreme Court maintained that Sandra Torres's candidacy was unconstitutional. The Court's decision left the UNE without a presidential candidate.[93] Nevertheless, legislators imposed restrictions on the federal budget to ensure that the cash transfer program could not receive resources from other agencies in the federal bureaucracy, to limit the likelihood that the program would be used to boost the political support of the incumbent party.[94]

In sum, the original design of MIFAPRO did not include transparency mechanisms or effective monitoring systems. Provisions to make program operations more transparent were included as a response to explicit demands from congress. Other program procedures have since been modified as a result of pressure from legislators. For example, in 2010 the program revised its communication strategy to improve the flow of information to poor households. The new strategy now includes more aggressive dissemination of information related to the criteria used by the program to select recipients.

Argentina

President Néstor Kirchner, who served from 2003 to 2007, and his successor Cristina Fernández de Kirchner, who was the president at the time this book was being written, established three flagship cash transfer programs: *Plan Jefes y Jefas de Hogar, Plan Familias,* and *Asignación Universal por Hijo* (AUH). In the discussion that follows, I review the evolution of these programs with particular attention to the debates that took place in congress surrounding these programs. Through most of the period under study, the president in Argentina had a majority of support among legislators. It was not until the 2009 congressional elections that president Cristina Fernández de Kirchner faced a divided congress.

The economic crisis that Argentina faced in the early 2000s created a coalition in support of the emergency social assistance program, *Plan Jefes y Jefas de Hogar*. The policy was welcomed by congress, where legislators recognized that the more than seventy social programs in operation at the time were ineffective

---

[93] The Economist, March 15, 2011.
[94] "Bancadas acuerdan candados para Mifapro en el 2011." *Prensa Libre*, November 30 2010. http://www.prensalibre.com/noticias/Bancadas-acuerdan-candados-Mifapro_0_381562061.html

in dealing with the economic crisis, required large bureaucracies to operate them, and captured an important share of the federal budget. Legislators from the opposition, however, expected that the program would become a universal unemployment insurance program that circumvented the bureaucracy and local party machines.[95] When *Plan Jefes y Jefas de Hogar* began operations, it was clear that the program did not meet the expectations of the opposition.

In February 2002, months after the program had begun, one opposition legislator remarked to congress: "With respect to the program *Plan Jefes y Jefas* there is much imprecision about the budget of the program. We still do not know how it will be implemented, but we believe it is on the right track, and we need to work on it. We consider that the 800 million [pesos], more or less, that are in the budget are insufficient, and we presume that [the government] is trying to get loans from multilateral organizations. But most fundamentally we care about how the program will be implemented; we don't want it to be paternalism, or to have a clientelist component... we want to take a step toward modern social security."[96]

Two years later, in 2004, legislators from opposition parties were still dissatisfied with the program. One legislator remarked: "I want to make clear that I am not questioning the financial aid allocated to the provinces for social expenditure. I do not question spending in non-contributory pensions, or in the program *Plan Jefes y Jefas*. I do question the lack of mechanisms to evaluate, verify, and oversee [the program]. I question the discretion in the allocation of program resources."[97]

Calls by legislators to reform the program continued. Some legislators proposed to transfer the resources directly to the unemployed through debit cards, so that the money would circumvent political and social leaders, as well as *punteros*.[98] A few suggested dismantling the program and replacing it with a universal unemployment insurance scheme conditional on full-time employment.[99] Still others suggested replacing the program with a universal system of allocation of money to children whose parents work in the informal economy.[100]

In 2005, after more than two years of debate, the government reformed the program. Although the chief of ministers announced these changes to Congress, legislators were not provided with details of the reforms.[101] Shortly thereafter, the president announced that a large share of beneficiaries of *Plan Jefes y Jefas* had been transferred to a program of wider scope: *Plan Familias*.[102]

---

[95] Parliament debates, federal budget 20/07/2001.
[96] Parliament debates, federal budget 28/02/2002.
[97] Parliament debates, federal budget 2004 37966.
[98] Parliament debates, federal budget 2004, 37966.
[99] Parliament debates, federal budget 2005, 38057.
[100] Parliament debates, federal budget 2004, 37966.
[101] Parliament debates, federal budget 15/12/2005.
[102] Parliament debates, federal budget 15/12/2005.

Legislators from the opposition questioned the new program as much as they had questioned its predecessor. One legislator explained that enrollment in social programs "has not increased since 2003. So it could be that the funds go to places where political *punteros* can include or exclude recipients... this means that his program is not an entitlement, but a benefit granted by the *punteros*."[103] Calls for insulating the program from clientelist pressures continued. One legislator expressed the frustration of the opposition in congress by stating: "It is evident that in this budget we are missing the opportunity to change the trend... toward social programs that directly transfer income in a transparent way, with clear criteria to allocate the benefits."[104]

In 2009, facing a divided government, President Cristina Fernández de Kirchner launched the program AUH. AUH aims to improve the well-being of impoverished children who are not enrolled in other social programs, and whose parents are either unemployed or working in the informal sector of the economy and earning less than minimum wage.[105] Like other CCT programs in Latin America, the cash transfer households receive through AUH is conditional on parents taking their children to medical checkups and children's school attendance. Three characteristics set AUH apart from other cash transfer programs in Argentina. First, AUH is accessed using a debit card. Second, AUH's operational rules specify directly that there is no need for intermediaries to register for the program or receive the transfers. That AUH circumvents *punteros* is publicly available and is a core component of the communication strategy of the program. Finally, shortly after the launch of the program, preparations for an independent evaluation began. As of 2011, the program had been evaluated by a research center based at the National University of La Plata.[106]

---

[103] Parliament debates, Extension of the Economic Emergency Law, 26/11/2008.
[104] Parliament debates, federal budget 4/11/2004.
[105] Decree No. 1602/2009.
[106] *Centro de Estudios Distributivos, Laborales y Sociales, Facultad de Ciencias Ecónmicas.*

5

Explaining Policy Outcomes

Scholars of the welfare state have traditionally neglected questions about policy implementation. This chapter offers evidence on the political determinants of the implementation of CCTs. First, I show that the same factors that lead to strict operational rules also lead to a robust implementation. Second, I test the assertion that the political factors that lead to strong policy design also lead to the elimination of political-economic cycles that result from the expansion of conditional cash transfer programs during election years. Finally, the last test in this chapter aims to prove that programs with weaker designs – and more flawed implementations – are more likely to be dismantled than programs with stronger designs and more exacting implementations. The evidence in this chapter confirms that the dynamics among presidents and legislators influence important policy outcomes that directly relate to the effectiveness of programs to eradicate poverty.

IMPLEMENTATION

The operational rules of programs regulate the actions undertaken by program agencies, from the selection of recipients to the evaluation of program impacts. This chapter examines the political determinants of the variation in program operations using the implementation index I constructed, which measures the degree to which program implementation complies with the design along each of the dimensions of CCTs' operation: targeting of beneficiaries, conditions to receive program benefits, mechanisms to verify eligibility status, monitoring and transparency systems, and evaluation mechanisms.

As noted in Chapter 2, measuring how closely program agencies adhere to CCTs' operation rules is a challenging tasks. The implementation index measures minimum compliance with operational rules. As a brief reminder, a CCT's implementation is deemed more robust if program documentation includes

Explaining Policy Outcomes

errors of inclusion and exclusion in the targeting system; verification of household compliance with program conditions (related to health and education) and evidence that households that do not comply with program conditions are penalized; evidence that a recertification process takes place periodically and families graduate from the program; evidence that a system of monitoring is in place (for example, an audit system) and program expenses, schedules of transfers, and enrollment updates are regularly published and made available to the public; and finally, a report produced by an international or domestic nongovernmental organization based on an impact evaluation of the program. The implementation index is the sum of the scores for each component of CCT operations. All CCT programs have more than one set of operational rules; therefore, I score the implementation of programs for each set of operational rules.[1]

Chapter 3 argues that the extent to which presidents face resistance from legislators has implications for a variety of policy outcomes. In particular, presidents who face checks on their power from congress design more intricate policies, which get funded precisely because their design ensures that agencies operate programs in a less political way. It follows, therefore, that the same factors that lead to a strict policy design also lead to a more robust program implementation. That politicians bother to discuss programs' rules and agency structures because they ultimately care about policy outcomes has been elusive to scholars.

Among observers of Latin America, it is frequent to hear that variation in program implementation relates first and foremost to a given country's state capacity, which is known to vary considerably in the region. In particular, in the case of CCTs there are administrative factors that can cause program implementation to lag behind. For example, the implementation of a program may require management capabilities that bureaucracies are not prepared to handle, or unexpected operational complications may cause delays for program processes. Following this argument, state capacity should explain why the program that gets implemented is not a perfect reflection of the program's original blueprints. State capacity, however, is endogenous to the political processes described in Chapter 3.

To see why this is the case, it is helpful to review how scholars have defined state capacity. Because capacity is a concept that is difficult to define and measure, there is no scholarly consensus on how to study it. One common definition relates state capacity to bureaucratic quality. Bureaucracies with meritocratic recruitment and standardized processes, with insulation from political pressure, and with the ability to provide services are a sign of high state capacity. If we accept this definition, then state capacity is analytically close to the concept measured in my implementation index. For example, if a program scores a high value in the implementation index, then the operating agency has standardized

---

[1] For details on the implementation index, its advantages, and its limitations, please see Chapter 2.

procedures to select program recipients, monitor program operations, evaluate program impacts, and so on. All of these procedures insulate the agency from political pressure. Thus, a higher index score implies a higher capacity. Yet, both the implementation score and the added capacity it implies are a consequence of constraints on executives. When facing resistance to their policies in congress, governments design more robust programs and invest in developing the capacity to implement them. Therefore, conflict between the executive and the legislative branches of government shapes the incentives of the government to design and implement more robust policies and, in the process, enhances the government's administrative capacity.

An alternative argument is that presidents design policies with the expectation that regardless of the compromises they make in the design, they will be able to implement policies in any way they want. This argument would be more plausible if the interaction between presidents and legislators were a one-shot game where presidents could fool legislators into funding a policy with rules, but then implement any variation that they desired. In reality, however, presidents and legislators interact constantly. Given that conditional cash transfers are not entitlements, presidents need to negotiate CCTs' budgets each year. If legislators feel that a president has cheated and moved a policy too far away from its design, then they may choose to revise the program's budget, which in an extreme case could lead to the discontinuation of a policy. For this reason, we can expect presidents to have a particular interest in keeping program implementation in line with program design as much as possible, even if this means monitoring their own bureaucracies or making continuous investments in administrative capacity. The expectation then is that although there may be some discrepancies, program design and implementation will be highly correlated, and the same factors that lead to stricter designs will lead to more robust implementation.

To further test the plausibility of this argument, I examine the determinants of CCTs' implementation, drawing from data across countries and over time in Latin America. As I demonstrate in the previous chapter, program design is a function of the presence of divided government, as well as checks and balances to presidential power. In the analysis that follows, I focus on program implementation.

The dependent variable is the implementation score, which takes the value of 0 when no CCT program is in operation. The value of the score increases by one unit for each of the six dimensions of compliance with program design. The two main independent variables are *Divided* and *Checks*, which are available in the database of political institutions (Beck et al. 2001, Keefer 2010, Keefer and Stasavage 2003). As I have mentioned, *Divided* measures whether the president controls the lower and upper houses in congress for each of the years (1990–2011) included in the data. If the party of the president has a majority of the seats in congress, *Divided* takes the value 0; otherwise, *Divided* takes the value 1. *Divided* takes the value 1 for half of the country-years in the data set. Chile experienced a divided government for 62 percent of the years in this study, making it the country with the longest exposure to this political phenomenon. Many other countries in the study, however, have also had substantial experience with divided governments. In Mexico and Peru, for example, the president's party controlled the majority of seats in congress 52 percent of the time. Finally, there are some countries with less experience with divided governments, such as Argentina, where the president's party controlled congress for 62 percent of the years in the study.

The second variable, *Checks*, was originally developed by Keefer (2002) and measures the degree to which the president's power is subject to checks and balances. *Checks* combines the existence of divided control between two chambers in a bicameral system with the number of veto players. *Checks* takes values from 1 to 7, and increases if the chief executive is competitively elected, if multiple parties won seats in the legislature, or if the opposition controls the legislature. It also increases for each chamber of the legislature unless the president's party has a majority in the lower house and a closed list system is in effect[2] and for each party coded as allied with the president's party and that has an ideological orientation closer to that of the main opposition party than to that of the president's party. For Cuba, for example, *Checks* takes the value 1 for all years. With the exception of Cuba, however, all countries have experienced varying degrees of checks to presidential power between 1990 and 2011. For example, *Checks* takes the value 2 in Mexico from 1990 to 1996, but in 1997, when the PRI lost control of the lower house of congress, it increases to 5. Checks on presidential power, however, do not consistently increase (or decrease) over time. In Peru, for example, *Checks* takes the value 4 in 1990 and 1991, decreases to 3 in 1992, further decreases to 2 from 1996 to 2000, and then increases to 4 again in 2001.[3]

The empirical study of policy implementation presents challenges similar to those described in the previous chapter. Comparisons across countries tend to confound the effects of observable and unobservable characteristics, which can lead to erroneous conclusions about the causal relationships among the measured variables. To mitigate this problem, at least to some extent, I include country-fixed effects in the analysis, which capture characteristics at the country level that are fixed throughout the period under study. My argument posits that state capacity is closely related to the implementation score, and therefore it is best to think of capacity as endogenous to the same political processes that explain policy implementation. If, however, countries have an endowment of fixed state capacity that could explain variation in program implementation, such time-invariant state capacity would be capture by the country-fixed effects.

In addition, I show the effects of *Divided* and *Checks* on cash transfer programs' implementation while controlling for factors that previous work has

---

[2] This implies stronger presidential control of his or her party, and therefore of the legislature.
[3] The average value of *Checks* for the entire data set is 3.3.

TABLE 5.1 *Effects of Divided Government and Checks on CCTs' Implementation*

	Implementation Score			
	(1)	(2)	(3)	(4)
Divided	1.006***	0.731***		
	(0.209)	(0.225)		
Checks			0.307***	0.380***
			(0.075)	(0.073)
Left		0.018		0.090
		(0.221)		(0.211)
GDP		0.221*		0.208**
		(0.117)		(0.098)
Openness		0.006		0.003
		(0.005)		(0.006)
Inflation (log)		0.060		0.038
		(0.067)		(0.063)
Population (log)		7.563***		8.562***
		(1.138)		(1.112)
Deindustrialization		0.084***		0.062**
		(0.029)		(0.029)
Child labor		0.084*		0.100**
		(0.043)		(0.039)
Constant	0.324***	−26.315***	−0.206	−27.791***
	(0.118)	(2.554)	(0.261)	(2.368)
Observations	580	326	572	326
R-squared	0.305	0.552	0.297	0.575
Country-fixed effects	yes	yes	yes	yes

Robust standard errors in parentheses.
***p < 0.01, **p < 0.05, *p < 0.1.

considered relevant to country-level explanations of welfare programs, such as the ideological orientation of the executive, GDP per capita, trade openness, inflation, total population, deindustrialization, and the extent of child labor. All of these variables, with the exception of the ideology of the executive, are available from the World Development Indicators and Global Development Finance data banks published by the World Bank (World Bank, 2010). The ideology of the executive comes from the database of political institutions (Beck et al. 2001, Keefer 2010). For a discussion of why these variables are relevant, please see Chapter 4.

Table 5.1 displays the results from the analysis of the effect of *Divided* and *Checks* on program implementation. Columns 1 and 2 present evidence that presidents with divided governments implement programs that are approximately one point more robust (on a scale that goes from 0 to 6) than presidents with unified governments. This result is statistically significant and robust to

Explaining Policy Outcomes

the inclusion of all control variables. The estimation in column 2 shows that even after controlling for country-fixed effects, the president's ideology, and economic and demographic variables, *Divided* still has a significant and substantive effect on program implementation scores. To better illustrate the magnitude of the effect, note that the average implementation score for countries with a CCT where *Divided* equals 0 is 2.8. Off of this baseline, a change in *Divided* from 0 to 1 is associated with a 35 percent increase in the implementation score. In other words, going from a unified to a divided government is associated with an improvement in implementation from a program like *Programa Familias* in Argentina, where there is minimum compliance with the schooling and health conditionalities, to a program like *Advancement through Health and Education* in Jamaica, where there is compliance with conditionalities, targeting of resources, and impact evaluations.

Checks on presidents have a similar effect to divided government. Columns 3 and 4 of Table 5.1 show that, consistent with previous results, *Checks* improves the implementation of programs in a statistically significant way. A country that experiences an increase in *Checks* from 2 to 5, which corresponds to a change from the minimum to the maximum value of *Checks* among countries that had a CCT operating, increases its implementation score by 1.14 points. If we take into account that the average implementation score among countries with *Checks* equal to 2 is 1.8, then an increase in *Checks* of three points is associated with a 63 percent increase in the implementation score.

Thus, politicians care about program design, and they care about policy implementation and policy outcomes. The similarity of the magnitude of the effect of *Divided* and *Checks* on program design and implementation lends credence to this. (See Chapter 4 for more details on the effect of *Divided* and *Checks* on program design.)

In terms of other factors associated with program implementation, a left-leaning president is not more likely to implement a robust program than a right, or center-leaning president, as Table 5.1 shows. Similarly, trade openness and inflation are not statistically associated with program implementation. On the other hand, higher GDP per capita significantly increases the implementation score. If GDP per capita increases by a thousand dollars, we would expect an increase of 0.22 point in the implementation score. Countries with more population, higher deindustrialization, and more child labor also implement more robust programs. The magnitude of the effect of these variables, however, is far less than the magnitude of the effect of *Divided*. For example, a 1 percent increase in population is associated with a 0.07-point increase in the implementation score.[4] A 1 percent increase in deindustrialization and a 1 percent increase in child labor are each associated with a 0.08-point increase in implementation.

---

[4] Because population is logged, I divide the coefficient on *Population (log)* by 100 to interpret the effect, as in any level-log regression.

In sum, the previous analysis produces results that are consistent with this book's argument. Whereas executives who face very few checks on their power from congress adopt less strict operational rules for CCT programs and operate less robust programs, presidents who do not control the legislature and face greater opposition in congress adopt more exhaustive operational rules and implement more robust programs.

POLITICAL-ECONOMIC CYCLES

Among the various aspects of implementation, the expansion of programs, especially during election years, has constituted an important issue on which opposition parties in congresses across Latin America consistently agitate. Speculations about presidents using conditional cash transfer programs to boost their electoral support abound in the media. Yet there are no studies that provide systematic evidence for the presence of political-economic cycles in the operation of cash transfer programs. Thus, the question that remains is whether presidents are manipulating program enrollment to improve their electoral fortunes. This is perhaps one of the most relevant questions for understanding the politics surrounding cash transfers.

I argue that legislators are concerned that presidents use cash transfer programs to the detriment of legislators' interests. The biggest concern of legislators from opposition parties could likely be that the programs fuel the president's electioneering strategies. When presidents face few checks on their power, opposition parties have no means by which they can prevent cycles of program expansion and contraction from following electoral cycles. With congressional checks in place, however, presidents have less room to manipulate cash transfer program enrollments according to the schedule of elections.

To explore this question, I collect data on expansion for all cash transfer programs implemented in Latin America from 1990 to 2011. Most programs follow a similar pattern of growth – programs often start out small and grow considerably during the first five or six years of operation, and then enrollment stabilizes. I calculate the fraction of recipient households that are newly enrolled in a program in any given year with respect to the total number of households in the program (according to the most recent available data). This measure takes into account the way a program typically evolves.

If presidents expand conditional cash transfer programs to boost their support before elections, we should see the largest expansions taking place close to an election period. To measure the role of elections in program expansion, I specify a regression model where the dependent variable is the fraction of CCT program recipients newly enrolled in a given year. The independent variables of interest are whether presidents face a divided government, whether there is a federal election that year, and the interaction between these two variables. Columns 1 and 2 of Table 5.2 shows that enrollment into programs operating under presidents who face a divided government is lower during election years. The interaction between *Divided* and election year is negative and statistically

Explaining Policy Outcomes

TABLE 5.2 *Political Determinants of Program Expansion*

	Fraction of Households Enrolled			
	(1)	(2)	(3)	(4)
Divided	0.160	0.076		
	(0.111)	(0.153)		
High checks			−0.032	−0.229
			(0.124)	(0.139)
Executive election	0.301**	0.248*	0.247*	0.271*
	(0.125)	(0.145)	(0.146)	(0.158)
Divided × election	−0.323**	−0.277*		
	(0.142)	(0.163)		
High checks × election			−0.289*	−0.299*
			(0.161)	(0.175)
Left		0.251**		0.288**
		(0.115)		(0.133)
GDP		−0.089		−0.080
		(0.109)		(0.101)
Openness		0.004		0.009**
		(0.004)		(0.004)
Population (log)		1.275		0.647
		(1.394)		(1.209)
Deindustrialization		−0.022		−0.004
		(0.029)		(0.029)
Child labor		−0.019*		−0.023*
		(0.011)		(0.012)
Constant	0.049	−1.879	0.201**	−1.459
	(0.092)	(3.550)	(0.099)	(2.858)
Observations	95	73	100	73
R-squared	0.195	0.341	0.168	0.395
Country-fixed effects	yes	yes	yes	yes

Robust standard errors in parentheses.
***p < 0.01, **p < 0.05, *p < 0.1.

significant. By contrast, presidents facing a unified government increase enrollment into programs more during election years, as suggested by the positive coefficient on election year. These results are robust to the inclusion of control variables, including the ideology of the president, GDP per capita, trade openness, population (log), deindustrialization, and child labor.[5]

Thus, presidents whose party controls congress enroll a higher fraction of program recipients during election years. To be more precise, they enroll a 30 percentage point higher fraction of the total recipients in election years

---

[5] In this analysis, I do not include inflation because it could be an outcome of the interaction between election year and unified governments (see for example Keefer and Stasavage 2003). Therefore, its inclusion would lead to post-treatment bias.

compared to presidents with divided governments. On the other hand, presidents facing a divided government do not increase program enrollment during election years (adding the coefficients for the main effect of election and the interaction term). To illustrate the magnitude of the effect, a president with a divided government enrolls on average 18 percent of the total household recipients during election years. Off of that base, a president with a unified government enrolls 1.6 times more households during an election year (0.30/0.18).

Checks on presidents from the legislature have an interactive effect with election years similar to that for divided government. The interaction between *Checks* and election year raises a minor issue. The fixed effect model is most convincing because it controls for unobserved but fixed country characteristics. However, to estimate an effect for a fixed effect model requires in-country variation. For the interaction between election year and *Checks*, the data set does not have sufficient observations to interact election year with each category of *Checks*. To circumvent the issue of a small sample, I create the variable *High Checks*, which takes the value 1 when *Checks* is greater than 3, and 0 otherwise.[6] Columns 3 and 4 present evidence that confirms that programs operating under presidents who face *High Checks* do not expand during election years. By contrast, programs operated by presidents facing few checks on their authority from congress are more likely to grow during election years, as suggested by the positive coefficient on election year. These results are statistically significant and robust to the inclusion of control variables in the models. The magnitude of this effect is as substantively important as that of *Divided*. Thus, when unconstrained, presidents increase program enrollment substantially more during election years.

The quantitative analysis shows that program expansions during election years are common when the executive is free to act unilaterally – a freedom manifested by programs with loose operational rules. In contrast, executives who face checks on their power have more regulated CCT programs and do not expand CCTs significantly during election years. Thus, classical manifestations of presidents' discretion in Latin America, such as electoral business cycles, continue to exist in countries where presidents face few political constraints. In countries where checks and balances exist, however, presidents no longer use poverty relief funds, such as cash transfers, to boost their support before elections.

THE SURVIVAL OF POLICIES

Conditional cash transfer programs are of recent vintage, yet it is already noticeable that some programs are more durable than others. Ninety-six percent of programs survive their first year of operation. Survival rates, however,

---

[6] I chose 3 as the threshold for *High Checks* because it is the midpoint of the values that *Checks* takes in Latin America during the period under study.

Explaining Policy Outcomes

TABLE 5.3 *Program Survival: Descriptive Statistics*

Time (Years)	Beg. Total	Fail Fail	Net Lost	Survivor Function	Std. Error	95% Confidence Interval	
1	25	1	0	0.9600	0.0392	0.7484	0.9943
2	24	3	0	0.8400	0.0733	0.6281	0.9367
3	21	0	3	0.8400	0.0733	0.6281	0.9367
4	18	1	2	0.7933	0.0828	0.5712	0.9087
5	15	1	3	0.7404	0.0926	0.5069	0.8756
6	11	0	2	0.7404	0.0926	0.5069	0.8756
7	9	0	3	0.7404	0.0926	0.5069	0.8756
8	6	1	1	0.6170	0.1366	0.3055	0.8215
9	4	1	2	0.4628	0.1683	0.1432	0.7368
14	1	0	1	0.4628	0.1683	0.1432	0.7368

drop drastically when programs reach their fifth year of operation. By then, 74 percent of programs survive. By the tenth year, only 46 percent of programs survive. The survival statistics, summarized in Table 5.3, reveal variation among CCT programs that has remained unexplored.

In addition to the implementation and expansion of programs, limits and checks on presidents coming from legislators shape the likelihood that a policy survives through their effect on policy design and implementation. A conditional cash transfer program whose design is not robust and does not prevent the agency from being politicized is more vulnerable to political changes and less likely to survive.

To test this argument, I conducted survival analysis. The outcome of interest is program duration. The independent variables of interest are, as in previous analysis, *Divided* and *High Checks*. Figure 5.1 presents the results of two survival models. In the upper graph, program duration is explained by whether a president faces a divided government or not. The solid and dashed lines represent how a program survival rate changes as time, measured in years, increases for programs operated by a president not facing and facing a divided government, respectively. In the first year, programs under divided and unified governments have the same high survival rate (close to 100 percent of programs survive the first year). At year 5, however, the effect of *Divided* is noticeable. A program under a unified government has a 50 percent chance of surviving year 5 of operations, whereas a program under divided government has more than an 80 percent change of surviving. By year 10, a program under unified government has almost a 20 percent chance of survival, whereas a program under divided government has more than a 60 percent chance of survival. Therefore, programs under divided governments are more durable and the distance between the survival rate of programs under divided and unified governments only widens over time.

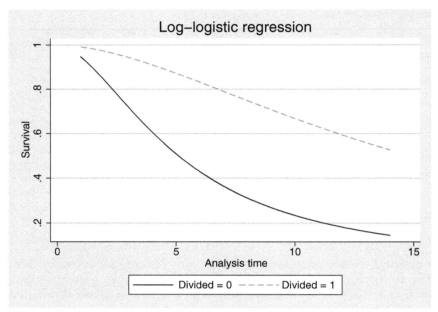

(a) Survival of CCT programs by divided government

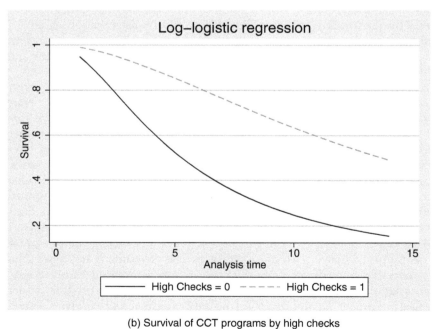

(b) Survival of CCT programs by high checks

FIGURE 5.1 Effects of divided government and checks on CCTs' duration.

TABLE 5.4 *What People Value in a Poverty Relief Program (by income groups)*

	Clear Selection Rules (1)	Prioritize Health and Education (2)	Avoid Clientelism (3)	Condition the Program to Increase Schooling (4)
Monthly Income (in pesos)				
1,500–3,000	0.118**	−0.085	0.034	−0.006
	(0.053)	(0.060)	(0.036)	(0.036)
3,001–6,000	0.080	−0.162***	0.094**	0.042
	(0.055)	(0.059)	(0.039)	(0.038)
6,001–12,000	0.114*	−0.115	0.059	−0.030
	(0.067)	(0.073)	(0.050)	(0.040)
more than 12,000	0.197**	−0.296***	0.150*	0.038
	(0.097)	(0.079)	(0.080)	(0.075)
Constant	0.253***	0.419***	0.111***	0.127***
	(0.041)	(0.051)	(0.026)	(0.029)
Observations	978	978	978	978
R-squared	0.013	0.022	0.012	0.005

Robust standard errors in parentheses.
***p < 0.01, **p < 0.05, *p < 0.1.

In the lower graph of Figure 5.1 program duration is explained by whether the president faced high checks from congress or not. The effect of *High Checks* on a program survival rate is similar to the effect of *Divided*. As years increase, the survival rate of programs under divided governments is greater than that of programs under unified governments.

A program under divided government has a more strict design and a more robust implementation compared to programs under unified governments. Thus, through its effects on program design and implementation, checks and limits on presidents improve the chances that a program survives. But why would a strict design and robust implementation increase program duration? One possibility is that citizens approve conditional cash transfer programs that have strict designs at higher rates than programs without a strict design. If governments take into account the opinions of citizens, then that strict programs garner broad support among the public could be directly linked to programs' survival rate. If this is the case, it is important to understand which program characteristics citizens consider to be most essential. In other words, understanding what people value in the poverty alleviation efforts undertaken by their governments may shed light on the bigger question of policy survival.

Table 5.4 presents evidence from a nationally representative survey conducted in Mexico in the summer of 2009. The survey asked respondents which characteristic of poverty relief programs they considered to be most important, and presented them with the following response options: (1) a program must have clear rules to select its recipients; (2) a program must invest in the health and education of children in poor households; (3) a program must avoid being used for electoral purposes; or (4) a program must condition benefits on parents sending their kids to school. This question provides insight into individuals' attitudes toward cash transfer programs.

Overall, 36 percent of survey participants said that the most important trait in a poverty relief program is the use of clear rules to select recipients. Thirty-two percent of respondents reported that they most value that a poverty relief program invests in the health and education of children in poor households. Seventeen percent of respondents said that the most important characteristic is that the program design prevents its resources from being used for electoral purposes. And, 14 percent of respondents said that the most important trait in a program that fights poverty is to condition benefits on parents changing their behavior for the benefit of their children. Thus, these statistics suggest that, overall, citizens care more about program rules being clear than they care about other program characteristics.

When examining preferences according to income levels, however, it becomes clear that rich and poor respondents value different program traits. Poor respondents indicated that they most value poverty relief programs that invest in the health and education of children, whereas wealthier respondents most valued programs that have clear rules and avoid clientelism. Table 5.4 presents an analysis that corroborates this pattern. Column 1 is a linear probability model where the dependent variable takes the value 1 when respondents reported that the most important trait in a poverty relief program is to have clear rules for selecting recipients, and takes the value 0, otherwise. Similarly, the dependent variable in column 2 takes the value 1 when respondents reported that a program's most important trait should be to prioritize investments in health and education of poor children. The dependent variable in column 3 takes the value 1 when respondents reported that programs should avoid clientelism first and foremost. Finally, the dependent variable in column 4 takes the value 1 when respondents said that they consider that making transfers conditional was the most important trait. The independent variables of interest in all models are dummy variables that capture five different income categories, where 1 represents households with monthly incomes equal to or less than $1,500 Mexican pesos (approximately 125 dollars), and 5 represents households with monthly incomes equal to or greater than $12,000 Mexican pesos (approximately 1,000 dollars). The reference group is the group of households with the lowest income category.

The starkest differences in the responses take place between the richest and poorest respondents. Row 4 of Table 5.4 shows that the wealthiest respondents are 20 percentage points more likely than the lowest income group to value that a poverty relief program has clear selection rules. This result is statistically significant at the 5 percent level. Similarly, the richest group is 15 percentage points more likely than the poorest group to value that a program avoids clientelism.

Explaining Policy Outcomes

This result is statistically significant at the 10 percent level. The richest group is also 30 percentage points less likely to value that a program invests in the health and education of children in poor households. This result is statistically significant at the 1 percent level. Finally, the highest income group is statistically indistinguishable from the lowest income group in terms of how important they think it is to condition program benefits on parents' behavior. These findings indicate that clear rules and avoiding clientelism are more a concern of the rich when it comes to cash transfer programs, and investments in human capital are more a concern of the poor. Thus, programs with a strict design, like Mexico's *Oportunidades* program, can potentially mobilize supporters from a range of income levels by investing in human capital and by having clear rules that suppress agency discretion.

These results are compatible with recent accounts of distributive politics in Latin America that emphasize the electoral cost of clientelism. Weitz-Shapiro (2012a), for example, argues that clientelism decreases support for the incumbent from non-poor constituents. People who do not benefit directly from clientelism, she argues, infer that the quality of government is lower if clientelism is prevalent, and as a consequence they are less likely to support politicians who offer favors and gifts in exchange for a vote. Alternatively, middle-class voters may disapprove of a clientelist politician on moral grounds (Weitz-Shapiro 2012b). In the context of antipoverty programs, the results here show that upper- and middle-class voters are clearly more supportive of programs with clear rules and programs that curb clientelism.

The circumstances in Argentina, Bolivia, Mexico, and Peru illustrate this point. Poverty relief programs in Argentina have been in constant flux since the economic and social crisis of 2001. From 2001 to 2002, GDP decreased almost 11 percent and unemployment reached 21 percent among the economically active population. In 2002, 57 percent of Argentineans lived in poverty, 27 percent lived in extreme poverty, and inequality reached a historical high (Agis et al. 2010). The government's first response to the crisis was to roll out the *Plan Jefes y Jefas de Hogar Desocupados* (PJJHD) program, a conditional cash transfer program for families with children eighteen years old or younger with one or more parents unemployed. Transfers to households were contingent on adults working at least four hours per day, as well as children's school attendance and children's vaccinations. In 2005, PJJHD was replaced by *Programa Familias*, where cash transfers were conditioned only on children's schooling and health care.[7] *Programa Familias* was initially financed by a loan from the Inter-American Development Bank for 700 million dollars.[8]

Programa Familias experienced its largest expansion between 2006 and 2007 when the number of children participating in the program grew from

---

[7] *Programa Familias por la Inclusión Social. Resumen Ejecutivo. Ministerio de Desarrollo Social,* 2007.
[8] Inter-American Development Bank, press release, October 26, 2005.

1.035 million to almost 2 million. The geographical coverage of the program also increased substantially, expanding from 258 mostly urban municipalities in 2006 to 357 municipalities in 2007 that included rural and semirural areas.[9] In 2007, Christina Fernández de Kirchner, wife of President Néstor Kirchner, was elected president in a landslide victory and asked her sister-in-law to continue to serve as the Minister of Social Development.[10] Speculation that this program expansion influenced the election abounded.

Policies like *Plan Familias* in Argentina, whose implementation is not robust and whose enrollment has followed a political-economic cycle, have a hard time surviving, for example. Although *Plan Familias* continues to operate, as of October 2009 the federal government was implementing a parallel transfer scheme called *Asignación Universal por Hijo para Protección Social* (AUH). This new and stricter conditional cash transfer program was created after the *Frente para la Victoria* lost its majority in both houses of congress in the 2009 congressional elections.

Similar to *Plan Familias*, AUH is a transfer scheme directed at children of unemployed parents, or parents working in the informal sector of the economy without access to social security benefits. One of the motivations behind AUH is that poverty levels remained high despite resources funneled through *Plan Familias*. The operational rules of the newly created AUH dictate that recipients cannot be enrolled in any other social program, and AUH is set up to progressively replace other cash transfer programs such as *Programa Familias*. Although AUH has only been in operation for a couple of years, it is already displaying more strict operational rules and a more robust implementation. As a consequence, the program is showing signs of effectively promoting investments in children. For example, Agis et al. (2010) find that AUH increases school enrollment by 25 percent and children's health care visits by 40 percent.

In Bolivia, the number of students participating in *Bono Juancito Pinto* increased by 38 percent in 2008. In the previous year, the number of beneficiaries had also increased but at a more modest rate of 18 percent. In August of 2008, a recall referendum proposed by President Morales was held to determine whether the president and vice president should remain in office. The aim of the referendum was to reduce the acute social and geo-political polarization, as well as to make the country more governable. At the root of the conflict was Morales's desire to approve a new constitution that would eventually bestow a greater share of Bolivia's natural gas wealth on the poorer, western regions, allocate more land to the country's indigenous majority, and allow

---

[9] *Programa Familias por la Inclusión Social. Resumen Ejecutivo. Ministerio de Desarrollo Social*, 2007.
[10] Dr. Alicia Kirchner was appointed Minister of Social Development in 2003 when her brother, Néstor Kirchner, won the presidency. Although she left this post briefly in 2005 to become a senator, she returned in August 2006 to lead the Ministry.

Morales to stand for reelection. If the percentage of votes in favor of a recall election exceeded the percentage of votes originally cast for the Movement toward Socialism, then Morales's presidency would have been at risk. President Morales won the referendum with more than 67 percent of the vote, which was almost ten percentage points more votes than he had won in the 2005 election.[11] As in Argentina, speculations in Bolivia that the government used the cash transfer program to boost support in the referendum were prominent in the media.[12]

In contrast to the Argentinean and Bolivian experiences, in Peru, the president delayed the launching of the *Juntos* program to avoid an overlap with the presidential election, and in Mexico, *Oportunidades*'s operational rules prohibit program expansions six months before federal elections.

In sum, this chapter has shown that the same factors that shape program design have an impact on policy outcomes such as the robustness of program implementation, the use of program enrollment to boost political support during election years, and program survival. Presidents who face checks on their power from congress not only design more strict policies, but implement more robust programs and are less likely to expand programs during electoral cycles.

New administrations, especially in cases where political power changes from one party to another, have incentives to dismantle the policy legacy of previous administrations. Poverty relief programs are particularly vulnerable because their constituencies tend to be disorganized. Understanding how policies that seek to provide assistance for the poor transform into institutions able to survive over time sheds light on enduring theoretical questions about institutional change. Thus, the findings in this chapter have direct implications for how we think about policymaking and the political development of Latin America.

---

[11] The referendum also asked whether nine elected regional governors, some of whom were Morales's fiercest political enemies, should remain in office. The referendum left six governors in office.

[12] "Divided Bolivia set for referendum." BBC News, August 9, 2008. http://news.bbc.co.uk/2/hi/americas/7547043.stm

6

Conditional Cash Transfers and Clientelism

There are two countervailing accounts in the literature about the relationship between social policy and clientelism. On the one hand, Scott describes how important welfare benefits were to the demise of clientelism in the United States (1969). In his account, the institutionalization of welfare replaced patrons' favors.

The services that tied the client to the machine were either no longer necessary or were performed by other agencies than the machine... With aid to dependent children and old age assistance becoming the formal responsibility of government agencies 'the precinct captain's hod of coal was a joke'. The protective and defensive function of the machine had simply ceased to be important political incentives (1156).

Along these lines, Weyland (1996) noted in the context of the return of democracy in Brazil that: "Only benefits guaranteed by the state through redistributive measures can break the hold of clientelist patrons and set the poor free to effectively exercise their citizen rights" (6).

On the other hand, Kitschelt argues that "some institutional designs to deliver social policy benefits facilitate the growth of clientelistic linkage practices between politicians and electoral constituencies and in some instances may well have been designed to deliver such consequences" (2007, 298). He observes that in both young and established democracies, social policy benefits -such as public housing, and to a lesser extent social insurance benefits for unemployment, old age, and illness- that are targeted directly at mass electoral constituencies are a core component of clientelistic practices (Kitschelt 2007).

Both accounts are useful for understanding the dynamics of conditional cash transfer programs in Latin America. In some countries in the region, the president exerts far greater power than other branches of government and can unilaterally design conditional cash transfer policies. Where this is the case, I argue that policies are more likely to serve the political interests of the president's party than the poor. In other contexts, where the president faces checks on his or her authority from congress, conditional cash transfer programs have more elaborate rules and more robust operations and are therefore more likely to be effective in fighting poverty. Where this is the case, conditional cash transfers erode patron-client relations.

Understanding the relationship between social assistance programs and clientelism is important for at least three reasons. First, clientelism influences the political development of a country. In the best-case scenario, social benefits may challenge and ultimately dismantle clientelistic structures, but in the worst-case scenario, social benefits can cement clientelistic ties and consequently obscure poor people's political preferences, deter political competition, and prevent the consolidation of a system of electoral accountability. Second, social policies that operate in clientelistic ways have detrimental consequences for the welfare of the poor (Díaz-Cayeros et al. 2007). Third, clientelistic social policies can hinder the evolution of the social sector, leading to long-term losses for human development.

The evidence presented thus far in the book has already shed some light on the relationship between a strict cash transfer program and the political manipulation of resources aimed to improve the well-being of the poor (see Chapter 4). This chapter explores the effects of the implementation of a strict conditional cash transfer program on patron-client relationships.

Conditional cash transfer programs with strict designs and robust implementation generate dynamics that resemble Scott's account of the demise of clientelism in the United States. In this chapter, I explore three mechanisms through which a strict cash transfer fosters the demise of clientelism. First, when programs include provisions to avoid mismanagement, they are more effective at increasing households' welfare. A wealthier household can, in turn, afford to distance themselves from local patrons, which makes vote buying more expensive for political parties' brokers.

Second, a program with strict operational rules has an informative effect on recipients. The more institutionalized a program is, the more information recipients have that program benefits do not depend on party brokers. This informative effect also makes vote buying more difficult, because voters learn that party brokers have less discretion to administer program resources. The income and informative effects together empower recipients to resist clientelism. Therefore, a strict CCT erodes patron-client relations.

Third, conditional cash transfer programs with strict operational guidelines reduce the discretion of party brokers. Such guidelines may include systems to monitor the implementing agency. For example, rules can be included to regularly detect errors of inclusion in and exclusion from the program, to detect when conditionalities are not properly verified, to detect when transfers are delayed, and so on. When such systems of monitoring and quality control are in place, party brokers have fewer opportunities to strategically manipulate program resources based on a system of rewards and punishments and to threaten to throw recipients off the program without being detected.

Thus, CCTs that reduce discretion make vote buying more difficult because brokers cannot bestow program benefits, nor can they punish (or credibly threaten to punish) recipients by discontinuing the stream of program benefits.[1]

Testing the argument that the implementation of a CCT with a strict design affects clientelism is challenging. Country-level data are not well suited to establishing the effects of enrollment in a cash transfer program on likelihood of engaging in clientelism for various reasons, including the difficulties of measuring clientelism at an aggregate level. Moreover, even with the ability to measure clientelism with aggregate data, using country-level variation would make it hard to disentangle the effects of enrollment in a CCT on recipients' political attitudes, as well as the effects of CCT presence on political parties and their brokers' responses. To circumvent these challenges, this chapter focuses on within-country comparisons, with particular attention to the Mexican case, where a strict program was put in practice in 1997. The chapter presents evidence on the effect of the Mexican CCT on the likelihood that recipients engage in clientelism using data from a national survey conducted in 2009, and the subgroup analysis of a list experiment included in the survey. The chapter also includes qualitative evidence from Mexico, Colombia, Peru, and Guatemala.

The evidence presented in this chapter strongly supports the argument that a strict cash transfer program erodes clientelism by empowering recipients to resist party broker's attempts to manipulate them in the case of Mexico, and shows that similar dynamics may take place in other countries in Latin America where a strict cash transfer program is in operation.[2]

The impact of strict conditional cash transfer programs on clientelism is surprising, given how resilient patron-client networks are. Previous work shows that not even grassroots movements (Sobrado Chavez and Stoller 2002), or state interventions explicitly designed to organize the poor (Abers 1997, Fox 1994) have been able to eradicate quid pro quo exchanges. Clientelism persists

---

[1] In this chapter, I focus only on strict conditional cash transfers. The effects of cash transfer programs when operational rules are lax, however, are more straightforward. Because presidents who face few checks on their power from congress often expand cash transfer programs during election years to bolster support for their party, whereas presidents who contend with a system of checks and balances do not (Chapter 4), and programs with less robust operations are not as effective at reaching poor households and have weaker effects on human capital, there is no reason why a conditional cash transfer program with a lax design would have the wealth, informative, and operative effects on clientelism that I described.

[2] My understanding of these developments is based on several types of qualitative research: (1) case studies of four Mexican villages: Santa María Citendejé (State of Mexico), Unión Ejidal and La Pedregoza (Tlaxcala), and El Chico (Hidalgo); (2) interviews with members of local governments at the National Conference of Local Development organized by the Ministry of Social Development; (3) interviews with *Oportunidades* staff from various levels, ranging from the national coordinator to local staff members; and (4) newspaper articles about the positions of all parties with respect to the program and the development of their campaigns from August 1997 to May 2000.

even after institutional changes, such as the introduction of electoral democracy, or even the introduction of the secret ballot (Escobar 2002). Remarkably, clientelism has survived class politics (Zuckerman 1983), as well as structural changes such as industrialization and globalization (Hytrek 2002, Lemarchand and Legg 1972).

THE EFFECTIVENESS OF A STRICT CCT AND CLIENTELISM

Although there is general agreement that voters would be better off in the long run if they punished clientelistic parties by withdrawing their support, history is full of examples of voters complying with clientelistic practices. Poverty may be an important part of the explanation for why voters rarely renege on their commitments to the political machines even when electoral markets present the opportunity.[3] Under the influence of poverty, individual constraints are even more binding. Scarcity of resources fosters risk aversion and impatience (Duflo 2006). This leads to a deadlock simply because the cost of siding with the wrong partisan group is high if it leads to the discontinuation of clientelist transfers (Lust and Masoud 2011).

A strict conditional cash transfer is more effective at improving households' welfare, because its operational rules include provisions to avoid mismanagement. Therefore a household enrolled in a strict conditional cash transfer program can afford to distance itself from party brokers.

The *Oportunidades* program in Mexico, for example, has been proven to have important positive effects on families' well-being, including improvements in children's health, nutrition, and school attendance. For a detailed review of the effects of *Oportunidades*, see Chapter 2. These improvements in human capital not only decreased the incidence of destabilizing shocks, such as illness, but also reduced the vulnerability of households to these shocks.

These improvements in well-being are also important because they are irreversible, in the sense that an additional year of schooling gained or a year spent without illness simply cannot be taken away. As these effects accumulate and poverty decreases, households become more risk tolerant and more patient. Thus families enrolled in *Oportunidades* can afford to distance themselves from local bosses. By providing some relief from poverty, and from the adverse shocks that come with it, strict cash transfer programs make party brokers' jobs more difficult.

CCT INFORMATION AVAILABILITY AND CLIENTELISM

Clientelism among beneficiaries of social programs works in part because voters are often unaware about where the funding for social programs comes from. In

---

[3] Recent work on clientelism, however, has challenged this long-standing assumption. For example, Lust and Masoud (2011) find that in Egypt and Jordan, poverty is not a strong predictor of participation in a clientelist network.

TABLE 6.1 *Survey Participants' Knowledge of Program Sources*

Program	Which Government is in Charge of CCT? (Percentages)				
	Federal	State	Municipal	Other	DK
None	63.91	20.96	7.5	3.36	4.27
CCT	69.93	16.99	7.19	4.58	1.31
Seguro Popular	58.46	27.69	12.31	1.54	0
Other programs	67.35	24.49	4.08	2.04	2.04

many cases, voters are also uncertain about the price of the goods and services they receive from government, which in many cases is below the market price. In contrast, *Oportunidades'* s monetary transfer and its source are clear. Doña Rosa, a resident of Santa María Citendejé in Mexico state, made this point clear. I encountered Doña Rosa in 2005 on the main road of the town pulling a small, battered cart from which she sells ice cream for a living. Doña Rosa is a member of the committee that serves as a bridge between *Oportunidades* and the program recipients in the village, and she herself has been enrolled in the program since 1998. When I eventually asked her where she thought the funds for the *Oportunidades* program came from (in 2005), she answered, "From President Fox." When I asked her who funded the program when it was called *Progresa*, Doña Rosa said it was "President Zedillo" and then said, "You see, this a federal program" (author's interview, Santa María Citendejé, August 31, 2005). Strictly speaking, the program's funds originate from an agency that is funded by three ministries of the federal government. But for practical purposes, Doña Rosa is correct in her assertion that the program falls under the responsibility of the executive.

Results from the 2009 national survey of Mexican households also support the conclusion that people are aware of which level of government operates *Oportunidades*. The survey conducted in 2009 is nationally representative, with an oversample in rural areas. Table 6.1 presents the responses to a survey question that asked participants which government authority is responsible for the operation of the Mexican CCT program. The first row of Table 6.1 indicates the responses from survey participants who, at the time of the survey, were not enrolled in any social program. The second row provides responses from respondents enrolled in the Mexican CCT, and the third row provides responses from respondents enrolled in *Seguro Popular*, a universal health insurance scheme. The fourth row shows responses from survey participants enrolled in some other social program at the time of the survey.

Survey respondents enrolled in *Oportunidades* are the group most informed about the sources of the program. Seventy percent of *Oportunidades* beneficiaries correctly identified the program as federally run, whereas 63 percent of respondents without any social program benefits correctly identified the CCT as a federal program. The second most common belief is that the program is operated by the state government, though there are three times fewer respondents who think of *Oportunidades* as a state-run program. In sum, for all individuals surveyed, knowledge that the CCT is a federal program was high, though it was particularly high for respondents actually enrolled in the program.

Not only are program beneficiaries aware that *Oportunidades* is a federally run program, they also understand the requirements that need to be met to remain enrolled in the program. In La Pedregoza, a rural village in the state of Tlaxcala, one recipient of the program told me, "We are not afraid. If kids stay in school, we stay in the program" (interview, La Pedregoza, Tlaxcala, July 2005). Program representatives in Tlaxcala also acknowledged that their work is facilitated by program recipients' knowledge of the conditions that they must meet to stay in the program. One program representative that I spoke with said, "Women know that missing the health talks or kids missing school results in the loss of the program" (interview with personnel, Tlaxcala, July 2005).[4]

In Peru, a survey conducted in 2007 by the National Committee of Monitoring and Transparency found that 94 percent of CCT program beneficiaries knew that to remain in the program, they were required to take their children to regular health checkups. A similar proportion of respondents knew that children's school attendance was also required.[5]

In Colombia, a survey conducted by the National Consulting Center in 2008 showed that among the population displaced by the violence in the countryside, 86 percent of CCT program recipients believed that the information they received about program enrollment clearly stated the time, place, and requirements for enrolling in the program. Only 15 percent believed that the information was incomplete because it only specified the date of enrollment. Nine percent reported that the information did not contain important details for the displaced population, 16 percent believed that the information was difficult to comprehend, 13 percent reported that the information did not contain enough details about the program benefits, and only 6 percent of respondents reported that they did not know the requirements for enrolling in the program (*Centro Nacional de Consultoría*, 2008).

The survey in Colombia also tested program recipients' knowledge about the conditions that households need to meet to receive program benefits regularly.

---

[4] The amount of the transfer varies depending on the size of the family, as well as the gender and age of the children. The formula for calculating the size of the transfer is somewhat complex, so it would not be surprising to find that recipients were confused by the differences in the amount of the transfer that each family receives. Nevertheless, I found that although recipients were aware of these differences, they knew the logic behind them. When asked why some families received more money than others, they answered correctly that cash transfers for girls are higher than for boys because parents tend to take girls out of school sooner. They also knew that being dropped from the program was directly related to their attendance at the health talks and children's school attendance (informational meeting at Unión Ejidal, July 2005).
[5] Report of the National Committee of Monitoring and Transparency, January–June 2007.

With regard to children's schooling, 87 percent of respondents correctly mentioned that school enrollment and attendance were required. The same number of respondents also correctly identified the conditions related to health and nutrition. In addition, 99 percent of respondents knew the amount of the transfer that corresponded to the education and health components, and 66 percent reported knowing where to file a complaint in the event that a payment was suspended or delayed. The one program component that respondents were less aware of is the portability of benefits. Only 23 percent of respondents knew that they were entitled to receive the cash transfers even if they relocated to another village or state in Colombia (*Centro Nacional de Consultoría*, 2008).

In Guatemala, Transparency International and *Acción Ciudadana* (2010) found through a survey that families enrolled in the program had a positive attitude toward the conditionalities and the verification process, and IDIES (2009) found that program recipients are informed about the program and its procedures. For example, 83 percent of program recipients indicated that the information about the program was good or very good, and 87 percent of recipients knew the person in charge of the program at the local level. Almost 70 percent of recipients knew that they were enrolled in the program as a result of income criteria, around 20 percent were unclear as to why they were in the program, 1.4 percent of recipients believed that they were enrolled in the program because they actively participate in their community, and 0.9 percent mentioned that they were in the program because the mayor enrolled them. Access to information about program conditionalities was also high among recipients: 82 percent of recipients mentioned the schooling requirement and 88 percent mentioned the requirement of taking children to health centers. IDIES also found that among the majority of program recipients, the program is positively viewed.

Despite the information available to beneficiaries, party brokers in all countries where a conditional cash transfer program is in operation have at some point tried to use the program to their benefit. During a conversation I had with a member of *Oportunidades*'s staff from the state of Sonora (a PRI-dominated state), he explained that "municipal authorities noticed early the political potential of the program and tried to take advantage of it."[6]

Program information, however, empowers beneficiaries to resist party brokers' attempts to manipulate them or involve them in a clientelistic exchange. Because beneficiaries know where the funding for the conditional cash transfer comes from and the requirements to receive programs' cash transfers, party brokers' opportunities to extort program recipients are limited.

In Mexico, for example, it is surprising that women not only are well informed about the program but actively protest against party brokers who

---

[6] Author's interview, August 2005.

try to intimidate them.[7] In Santa María Citendejé, a group of women told me that a broker in their village intended to use the program to advance her own political career by threatening people or promising to enroll families into the program. One of these women said, "But we know she does not have the last word on this. That is why we don't like her."[8]

Oportunidades's headquarters receives frequent complaints about party brokers and other politicians trying to use the program for political aims. During an interview I conducted with the national coordinator for the program during the Fox administration, Rogelio Gómez Hermosillo, he gave me the following example:

Program staff from Hidalgo brought me a video from a community that had a problem with the doctor at the local health center. The problem was that the doctor proposed to the recipients that instead of a usual informational talk she was going to send them to an event sponsored by the Minister of Health, because it was World AIDS Day. The recipients of the program were upset because they felt that the doctor was trying to manipulate them into attending a political event, so they called the program office in Pachuca (state capital) and asked them to send someone to intervene in the issue. When the program staff arrived, the doctor explained that the event she was proposing was not political but rather a non-partisan event at which the Minister of Health was going to talk about AIDS (interview, August 2005).

Two points are interesting about this anecdote. First, the doctor's proposal annoyed the recipients even though it was not a case of political pandering. Second, the recipients knew they were not required to comply with the doctor's request, and they knew whom they had to call to file their complaint.[9]

In Colombia, local brokers tried to take advantage of the widespread political manipulation of the first targeting system, SISBEN I, to falsely promise enrollment in the CCT program, *Familias en Acción*, in exchange for votes (for more details about the SISBEN I, see Chapter 2). Recipients of the CCT reported to the program headquarters that party brokers attempted to use the CCT for clientelist purposes. The national media closely followed the issue and gave frequent reminders that enrollment in the CCT program was free and did not require an intermediary. In 2010, the coordinator of the SISBEN II

---

[7] It is very likely that the requirement that the female head of the household attend talks at the local health center has contributed to a proper understanding of the program, as these gatherings have created an opportunity for women to meet on a frequent basis to interact and discuss matters related to the program, as well as, in many cases, more general issues related to their community. Impact evaluations have shown that participation in these talks induced a behavioral change. See Hoddinott and Skoufias (2004).

[8] Author's interview, Santa María Citendejé 2002.

[9] Hermosillo also mentioned in our interview that the highest number of complaints received by the *Oportunidades* program headquarters were about dubious practices on the part of the PAN. His hypothesis was that politicians in the PAN are less experienced manipulators, and therefore get caught more often than politicians from other parties. However, there are no data on the number and nature of complaints to further explore this issue.

targeting system told a reporter from *El Universal*, one of Colombia's biggest newspapers, that "the electoral authorities know about these types of activities. I remind the community that the process of enrollment in the program is free, and does not require an intermediary or political connections... Some candidates threaten people by saying that transfers will continue only if votes are delivered. This is false because *Familias en Acción* is not under the jurisdiction of anyone that is not the [federal] government." Colombia's anti-corruption czar was also interviewed for the article and reinforced the message by further explaining that the program was not a prerogative of local governments or political parties, but was a policy directly under the jurisdiction of the federal government.[10] Then, as in the Mexican case, the information available to recipients about program operations curbed the ability of local brokers to coerce CCT program recipients to vote in a certain way.

Even displaced people enrolled in the Colombian CCT suspect that party brokers have an incentive to distort the information about program enrollment opportunities; they are especially suspicious of local brokers with clear ties to political candidates. Thus, displaced communities do not trust local brokers when it comes to program enrollments.[11]

THE STANDARDIZATION OF PROGRAMS AND CLIENTELISM

In addition to the effect of a strict conditional cash transfer program on clientelism through an informative mechanism, such a program also affects clientelism in part because it is systematically implemented, which reduces the discretion of party brokers to operate a program. This makes vote buying more difficult because brokers cannot bestow program benefits, nor can they punish (or credibly threaten) recipients by discontinuing the stream of program benefits.

The *Oportunidades* program in Mexico, for example, had a large impact on local party brokers, who were circumvented by the program bureaucracy. When *Oportunidades* was first implemented in 1997, old-style *caciques* (local bosses) were no longer feudal chiefs with absolute economic, political, and social control over a region and its inhabitants, like the legendary figures of Gonzalo N. Santos in San Luis Potosí,[12] Leobardo Reynoso in Zacatecas, and Ruben Figueroa in Guerrero. The modernization of the country, electoral reforms, and the expansion of government welfare bureaucracies on the one hand and the frequent economic crises and pro-market economic reforms

---

[10] "Advierten engaños de políticos que prometen entrega de Sisbén." *El Universal*, Cartagena, Colombia February 21, 2010. http://www.eluniversal.com.co/cartagena/local/advierten-enganos-de-politicos-que-prometen-entrega-de-sisben.
[11] Centro Nacional de Consultoría 2008, p. 544.
[12] Bezdek (1995) wrote about Santos: "Virtually all sources report that he applied the law of the three ierros to his opponents: el encierro, el destierro and el entierro" (imprisonment, banishment, and burial) (35).

on the other hand sharply diminished the resources available to local bosses (Cornelius and Craig 1991). As a consequence, the ability of patronage machines to mobilize voters was already compromised, which is reflected in the steady drop in voter turnout that began in the 1960s and bottomed out in the closely – contested elections of 1988 (Lawson and Klesner 2004).

The evolution of welfare agencies, however, did not dilute machine politics in Mexico to the same degree as it did in the United States after the New Deal.[13] In Mexico, welfare agencies more often than not reproduced clientelistic relations. Thus, old-style caciques were replaced by (or transformed into) new patrons "positioned around occupants of the management offices of large state-owned companies, managers of agricultural banks, and federal delegations" (Aguilar Camín and Meyer 1993).

In large urban centers, the power of these new patrons was constrained.[14] In rural areas of the country, where patrons remained powerful, local politics was characterized by three features. First, public resources were distributed in the form of food, clothing, construction materials, and – when the machine was generous – even washing machines in exchange for explicit political support. Brokers often allocated resources close to an election period, and most accounts of how clientelism works in Mexico mention that resources are distributed contingent on a vote for the party in charge. Second, state representatives of welfare agencies conditioned the distribution of services on support for the ruling party (Williams 2001). Third, state representatives were more interested in turning people out to parades, rallies, and the polls than in ensuring the proper functioning of state agencies because their careers were determined mainly by their ability to respond to the political needs of the incumbent party. Many years ago an executive from the National Staple Products Company (CONASUPO) explained this succinctly:

The state representative is often sandwiched between his responsibilities as direct representative of CONASUPO or the general director in the state and the political pressures which are exerted upon him by the governor and local political forces. Many times he might be in a position of wishing to ignore or not hear about the malfunctioning or non-functioning of CONASUPO programs because of other pressures upon him (in Grindle 1977, 143).

Oportunidades directly challenged local governments' clientelistic control of federal resources because the operational rules of the program circumvented traditional mechanisms of resource distribution that were susceptible to pressure from governors and locally important political figures.[15]

---

[13] See Scott (1969).
[14] In Mexico City, for example, the insufficient response from the city government after the 1985 earthquake caused grassroots organizations to replace old-style PRI patronage machines as the political centers of poor neighborhoods (Aguilar Zinzer et al. 1986, Centeno 1999).
[15] Prior to *Oportunidades*, PRONASOL was seen by some as an effort to bypass both local authorities and traditional political bosses (for more on PRONASOL, see Chapter 2). Although the

Unlike state representatives for other social programs, whose careers were tied to their ability to get votes, *Oportunidades* personnel had a different set of incentives because of the decree that made using *Oportunidades* to gain votes a federal offense punishable by law. In addition, the clear and fixed criteria to select program recipients diminished federal government's ability to openly manipulate the program budget.

The program was further insulated from local politics by the inclusion of text stating that program participation was not contingent on affiliation with any party or voting for a specific candidate. This text appeared in all program materials (including the program identification card carried by all beneficiaries). In addition, program materials clearly stated that without exception, anyone who tried to use the program for electoral purposes would be prosecuted.[16]

The fact that recipients learned that resources should flow independent of the local boss or state governments made local brokers' jobs more difficult, if not impossible. In my interview with a PRI broker from the state of Tabasco, he explained his discontent with the program:

What the *Oportunidades* staff doesn't get is that they have to let us decide who enters and exits the program; otherwise, we can't punish people who didn't vote for us. And we know who didn't; we know because we know the people, where they work and what party they are loyal to. With the inflexibility of the program we can't include our people and take out the ones that are not with us. (Interview with PRI broker, Mexico City, August 2005)[17]

This broker was not the first to complain about the federal government intervening in the political life of municipalities. Before *Oportunidades*, however, this complaint often came not from PRI brokers but from the opposition. A notorious example was the opposition's antagonism to PRONASOL (see Fox and Moguel 1995, Acedo Angulo and Ruiz Suárez 1995). The fact that *Oportunidades* made both the PRI and opposition brokers' jobs more difficult strongly suggests that the political machines in the poorest rural areas in Mexico were finally eroded.

The brokers' feelings of displacement are shared by municipal presidents of all political affiliations throughout the country. *Oportunidades*'s features

---

extent to which PRONASOL challenged local bosses remains unclear, Fox and Moguel (1995) argue that many, but not all, opposition mayors were bypassed. The discretion with which PRONASOL funds were allocated gave the state and municipal agents room for bargaining. Thus, the degree to which municipalities were bypassed was a function of the state electoral context and local bargaining strategies.

[16] For the full text, see Chapter 3.

[17] The exact words in Spanish were "lo que los de oportunidades no entienden, es que nos tienen que dejar intervenir en la decisión de quién entra y quién no en el programa, si no nosotros (en el municipio) no tenemos manera de castigar a la gente que no estuvo con nosotros en la elección. Y nosotros sabemos quién no voto con nosotros, sabemos porque conocemos a la gente y donde trabajan y con qué partido se afilian de toda la vida, así que con lo estricto del programa no podemos meter a nuestra gente y sacar a la gente que no estuvo con nosotros."

Conditional Cash Transfers and Clientelism 123

disconnected governors, state delegates, local bosses, and local authorities from an important source of power by circumventing them and delivering resources directly to the pockets of the poor. At the National Convention for Local Development that took place in Mexico City in 2005, municipal presidents from around the country met with *Oportunidades* personnel to discuss the advantages and disadvantages of the program. The municipal presidents were divided into working groups to discuss program operations in their municipalities in detail. Although all the working groups recognized the importance of the program for addressing poverty, the groups also agreed on one chief demand: the decentralization of resources.[18] Many municipal presidents also requested an active role in the selection of recipients, full access to the list of program beneficiaries, and the power to purge this list at their discretion.[19]

Juntos, the cash transfer program in Peru, also faced resistance from local brokers. In a session of the regional government of Piura, the regional coordinator of the *Juntos* program expressed the following concern: "In [the districts of] Ayabaca and Pacaipampa...there are communities that have their own policies, and they don't allow access to the (*Juntos*) program. I have been concerned with signing agreements that allow the operation of the program, because *Juntos* is a state policy, we want that when this government is over, the program continues. We need the district councils to cooperate."[20]

Local brokers' discontent with the program in Peru was widespread. A few months after the inauguration of the program in 2005, 250 municipal presidents, who were members of the Network of Rural Municipalities in Peru, organized a rally to demand that congress transfer funding and administrative oversight for all social programs, including *Juntos*, to the municipalities. Although the mayors were invited to a meeting with legislators to further air their grievances, municipalities were ultimately denied their requests, and *Juntos* has remained a federal program.[21]

In Guatemala, the evaluation report of the MIFAPRO program conducted by the Institute of Economic and Social Studies (IDIES) revealed that members of local organizations saw the conditional cash transfer program as a threat because they anticipated that program recipients would no longer attend their events, given that they couldn't compete with the cash transfer offered by the MIFAPRO program (IDIES 2009). Local organizations also complained

---

[18] Would the program function more effectively if it were decentralized? Kitschelt (2000) has a pessimistic argument on this point: "Going beyond institutional contingencies, where socioeconomic development and state formation strongly pull a democratic polity toward clientelist linkage mechanism, at the margin of a new democracy, the power of the presidency may be the only available institutional antidote to the reign of special interest in clientelist networks" (861).
[19] Author's notes and observations at the 2005 Convention.
[20] Special Session Number 14 2009, Sede del Gobierno Regional Piura.
[21] "*Alcaldes piden administrar programa Juntos.*" *La República*, September 21, 2005. http://www.larepublica.pe/21-09-2005/alcaldes-piden-administrar-programa-juntos.

about their lack of information about program enrollment and compliance with program requirements, because most of this information flows through the local health and education institutions, and about the little influence they have on the enrollment process. These groups also felt that they should play a larger role as intermediaries between program administrators and local communities, and have a say in how program resources are allocated.

The evaluation report also documents that municipal presidents around the country also expressed concern about how data were collected for determining program eligibility. Their concern was that municipal authorities were not involved in the process, and they felt deceived because they thought the government was only collecting census data (IDIES 2009, 18). Several municipal presidents indicated that program personnel invited their communities to attend local meetings where information about MIFAPRO and the method for determining program eligibility was disseminated, but that the selection of program recipients was done in the capital city (18). Similarly, local leaders also complained that they were excluded from participating in the process of selecting program beneficiaries.

In sum, the systematic implementation of a strict conditional cash transfer program reduces the discretion of party brokers to operate a program based on a system of rewards and punishments. In turn, reducing party brokers' discretion erodes clientelism.

TESTING THE ARGUMENT

In this section I present an analysis based on data from a nationally representative survey conducted with Mexican households in 2009 to test the argument that the robust implementation of a strict CCT program such as *Oportunidades* weakens clientelism. The survey oversamples the rural areas where more of the program's recipients are located, and also where clientelism is thought to be more pervasive.

Table 6.2 presents descriptive statistics on respondents according to their social policy enrollment status. Column 1 includes respondents enrolled in *Oportunidades*, column 2 includes people enrolled in *Seguro Popular*, column 3 includes respondents enrolled in some other social program, and column 4 includes people who are not enrolled in any social program. Among these social programs, *Oportunidades* has the most targeted allocation of resources. As explained in Chapter 2, like other CCT programs in Latin America, *Oportunidades* focuses its resources on the poorest regions in the country and targets households living under the poverty line. *Seguro Popular*, on the other hand, is a universal health insurance scheme that was designed to grant poor families access to health services. Finally, the other social programs that respondents participate in include programs different from *Oportunidades* or *Seguro Popular* operated at the federal and state levels, most of which have less clear selection mechanisms and less robust implementations than *Oportunidades*.

TABLE 6.2 *Education, Income, and Party Identification of Survey Sample*

	(1) CCT	(2) SP	(3) Other	(4) No Program	(5) (1)–(4)	(6) (2)–(4)	(7) (3)–(4)
Education	3.49	4.11	4.59	4.86	−1.37 (0.24)***	−0.75 (0.36)	−0.27 (0.39)
Primary education or less	0.67	0.47	0.52	0.44	0.23 (0.04)***	0.03 (0.06)	0.08 (0.06)
Income	2.01	2.04	2.39	2.61	−0.60 (0.09)***	−0.57 (0.13)***	−0.22 (0.16)
Poor	0.58	0.60	0.38	0.36	0.22 (0.04)***	0.24 (0.06)***	0.02 (0.06)
Phone	0.25	0.21	0.55	0.46	−0.21 (0.04)***	−0.25 (0.06)***	0.09 (0.06)**
Cell phone	0.23	0.37	0.44	0.38	−0.15 (0.04)***	−0.01 (0.05)	0.06 (0.06)
Internet	0.05	0.17	0.13	0.17	−0.12 (0.02)***	0 (0.04)	−0.04 (0.04)
Party ID: PAN	0.10	0.04	0.08	0.11	−0.01 (0.02)	−0.07 (0.04)*	−0.03 (0.04)
Party ID: PRI	0.22	0.30	0.30	0.21	0.01 (0.003)	0.09 (0.05)	0.09 (0.05)
Party ID: PRD	0.03	0.03	0.06	0.03	0 (0.01)	0 (0.02)	0.03 (0.02)

Standard errors in parentheses.
*** p < 0.01, ** p < 0.05, * p < 0.1.

Previous work has convincingly shown that the targeting mechanism of *Oportunidades* was effective in reaching poor households (see Chapter 2). Table 6.2 presents further evidence of this. In this nationally representative sample, *Oportunidades*'s recipients are the poorest of those surveyed. For example, in terms of education, *Oportunidades* recipients reported at average score of 3.5 on a scale that goes from 1 to 12, where 1 indicates that a respondent has no formal education and 12 indicates that a respondent has graduate-level education. On this scale, 3.5 is equivalent to slightly more schooling than primary education. Respondents enrolled in *Seguro Popular* reported a slightly higher average score for education at 4.11. Respondents enrolled in other social programs reported an average score of 4.6, and respondents not enrolled in any social program reported a score of 4.9, which is equivalent to having completed secondary school.

Column 5 presents the differences in means between respondents enrolled in the CCT program and respondents not enrolled in the program. This difference is statistically significant at the 1 percent level, which confirms that *Oportunidades* recipients are poorer on average than those individuals not enrolled in a social program. Column 6 presents the differences in means between respondents enrolled in *Seguro Popular* and respondents not enrolled in any social program, and Column 7 presents the differences between respondents enrolled in other programs and respondents not enrolled in social programs. Neither of these differences is statistically significant.

To further strengthen this result, Row 2 in Table 6.2 presents the proportion of respondents who have primary school education or less according to social program status. Among respondents with *Oportunidades*, 67 percent have no education past primary school. Among respondents with *Seguro Popular*, 47 percent are at this level, and among respondents with other programs or no program, 52 percent and 44 percent, respectively, have primary school education or less.

Respondents enrolled in *Oportunidades* also report less income on average than any other group of respondents. The survey measures household income in five categories: 1 represents an income of 1,500 pesos a month or less, 2 represents an income between 1,501 and 3,000 pesos, 3 represents an income between 3,001 and 6,000 pesos, 4 represents an income between 6,001 and 12,000 pesos, and 5 represents an income greater than 12,000 pesos per month. *Oportunidades* respondents report an average of 2 on this income scale. *Seguro Popular* respondents report an average of 2.04, respondents with other social program benefits report an average income of 2.39, and respondents without social programs report an average income of 2.6. In other words, if we define a household as extremely poor when their income is 1,500 pesos a month or less, then the proportion of *Oportunidades* recipients who report income levels that qualify them as extremely poor is almost 60 percent. Among *Seguro Popular* respondents, the proportion of extremely poor is also around 60 percent. In contrast, the proportion of respondents enrolled in other programs who report being extremely poor is 38 percent, and the proportion of extremely poor in the group of respondents without social programs is 36 percent.

The differences in means between respondents with *Oportunidades* and respondents without a program, and respondents with *Seguro Popular* and respondents without a program, are statistically significant. In contrast, the differences in means between the respondents enrolled in other programs and respondents without a program, are not statistically significant. Rows 5 through 7 of Table 6.2 present complementary measures of wealth differences among groups, including the proportion of respondents with a fixed telephone at home, with a cellular phone, and with access to the Internet. Consistent with the education and income measures, a smaller proportion of *Oportunidades* respondents have a telephone at home, a cellular phone, and access to the Internet than respondents not enrolled in a social program. All these differences are statistically significant at the 1 percent level. The proportion of respondents with *Seguro Popular* who have fixed telephones and cell phones is also smaller than the proportion of respondents not enrolled in programs who have access to these items, and these differences are statistically significant. These groups have statistically indistinguishable access to the Internet, however. In contrast, respondents enrolled in other social programs are equally as likely to have a telephone and access to the Internet than respondents without a social program. Surprisingly, respondents enrolled in other programs are more likely to say that they have a telephone at home than respondents without a social program.

Finally, Table 6.2 shows the descriptive statistics of partisan identification among respondents enrolled in the various social programs. Respondents in *Oportunidades* have a statistically indistinguishable partisan identification profile compared to respondents without a social program. In both groups, approximately 10 percent of respondents identify strongly with the PAN, 22 percent with the PRI, and 3 percent with the PRD. Respondents with *Seguro Popular* and other programs are also, for the most part, statistically indistinguishable from individuals with no social program with respect to partisan identification, except that the proportion of respondents with *Seguro Popular* who identify with the PAN is smaller than the proportion who do among individuals with no social program.

In sum, these descriptive statistics suggest that *Oportunidades* effectively targeted the poorest members of the population. Similarly, *Seguro Popular*, although universal, seems to reach the poor. In contrast, it appears other social programs do not effectively target the poor, as respondents benefiting from these programs are not more likely to report that they are poor or less educated than respondents without social programs. In terms of party identification, these descriptive statistics suggest that there is no apparent partisan bias among respondents enrolled in the CCT program.

One of the most robust findings in the literature on clientelism is that parties target poor voters because they can buy their votes for less money (Auyero 2000; Stokes 2005). Following this argument, if it were just for their poverty, respondents enrolled in *Oportunidades* should report the highest levels of vote buying because they are the poorest group in the sample. *Oportunidades* recipients' experiences of vote buying, patronage, and coercion reveal a different pattern, however.

Table 6.3 reports the coefficients and standard errors of various linear probability models where the dependent variables are measures of respondents' reports of vote buying, patronage, and coercion, as well as respondents' beliefs in the secrecy of the ballot and how free they felt when casting their vote. The independent variables of interest are three dummy variables that capture a respondent's social program enrollment status (CCT, *Seguro Popular*, or other program). The reference group is made up of respondents who are not enrolled in any social program. To take into account that respondents enrolled in *Oportunidades* are poorer and have fewer years of schooling than other respondents, Table 6.3 presents the results of the linear probability models with and without socio-demographic characteristics. All models include district fixed effects to capture factors that affect clientelism but that are constant within districts. The results of all these models, however, are robust to the exclusion of these fixed effects.

In the first two models, the dependent variable is a dummy that takes the value 1 for respondents who agree with the statement that political parties always buy votes, and 0 otherwise. Respondents enrolled in *Oportunidades* are 8 percentage points less likely than respondents not enrolled in a social program to report that political parties always buy votes. This result is statistically significant at the 5 percent level, and it is robust to the inclusion of socio-demographic characteristics as control variables. Enrollment in *Seguro Popular* or in other social programs has no statistically effect distinguishable from 0 on the likelihood that respondents report vote buying as a frequent phenomenon.

In models (3) and (4), the dependent variable is a dummy variable that takes the value 1 when respondents report that they received a gift or a favor in exchange for their vote. Respondents enrolled in *Oportunidades* or in *Seguro Popular* are as likely to report receiving a gift or favor as are respondents not enrolled in a social program. In contrast, respondents enrolled in other programs are 17 percentage points more likely to report selling their votes. These results are statistically significant at the 10 percent level and are also robust to the inclusion of socio-demographic control variables.

In the next two models, (5) and (6), the dependent variable is an indicator that takes the value 1 when respondents report that parties offered them a job in exchange for their vote, and 0 otherwise. Respondents enrolled in *Oportunidades* report 3 percentage points fewer patronage offers than respondents with no social program. This result is statistically significant at the 1 percent level and continues to be significant at the 5 percent level after the introduction of baseline characteristics. Enrollment in neither *Seguro Popular* nor other social programs has an effect on participation in patronage. In models (7) and

TABLE 6.3 Oportunidades and Clientelism (Survey Data)

Variables	Parties Always Buy Votes (1)	(2)	Received Gift (3)	(4)	Offered Job (5)	(6)
CCT	−0.085** (0.034)	−0.068** (0.035)	0.006 (0.024)	0.013 (0.025)	−0.029*** (0.010)	−0.023** (0.010)
Seguro Popular	−0.009 (0.060)	0.004 (0.062)	0.062 (0.041)	0.062 (0.042)	−0.022 (0.015)	−0.020 (0.015)
Other program	0.135 (0.088)	0.126 (0.085)	0.169* (0.100)	0.169* (0.096)	−0.008 (0.021)	−0.013 (0.022)
Controls	no	yes	no	yes	no	yes
Constant	0.210*** (0.016)	0.166*** (0.032)	0.053*** (0.009)	0.017 (0.019)	0.031*** (0.007)	0.005 (0.015)
Observations	1,233	1,219	1,233	1,219	1,233	1,219
R-squared	0.097	0.112	0.078	0.085	0.037	0.057

	Threat (7)	(8)	Vote is Secret (9)	(10)	Felt Free to Vote (11)	(12)	List Experiment (13)	(14)
CCT	−0.011 (0.007)	−0.004 (0.007)	0.125** (0.051)	0.127** (0.052)	0.128*** (0.044)	0.136*** (0.044)	−0.337* (0.177)	−0.341** (0.173)
Seguro Popular	0.007 (0.020)	0.013 (0.020)	0.138** (0.066)	0.146** (0.066)	0.018 (0.062)	0.032 (0.062)	−0.023 (0.254)	−0.034 (0.261)
Other program	−0.010 (0.011)	−0.015 (0.013)	−0.032 (0.099)	−0.022 (0.093)	−0.077 (0.087)	−0.067 (0.079)	−0.001 (0.238)	0.002 (0.253)
Controls	no	yes	no	yes	no	yes	no	yes
Constant	0.017*** (0.005)	0.012 (0.013)	0.513*** (0.021)	0.418*** (0.043)	0.693*** (0.019)	0.612*** (0.040)	2.020*** (0.049)	2.035*** (0.081)
Observations	1,233	1,219	1,233	1,219	1,233	1,219	1,169	1,157
R-squared	0.036	0.068	0.083	0.098	0.083	0.098	0.110	0.121

Robust standard errors in parentheses.
All models include district fixed effects.
*** p < 0.01, ** p < 0.05, * p < 0.1.

(8), the dependent variable is an indicator that takes the value 1 if respondents reported that a party threatened their jobs to coerce them to vote for them. Very few respondents reported being threatened, and social program enrollment status has no statistically significant effect on the probability of such a threat.

Together, models (1) through (8) show consistent evidence that respondents enrolled in *Oportunidades* are less likely to report witnessing or participating in vote buying and patronage. Models (9) through (12) explore a slightly different angle on the same issue. The literature on clientelism suggests that political parties are more likely to buy votes when they have ways to monitor the votes that they buy. One institutional feature that has received attention in scholarly work is the secrecy of the ballot. Voters are more vulnerable to participating in vote buying when they believe that parties can figure out how they voted. In models (9) and (10), the dependent variable is a dummy that takes the value 1 when respondents report that they believe strongly that their vote is secret, and 0 otherwise. Respondents enrolled in *Oportunidades* are 13 percentage points more likely to report that their vote is secret compared to respondents not enrolled in any program. This result is statistically significant at the 5 percent level, and it is robust to the inclusion of socio-demographic controls. Similarly, respondents enrolled in *Seguro Popular* are more likely to report that their vote is secret than individuals with no social program. This result is significant at the 5 percent level. In contrast, respondents enrolled in other social programs are statistically undistinguishable from respondents with no program.

Finally, models (11) and (12) have as dependent variable a dummy that takes the value 1 when respondents report that they felt completely free to cast their ballot according to their preferences, and 0 otherwise. Respondents enrolled in *Oportunidades* are 13 percentage points more likely to respond that they felt completely free to cast their vote compared to individuals with no social program. This result is statistically significant at the 1 percent level. When demographic characteristics are included as controls, the result becomes slightly stronger (14 percentage points) and is statistically significant at the 1 percent level. Enrollment in *Seguro Popular* and other programs does not have a statistically significant effect on the probability that a respondent feels free to vote for his or her choice.

In sum, Table 6.3 presents evidence that is consistent with the argument of this book that enrollment in a strict CCT program with a robust implementation erodes clientelism. Not only are individuals enrolled in *Oportunidades* less likely to report witnessing or participating in vote buying and patronage compared to individuals not enrolled in the CCT, but they also felt more strongly that their vote is secret and that they are free to cast their ballot according to their preferences. The effects of *Oportunidades* are also distinct from the effects of other social programs such as the universal *Seguro Popular* or other programs implemented locally.

Although the results in Table 6.3 are robust and consistent, one source of potential concern is that individuals enrolled in *Oportunidades* are more vulnerable to social desirability bias. In other words, *Oportunidades* recipients may be more prone to believe that vote buying is socially unacceptable. This belief may be a consequence of the effort of program operators of insulate the program from politics, such as including in all program materials a message explicitly stating that it is a federal offense to use the program for political purposes (for more details on this, see Chapter 2). If beneficiaries of *Oportunidades* are therefore more vulnerable to social desirability bias, they may be more likely to underreport their participation in vote buying and patronage, as well as misrepresent their beliefs about the secrecy of the ballot and how free they felt to cast a ballot. If systematic misreporting happens, inferences about the effects of enrollment in programs like *Oportunidades* would be invalid. To check the robustness of the result to this potential problem, I added two models in Table 6.3 that take advantage of a list experiment conducted in the nationally representative survey.

List experiments are a useful tool to circumvent problems associated with social desirability bias. In political science they have been used to study racial prejudice, corruption, and religious attendance. More recently (Gonzalez-Ocantos et al. 2012) conducted a list experiment to study vote buying.[22] The attractiveness of list experiments is that they grant respondents a certain degree of anonymity when answering sensitive questions. Following a commonly used list experiment to measure vote buying, the survey sample was split into two groups. During the interviews, one group of respondents (the control group) was handed a card with a list of activities that parties engage in to get votes, including placing campaign posters in the village, visiting the respondent's home, broadcasting campaign publicity on the radio and on television, and threatening the respondent to gain his or her vote. Respondents were not asked to report which of these activities were carried out by a party, but rather how many were. During interviews with the other half of the sample (the treatment group), respondents were handed a card with the same list of party activities, except that the card included an additional item in third place on the list that explicitly referred to vote buying: Parties gave you a gift or did you a favor. As with the control group, respondents in the treatment group were asked to report how many activities parties engaged in to get her vote. The difference between the average number of activities reported in the treatment and control groups is a measure of the extent of vote buying.

Survey respondents who were not enrolled in any social program reported witnessing 2.22 activities on average in the treatment group, and 1.98 activities in the control group. The difference in mean number of items is statistically significant at the 1 percent level and suggests that among this group 24 percent

[22] See Blair and Imai (2012) for more details on the benefits and drawbacks of list experiments.

TABLE 6.4 *List Experiment (Comparison of Means)*

Program	Treatment	Control	Difference
CCT	1.94	2.14	−0.19
			(0.13)
SP	1.88	1.91	−0.03
			(0.20)
Other	2.46	2	0.46
			(0.24)**
None	2.22	1.98	0.25
			(0.06)***

of individuals ((2.22 − 1.98) × 100) participated in vote buying. Among respondents who were enrolled in a social program other than *Oportunidades* or *Seguro Popular*, the treatment group reported an average of 2.46 activities, and the control group reported an average of 2 activities. Thus, among respondents enrolled in other social programs, these findings suggest that 46 percent ((2.46 − 2) × 100) participated in vote buying. These differences are statistically significant at the 10 percent level (see Table 6.4).

These rates of vote buying are in sharp contrast with the vote buying rates among respondents enrolled in the CCT program and *Seguro Popular*. Respondents enrolled in the CCT program report an average of 1.9 activities in the treatment group and 2.1 activities in the control group, but this difference in means is not statistically significant, suggesting that anonymity does not change the answers recipients of the CCT give to the question about vote buying. Similarly, respondents enrolled in *Seguro Popular* report 1.88 activities in the treatment group and 1.9 activities in the control group, and the difference in means is not statistically significant. Thus, respondents who are not enrolled in any social program or who are enrolled in programs other than *Oportunidades* and *Seguro Popular* participate in vote buying at higher rates, even when vote buying is measured with a list experiment.

The last two models in Table 6.3 test whether enrollment in different social programs has a robust effect on vote buying as measured with the list experiment. The dependent variable in these models is the number of party activities reported by respondents. The independent variables of interest are the interaction terms between social policy status and treatment group. For example, in model (13) the row corresponding to CCT gives the coefficient of the interaction between treatment and enrollment in the CCT program. In other words, this row reports the effect of being in the treatment group and enrolled in the CCT on the number of activities reported in the list experiment. The main effects of all interactions are included in the specification, but not reported in Table 6.3 for expositional reasons.[23]

---

[23] The full table is available upon request to the author.

Conditional Cash Transfers and Clientelism

The estimates of models (13) and (14) provide further evidence that recipients of *Oportunidades* witness less vote buying than individuals who are not enrolled in any social program. More specifically, results from the list experiment indicate that CCT recipients witness 33 percentage points less vote buying than individuals with no social program. This result is statistically significant at the 10 percent level. Model (14) shows that the result is robust to the inclusion of baseline control variables. In fact, once baseline characteristics are included in the specification, vote buying among *Oportunidades* recipients decreases by 34 percentage points. Enrollment in a CCT program is the only social policy status that produces statistically significant estimates with respect to vote buying measured with the list experiment.

In sum, Tables 6.3 and 6.4 present evidence confirming that enrollment in a strict CCT program reduces the frequency of vote buying, increases recipients' perceptions that their vote is secret, and increases the probability that recipients feel free to cast their vote according to their preferences. These results are robust to the inclusion of demographic covariates and even to the measurement of vote buying through a list experiment that grants respondents anonymity. The results also corroborate that the effects of enrollment in a strict CCT program are distinct from the effects of enrollment in other social programs. In this particular case, the effects of the Mexican CCT program are distinguishable from the effects of enrollment in Mexico's universal health insurance and enrollment in other social programs.

7

The Electoral Bonus of Conditional Cash Transfers

The increasing popularity among Latin American governments of conditional cash transfers raises a fundamental question about the electoral returns of government spending in general, and targeted benefits in particular. When a traditionally clientelistic party shifts away from discretionary spending to programmatic politics, can it retain the support of targeted voters? To date, the burgeoning distributive politics literature has given more attention to how politicians optimize their electoral prospects than to the conditions under which such strategies successfully increase support for incumbents.[1] This focus on discretionary spending leaves out a subset of allocation strategies in which targeting is based on technical criteria, as is the case for many conditional cash transfers, as opposed to electoral criteria.[2]

Although speculations about CCTs' proincumbent effects abound in the media,[3] scholarly work on the subject is inconclusive, as I describe in more detail in this chapter (Cerda and Vergara 2008; Cornelius 2004; Díaz-Cayeros et al. 2007; Díaz-Cayeros and Magaloni 2009; Green 2006; Zucco 2013). The empirical conundrum that has bedeviled previous attempts to uncover the causal effect of targeted government programs is that if incumbents strategically funnel resources to areas where they are electorally vulnerable (or strong), then estimates of electoral returns are biased downward (or upward). If we could observe the process that incumbents use to allocate resources, then accounting for it would be enough. However, in most cases we can only approximate the process with some error. Thus, the concern that remains is that an unobserved omitted variable biases the estimations (Levitt and Snyder 1997). In addition,

---

[1] For an insightful review of this literature, see Cox (2010).
[2] Two recent papers are exceptions to this trend. Brusco et al. (2006) and Calvo and Murillo (2004) evaluate both allocation strategies and its effectiveness in Argentina.
[3] BBC (2009), The *Washington Post* (2006), Lindert and Vincensini (2008).

non-recipients' responses to targeted programs (Humphreys and Weinstein 2009) and social desirability response bias when estimating the effects of CCT with survey data can render inferences invalid.[4]

To overcome these challenges, in this chapter I take advantage of the fact that Progresa's randomized impact evaluation offers exogenous variation in the duration of exposure to program benefits. The experiment, together with data on election outcomes at the polling precinct level, reveals that assignment to early program enrollment led to a 7 percent increase in voter turnout and a 9 percent increase in incumbent vote share in the 2000 presidential election.[5] The experiment also reveals that exposure to program benefits had no influence on support for opposition parties. Together, these findings lend evidence to Progresa's pro-incumbent mobilizing effects. The findings in this chapter suggest that CCT programs' ability to foster support for the incumbent could explain, in part, the popularity of these social programs among left- and right-leaning governments alike.

Progresa's effect on electoral behavior among the experimental groups also speaks to the broader question of how compatible targeted government programs are with democracy. Existing research has staked out contradictory claims in this regard. Some argue that targeted programs persuade recipients to change their vote choice for programmatic reasons, such as retrospective voting (Díaz-Cayeros and Magaloni 2009). Others, however, posit that targeted programs are detrimental to democracy because they perpetuate a clientelist linkage between incumbents and recipients. In particular, the concern is that beneficiaries of targeted programs may be persuaded to vote against their preferences in response to threats of program discontinuation (Cornelius 2004; Schedler 2000). Chapter 6 already showed that enrollment on the Mexican CCT eroded clientelism through multiple avenues. In this chapter, I document that the electoral bonus of CCT is closer to programmatic politics than clientelism.

This chapter contributes to the vast literature on the effects of welfare programs on political participation (Campbell 2003; Mettler and Soss 2004; Soss 1999; Soss et al. 2007). Lessons from the American context show that public policies affect a wide range of social outcomes, from group identification to individual mobilization. Specifically, "individuals affected by a program may become active on related political issues, presumably to protect or expand benefits" (Mettler and Soss 2004, 62). Campbell (2003) argues that social groups develop organizational capacity in response to the creation of a relevant public policy. For instance, she finds mobilization to be strongest among low-income beneficiaries of old-age insurance – the group most likely to be dependent on social security income.

---

[4] For an insightful review of social desirability bias, as well as ways to circumvent it, see Gonzalez-Ocantos et al. (2012).
[5] For a detailed account of the 2000 presidential election in Mexico, see Domínguez (2012).

Research on the effect of means-tested programs on political participation has found evidence of negative or no mobilization. Soss (1999) presents evidence that Aid to Families with Dependent Children (AFDC) has a negative effect on the likelihood that an individual will vote. In addition, Social Security Disability Insurance (SSDI) is not correlated with a voter's intention to vote. This divergent effect is related to differences in the information each program conveys about governmental performance. SSDI's complexity and responsiveness produce a sense of internal efficacy of political action. In contrast, AFDC bureaucracy fosters low levels of political participation (364). Soss highlights the importance of welfare participation itself as an educative process. Recipients of welfare programs learn about the public life and their role in it through their experiences with welfare agencies (376). In some cases this experience is empowering, and in others it is not. Beyond the design of particular means-tested programs, scholars who study American programs have emphasized that targeting poor minorities is harmful for political engagement because dependents on government aid are stigmatized (Rogers-Dillon 2004).

The relevance of studies based on American programs is not the specific direction of the effect of programs on political behavior. Rather, the key lesson is that there is an important "policy feedback loop" that should be taken into account when explaining the political behavior of the poor (Mettler 2002; Skocpol 1992). When thinking about the effect of programs targeted at the poor in developing countries, in contrast to the United States, there is a radical difference in the number of people living in poverty. Means-tested programs in the developing world are not tailored to the needs of minorities; on the contrary, they are tailored to majorities. In a way, targeting the poor in a developing country is an example of Skocpol (1991) classification of a semi-targeted or semi-universal approach. Thus, it makes sense to think that the arguments about stigma or a low internal sense of efficacy caused by being part of an underprivileged minority simply are not as relevant when being underprivileged is not the exception, but the rule.

CALCULATING PROGRESA'S ELECTORAL RETURNS

Scholarly work on CCTs' electoral returns has made rapid progress in recent years. The earliest and most common empirical approach relies on survey data. Drawing on the Mexico 2000 Panel Study, Cornelius (2004) finds that respondents enrolled in Progresa were 12 and 26 percent more likely to vote for the incumbent (PRI) candidate than the right- and left-wing candidates, respectively. However, he finds no effect on turnout. Since then, CCT's persuasive effects have dominated the literature. Analysis by (Díaz-Cayeros et al. 2007; Díaz-Cayeros and Magaloni 2009) of the national exit polls fielded by the newspaper *Reforma* in 2000 and 2006 shows that voters enrolled in Progresa were 17 and 11 percent more likely to vote for the incumbent party in each election. They also find that program enrollment decreased the vote of the right-wing party in the 2000 election and decreased the vote of the left-wing candidate in the 2006 election. For the Brazilian CCT, Zucco (2013) uses the first Vox Populi survey in 2006 and finds that program enrollment increases the probability of voting for the incumbent by 30 and 43 percent among respondents in the two lowest brackets of income, respectively.

The appeal of using survey data is that a direct comparison can be made between recipients and nonrecipients. However, a variety of methodological challenges arise. Perhaps the most pressing issue is that self-reported turnout and vote choice are prone to social desirability response bias (Gonzalez-Ocantos et al. 2012). If program recipients are more eager to manifest support for the incumbent when responding a survey than when casting a ballot, or are reluctant to declare that they did not turn out, then conformity bias leads to erroneous estimations.

Another concern with survey data relates to measurement error. Previous work is cognizant of the possibility that recipients are unlike nonrecipients. This is especially troublesome for the study of Progresa because the traits that set recipients apart, such as poverty, shape electoral behavior directly. Methods of covariate adjustment, such as regression (Cornelius 2004) or propensity score matching (Díaz-Cayeros et al. 2007, 2009; Zucco 2013), are the most prominent approach to avoid comparisons that conflate program impacts with preexisting differences. The remaining challenge is that traits such as income are likely measured with error in surveys. If noise in the measurement of income correlates with program enrollment and also has a direct effect on electoral outcomes, then estimates will be biased. To mitigate this concern (Díaz-Cayeros et al. 2007; Díaz-Cayeros and Magaloni 2009) include in the propensity score additional community-level characteristics.

Concerns about unbalanced observed demographics, however, pale beside concerns about hidden bias and endogenous program enrollment. That clientelism abounds in countries where most CCTs operate exacerbates the concern that incumbents use unobserved strategic criteria to allocate program resources. Consequently, unobserved omitted variables and reverse causality remain problematic because "perfect balance on important covariates does not necessarily warrant causal claims" (Morgan and Winship 2007, 122). Even in cases when a rich set of covariates are available, if unobserved heterogeneity remains, then matching can lead to different results than an experimental benchmark (Arceneaux et al. 2010).

Estimates based on aggregate data so far have produced mixed results. Using propensity score matching in two cross-sections of data, Zucco (2013) finds that the Brazilian CCT increased incumbent vote share in 2002 by 0.12 percent and in 2006 by 0.2 percent. On the other hand, Green (2006) finds no effects of the Mexican CCT using a regression discontinuity design.[6] In this innovative approach, a comparison is made between localities right below and above the program's eligibility threshold. The appeal of this design is that, because

---

[6] Manacorda et al. (2011) find a pro-incumbent effect in Uruguay using a similar regression discontinuity design.

the threshold is arbitrary, localities around it are similar in many respects. The drawback is that villages close to the threshold are more populous and wealthier than the average eligible village. Thus, it is unclear if the results can be extrapolated to all eligible villages.[7]

Using the Randomization

Progresa's randomized component offers exogenous variation in exposure to program benefits that allows the methodological challenges previously discussed to be circumvented. The randomized experiment was implemented in seven states where the program was first scaled up.[8] The sample selection process followed Progresa's targeting method closely. The first step was the selection of villages eligible for the program based on a poverty measure created with the 1990 census data and the 1995 partial census data. The poverty index was divided into five categories that go from very low poverty to very high. Localities deemed to have a high or very high degree of poverty were considered priorities to be included in the program.

The second step was a result of the program's conditionalities. Those localities with access to school and health services (or with available roads when the services were not located in the same community) were considered eligible. In addition, localities with fewer than fifty or more than 2,500 inhabitants were excluded. Finally, using Geographic Information System (GIS) software, remaining localities were grouped based on geographical proximity. Isolated localities were excluded from the selection process (Progresa 1998).[9]

---

[7] This problem is exacerbated by the restriction of the sample to localities that either correspond one-to-one to electoral precincts or localities that were contained in two electoral precincts. More generally, RDD faces a trade-off between precision and bias because around the discontinuity point, data may be sparse. Although expanding the interval around the eligibility threshold would increase precision, it would also increase the probability of bias (Green et al. 2009). Also, RDD's assumption is that unobservable variables that affect voting behavior are not discontinuous functions at the eligibility threshold.

[8] The states are Guerrero, Hidalgo, Michoacán, Querétaro, Puebla, San Luis Potosí, and Veracruz. The selection of states responded largely to logistical and financial restrictions. The exclusion of two of the poorest states in the country from both the experiment and the first phases of the program deserves a few words. In the case of Chiapas, 1,720 villages lacked data from the 1995 Partial Census, probably because of the uprising of the guerrilla movement the previous year. In Oaxaca, political considerations prevented the implementation of the experiment. As the director of the program lamented: "In the early stages of Progresa, we could not make the program work in Oaxaca, our representatives ended up hurt most of the time when trying to do their job. We had to change our team because it was completely subordinated to the governor's interest at that time" (author's interview, Mexico City, August 2005).

[9] According to the program's operational rules, after eligible households had been identified, the list of beneficiaries was meant to be presented to community assemblies, and their feedback should have been used to correct any inclusion or exclusion errors. Yet, this stage of selection was in practice irrelevant both for the experiment and the large-scale operation of the program. As of 2000 "the number of households whose selection into Progresa was disputed at this stage of the selection process was minute (0.1 percent of the total number of selected households)" (Skoufias et al. 1999).

Randomization was implemented at the village level.[10] Families in 320 villages were randomly selected to receive benefits in September 1998, whereas 186 villages were excluded from the program until January 2000 (Schultz 2001). There was a 60 percent probability of being assigned to the early-treatment group, and a 40 percent probability of being assigned to the late-treatment group. In villages assigned to early treatment, all eligible households within each village, identified by the Household Socio-economic Characteristics Survey (ENCASEH), were offered enrollment in Progresa. In villages assigned to the late-treatment group, none of the households received program benefits until January 2000 (Progresa, Methodological note: General Rural, 2006). By the 2000 presidential election, villages in the early and late treatment groups had been assigned to treatment for twenty-one months and six months, respectively.

Program officials expected that an impartial program evaluation would help the program to survive the change in federal administration in 2000. However, it was also clear that delaying enrollment of eligible villages for the sake of the evaluation was politically sensitive. To avoid confrontations, program officials waited to publicize the evaluation until December 2000. Media reactions proved that concerns were justified, as the evaluation was criticized on ethical and budgetary grounds (Parker and Teruel 2005). Media exposure, however, came after the presidential election, so it did not alter information available to experimental groups during the period of study of this chapter.

Data

As in many countries, in Mexico, election results are not reported at the village level. Instead, election outcomes are reported at levels defined by the electoral law. To take advantage of the random assignment, I overlaid the 506 experimental villages to the smallest unit of outcome measure for which census, program, and electoral data roughly coincide: the *sección electoral* (precinct).[11] Neither villages nor precincts have fixed population size, and generally they do not correspond one to one.[12]

---

[10] The methodological note of the evaluation mentions that the sample was stratified by population. However, the details of such population strata are not included, and none of the evaluation data sets or the articles using the evaluation include them.
[11] The Federal Electoral Institute (IFE) and INEGI use different identifiers for states, municipalities, and villages. All merges were done first by hand based on the village names taken from the ENCASEH (1997). I corroborated the match by overlaying the geographical boundaries of the electoral precincts, and the position of the villages with GIS. Of the 506 villages in the experiment, GIS located only 27 in a different precinct because of their proximity to the electoral precinct boundary. I kept the manual coding for these 27 villages. Four of the experimental villages were not found in the IFE records. The remaining experimental villages were located in 465 precincts. Ten of these precincts contained special voting booths where by law out-of-precinct voters can cast a ballot (in these precincts turnout often exceeded 100 percent).
[12] I excluded from the analysis three precincts that were clear outliers in terms of population and the number of villages. For example, one of the precincts (located in Veracruz) has 66 villages,

TABLE 7.1 *Descriptive Statistics of Experimental Villages and Electoral Precincts*

	1995	2000
Panel A: Villages in the random assignment N = 502		
Average population	260	254
Average population 18 years old or above	132	131
Average poverty	4.66	
Panel B: Electoral precincts N = 462		
	1995	2000
Average population	1977	2065
Average number of voters	1055	1099
Average poverty	4.58	
Average share of eligible population	0.87	
	1994	2000
Turnout	0.65	0.67
PRI vote share	0.42	0.37
PAN vote share	0.05	0.14
PRD vote share	0.10	0.12

Notes: Poverty and population measures taken from CONAPO 1995 and 2000. Electoral data taken from *Atlas Electoral de México*, IFE 1991–2000. The original number of villages in the experiment was 506; I excluded 4 villages because they were not found in the IFE records. The original number of precincts with randomized villages was 465. I excluded from the analysis 3 precincts that were outliers in terms of population and number of villages in 1994.

Because the units of assignment to treatment and outcome measure do not overlap perfectly, the aggregation of villages into precincts brought in villages that were originally excluded from the experiment. Precincts in the sample contained six villages on average. Thus, experimental precincts were more populous than experimental villages, but they were very similar in terms of poverty, with villages having an average poverty of 4.66 and precincts of 4.58 on a scale that goes from 1 to 5.[13] Summary statistics of villages and precincts are presented in Table 7.1.

whereas the rest of the sample has on average 6 villages. Another precinct (located in Michoacan) has a population of 550,473 inhabitants, whereas the rest of the precincts have an average population of 2,065 inhabitants. Including these outliers in the analysis, however, does not change the results (estimations with outliers are available on request). In addition, five precincts belonged to districts that were affected by the 1996 redistricting process; thus they have no election results in 1994.

[13] Population data comes from the Census of Population and Housing (1990, 2000) and the Partial Census (1995) produced by INEGI. To replicate the eligibility criteria, I used the same Poverty Index (1995) used by program officials. Following the original randomization process, I defined a village as eligible if it scored a 4 or higher in the measure of poverty and had a population larger than 50 but smaller than 2,500 inhabitants.

TABLE 7.2 *Baseline Characteristics (Means and Standard Deviations)*

	Early	Late	Difference
Poverty	4.57	4.59	0.01
			(0.04)
Population	2040.10	1851.35	−188.49
			(651.98)
Population eligible	0.88	0.85	−0.03
			(0.03)
Number of villages	6.08	6.37	0.29
			(0.37)
Randomly assigned villages = 1	0.90	0.90	0.002
			(0.02)
Randomly assigned villages = 2	0.09	0.08	−0.006
			(0.02)
Turnout 1994	0.65	0.64	−0.01
			(0.03)
PRI vote share 1994	0.43	0.41	−0.02
			(0.02)
PAN vote share 1994	0.05	0.06	0.01
			(0.009)
PRD vote share 1994	0.10	0.09	−0.004
			(0.012)

Notes: The third column reports the difference in means between the late and early groups. Standard errors in parentheses. ***$p < 0.01$, **$p < 0.05$, *$p < 0.1$.

For the original randomization, Behrman and Todd (1999) show that villages in the late-treatment group are a valid counterfactual for villages in the early-treatment group, as there are no systematic differences between them in terms of population size, age distribution, education levels, access to health services, and income. Once villages are aggregated into precincts, randomization still implies that assignment to receive early Progresa benefits is exogenous and, in principle, the baseline characteristics of the early and late treatment group should be balanced. The data support these claims. When comparing the baseline characteristics of the early and late treatment groups at the precinct level, there are no statistically significant differences between them in poverty, population, population living in an eligible village, and number of villages.

If Progresa's experimental sample was a discretionary allocation strategy, as opposed to a random allocation, its distribution would reveal some form of electoral bias. The data give no evidence of this as there are no statistically significant differences between early and late treatment groups in terms of pre-program electoral behavior (Column 3 of Table 7.2). To further test the validity of randomization, I estimated a logistic regression to predict early treatment based on turnout in 1994, vote shares of the three largest parties in 1994, average poverty, and population in 1995. As expected, none of the baseline characteristics is statistically different from zero, and the chi-square is nonsignificant (p = 0.29). Similarly, baseline demographics and the chi-square remain nonsignificant after the inclusion of a fixed effect by the number of villages in the precinct (p = 0.49).

Beyond balance in baseline covariates, random assignment means that each entity in the study has an equal chance to be in a particular treatment or control condition (Druckman et al. 2011). In the original experiment, each village had the same probability of being part of the early treatment group. To see the consequences of the aggregation of villages into precincts for the probability of treatment, consider the hypothetical example where ten villages form part of the experiment. One set of villages corresponds one-to-one into precincts, another set corresponds two-to-one. Each village has a 50 percent chance of being assigned to the treatment. In the first set of hypothetical precincts, this means that 50 percent are in treatment and 50 percent are in control. In the second set, 25 percent are in control, 50 percent are in half-treatment, and 25 percent are in treatment. Precincts in the two sets have different probabilities of treatment, but these differences are captured perfectly by the set to which they belong. Moreover, for precincts in the second set there are two alternative treatments available: treatment and half-treatment, but this can also be captured by the set to which precincts belong. Thus, taking into account the sets that villages belong to allows for appropriate estimations.

Going back to Progresa's experiment, the aggregation of villages into precincts influences the probability of treatment in two ways. First, 90 percent of precincts assigned to early treatment as well as 90 percent of precincts assigned to late treatment included only one experimental village. The remaining 10 percent of precincts included two experimental villages.[14] Second, the number of villages in the experimental precincts varies. To take into account that these two factors influence the probability of treatment, the analysis throughout includes fixed effects by the number of villages, and I split precincts into two groups based on whether they include one or two randomized villages. For ease of presentation, I include the results based on the 90 percent of the sample. The analysis pertaining to the remaining 10 percent of the precincts is available on request from the author.

Finally, the aggregation of villages into precincts together with the roll-out of the program outside of the experiment present a challenge that is analogous to the standard issue of experimental crossover. In experimental work, it is common that not all subjects assigned to one treatment regime accept it. In this application, because of the roll-out of the program, not all households in precincts assigned to early treatment were enrolled early, and not all households

---

[14] Two precincts in the late-treatment group included three experimental villages. Because there is no counterfactual in the early-treatment group, these two precincts are not included in the analysis.

in precincts assigned to late treatment were enrolled late (more details on this are discussed in the next section). To take into account these crossovers (and any failure to treat at the village level), the next section presents first the intent-to-treat (ITT) estimates of assignment to early treatment, which involve the purest experimental comparison. ITT is a robust way to analyze experimental data; however, it tends to produce conservative estimates of the effect of an intervention because crossovers from one treatment condition to the another dilute the effect (Dunning and Hyde 2008). I then present instrumental variable estimations of the effect of early coverage, where the instrument for early coverage is the random assignment to early treatment.

EXPERIMENTAL RESULTS

In the following analysis there are four dependent variables: turnout, incumbent (PRI) vote share, and party vote shares for the two largest opposition parties (National Action Party [PAN] and Party of the Democratic Revolution [PRD]) in 2000. Turnout is calculated as total number of votes as a share of the voting-age population (eighteen years or older). Similarly, vote shares are calculated as total number of votes for a given party as a share of the voting-age population in the precinct. The reason to measure all outcome variables with respect to potential voters, as opposed to with respect to registered voters, is that the program asked the female head of the household for an identification. Because the most common identification card is issued by the Electoral Institute, enrollment in the program could have the automatic effect of increasing the number of registered voters.[15]

Assignment to treatment status is captured by the dummy variable *Treatment*, which takes the value 1 when the precinct includes a village assigned to early treatment, and 0 when the precinct includes a village assigned to late treatment. Because of randomization, consistent estimates of the effects of assignment to different durations of Progresa's benefits, or the ITT effect, can be calculated as the average outcome for the early-treatment group minus the average outcome for the late-treatment group. For the moment, the ITT analysis leaves aside the question of compliance. The upper panel of Table 7.3 presents the estimates of the effect of assignment to early treatment starting with turnout in Column 1, and the party vote shares in columns 2 through 4. The specifications include number of villages fixed effect to take into account the aggregation of villages into precincts as explained earlier. The models also include a set of baseline covariates (poverty, population, total number of votes, votes cast for the PRI, PAN, and PRD).

The effect of being assigned to the early-treatment group, as opposed to the late-treatment group, on turnout is positive and statistically significant at the

[15] The electoral data is compiled by IFE and reported in the Atlas of Federal Elections 1991–2000, and Statistics of the 2003 Federal Election.

TABLE 7.3 *Impact of* Progresa *on Turnout and Party Vote Shares*

	ITT Estimates of the Assignment to Early versus Late Treatment			
	(1) Turnout	(2) PRI	(3) PAN	(4) PRD
Treatment	0.053*	0.037**	0.007	0.002
	(0.030)	(0.015)	(0.012)	(0.014)
Constant	0.580***	0.233***	0.191***	0.166**
	(0.172)	(0.086)	(0.072)	(0.074)
Controls	yes	yes	yes	yes
# Villages Fixed effects	yes	yes	yes	yes
Observations	417	417	417	417
R-squared	0.116	0.288	0.197	0.318
	IV Estimates of Early Progresa Coverage			
	Turnout	PRI	PAN	PRD
Early Progresa	0.156*	0.108**	0.021	0.006
	(0.087)	(0.045)	(0.035)	(0.040)
Constant	0.702***	0.414***	0.146**	0.140**
	(0.154)	(0.080)	(0.069)	(0.068)
Controls	yes	yes	yes	yes
# Villages Fixed effects	yes	yes	yes	yes
Observations	417	417	417	417
R-squared	0.095	0.275	0.192	0.317

Note: In the upper panel, this table presents the Intent-to-Treat estimates of early versus late assignment to treatment. In the lower panel, the table presents the IV estimates of early Progresa coverage on turnout and party vote shares. The instrument is the assignment to early or late treatment. All columns include number of villages fixed effects, and the following controls: poverty in 1995, population 1995, total votes 1994, votes for the PRI, PAN, and PRD in 1994. Robust standard errors in parentheses. The estimates are robust to the exclusion of controls. ***p < 0.01, **p < 0.05, *p < 0.1.

10 percent level on a two-sided test. Assignment to early treatment leads to a 5 percentage point increase in turnout. Because base turnout in the late treatment group was 64 percent, the effect of assignment to early treatment represents a 7 percent increase in turnout.

Column 2 in Table 7.3 displays the results when PRI vote share is the dependent variable. As with turnout, assignment to early enrollment in Progresa had a positive and significant effect on incumbent support. A precinct assigned to be enrolled in the program twenty-one months before election time led to a 3.7 percentage point increase in PRI vote share, significant at the 5 percent level in a two-sided test. Because in the late treatment group base support for the incumbent was 41 percent, the effect of early enrollment represents a 9 percent increase. Turning to the causal effect of the program on opposition parties' support, Progresa had no statistically significant effect on either the right- or left-wing parties (Columns 3 and 4).

To estimate the effect of early enrollment in Progresa, as opposed to assignment, I use an instrumental variable estimator where random assignment is an instrument for early enrollment. Outside of the experiment, program coverage expanded according to program rules giving priority to the poorest and eligible villages. Because precincts in the early and late treatment groups had an equal number of eligible villages, the experiment created a substantive difference in terms of early coverage between these two groups. In the early-treatment group, 86 percent of precinct households receiving program benefits in July 2000 were enrolled early. In contrast, in the late-treatment group, only 52 percent of households were enrolled early in the program.[16]

The first stage of the IV estimation corroborates that assignment to treatment is a valid instrument for early Progresa coverage. *Treatment* has a positive and statistically significant effect at the 1 percent level on early coverage. The magnitude of the effect is substantive (being assigned to early treatment increases early coverage by 34 percentage points). The F test of *Treatment* of 153 suggests that the instrument is far from weak (Staiger and Stock 1997; Stock and Yogo 2002). The lower panel of Table 7.3 shows the IV estimates. The effect of early coverage is three times greater than the ITT effect. Similarly, the effect of early Progresa coverage on the incumbent vote share is more than double the ITT estimate. Finally, the IV estimates show no effect of Progresa coverage on opposition parties' vote shares.

WHY DID PROGRESA AFFECT ELECTORAL OUTCOMES?

Why did early enrollment in the program have such proincumbent mobilizing effects? Proving a particular mechanism is a daunting task. Instead of attempting to do so, I provide a discussion of mechanisms that seem to be at odds with the experimental evidence and discuss some other channels that seem to be at work.

When combining cash and votes in the same sentence, inevitably vote buying comes to mind. Chapter 6 showed that enrollment in the Mexican CCT eroded clientelism through multiple avenues. Here I further explore whether the electoral bonus of CCT is closer to programmatic politics than clientelism.

Is vote buying then responsible for Progresa's electoral returns? Stokes (2007) succinctly explains why it is difficult to answer this question: "Both vote buying and programmatic mobilization entail exchanges; in both, parties can be thought as paying a price per vote" (6). Vote buying, however, is distinct

---

[16] Early coverage is calculated as the share of households enrolled during the first four phases of the program's expansion with respect to the total households in the program by the eleventh phase of the expansion. In practice, among precincts in the early-treatment group, enrollment grew faster in the fourth and fifth expansions, which closely coincide with the experiment.

in at least three ways. First, "politicians [buying votes] target a range of benefits only to individuals who have already delivered, or who promise to deliver their electoral support to their partisan benefactor" (Kitschelt and Wilkinson 2007, 10). In contrast, politicians engage in programmatic mobilization when "they devise policy packages knowing that they are likely to benefit particular groups of voters, and that this in turn will make it more likely in general that members of these groups will vote for the party ... but the party does not have the precise knowledge of who in the target constituency will vote for them"(Kitschelt and Wilkinson 2007, 10). In this first dimension, the experimental results are closer to programmatic mobilization than clientelism because we know with certainty that program benefits were explicitly noncontingent on recipients' vote choice.

The second distinctive feature of vote buying is that the exchange is accompanied by sanctioning of voters who defect from the politician's partisan camp (Kitschelt and Wilkinson 2007). There are two equally detrimental corollaries to this feature. Clientelistic parties can punish voters who fail to vote by excluding them from the flow of goods or services (Stokes 2007), and parties can simply threaten voters to guarantee their compliance. Regarding the former, I argued in Chapter 6 that the regularized operation of the program in the hands of a new agency that circumvented governors, state delegates, and mayors prevented party brokers from effectively punishing program recipients who voted against the incumbent. Thus, if anything, Progresa eroded brokers' ability to sanction voters.

The experiment allows me to say something more specific about the second corollary. Both the early and late treatment groups received cash from the federal government. Therefore, both groups were susceptible to threats of program discontinuation. Yet, turnout is higher in the early than the late treatment group. For this pattern to be compatible with a prospective story based on threats, we would have to assume that the incumbent party was able and, more importantly, willing to use fine-grained information to prioritize the 320 villages in one group, and not the 186 villages in the other. Although it is not impossible, it is highly unlikely that a party that could target one group would not target the other because the experimental villages represent only 0.5 percent of the total villages in the country. Thus, threats are unlikely to explain the experimental results.

Table 7.4 lends additional support to this claim. I collected information on the number of party observers present at the polling station in the 2000 election. Party observers are a finite resource that parties allocate across polling stations.[17] If precincts in the early-treatment group were a priority for the incumbent party, then we would expect to see a higher number of observers

---

[17] Party observer data come from IFE. Total party observers have a mean of 11 and standard deviation of 5. In 2000, the PRI had the highest number of observers with a mean of 5 and a standard deviation of 2, followed by the PAN with a mean of 3.4 (std. dev. 2), and finally, the PRD had in average 3 party observers (std. dev. 1.5)

TABLE 7.4 *Impact of Assignment to Early and Late Treatment on Number of Party Observers*

Variables	(1) Total	(2) PRI	(3) PAN	(4) PRD
Treatment	−0.478	−0.167	−0.031	−0.125
	(0.471)	(0.190)	(0.197)	(0.151)
Constant	11.245***	4.635***	3.401***	3.044***
	(0.372)	(0.155)	(0.157)	(0.124)
# Villages Fixed effects	yes	yes	yes	yes
Observations	420	420	402	411
R-squared	0.140	0.116	0.089	0.120

Notes: This table presents the intent-to-treat effects of early versus late treatment on the number of party observers at the polling precinct in the 2000 election. Robust standard errors in parentheses. ***p < 0.01, **p < 0.05, *p < 0.1.

in those areas. Table 7.4 shows that this is not the case; precincts assigned to early and late enrollment had the same number of party observers.[18]

Finally, it is well established that clientlistic parties target poor voters because they are most responsive (Stokes 2007). The early-treatment group was exposed longer to program benefits; thus they were healthier and had additional disposable income for longer. The clientelistic party would not target the better-off early-treatment group, but the more vulnerable late-treatment group. If the party followed such a strategy, it was clearly unsuccessful, because we know empirically that the better-off group cast more ballots in favor of the incumbent.

Other theories are compatible with the mobilization result but fall short of explaining Progresa's proincumbent effects. For example, a resource model predicts that participation is increasing with income (Brady et al. 1995). In Mexico, for decades high participation was a feature of poor and rural regions, but by Progresa's time, turnout patterns resembled more closely those of establish democracies with more affluent people participating more in elections (Klesner and Lawson 2001). Thus, a resource model is compatible with the turnout result. However, if only an income effect was at work, we would expect that the more affluent a voter, the stronger their sympathy for the conservative party.[19] This argument finds no support in the data.

---

[18] In addition, it is unlikely that the party state delegations could target Progresa recipients because municipal governments did not have access to the list of program beneficiaries. This list was kept confidential until 2002 when the Access to Information Law was enacted.
[19] Several studies document a positive link between income and support for the conservative party in Mexico (Domínguez and Lawson 2004; Domínguez and McCann 1996; Moreno 2003). Cortina et al. (2009) also find that the PAN did better in richer states than in poorer states in the 1994, 2000, and 2006 elections.

Rational choice theories emphasize that the probability of turning out to vote decreases when the cost increases (Riker and Ordeshook 1968). It is possible that women enrolled in Progresa faced lower costs of voting, because to register in the program they were required to present an official identification card. The Federal Electoral Institute (IFE) issues a widely accepted identity card, so perhaps enrollment in Progresa fostered registration to vote, and women in the early-treatment group had more time to process the IFE identity card. Alternatively, the better health of children among the early-treatment group perhaps led to fewer impediments to turnout for women (and men) in this group. Yet, it is unlikely that a resource model or a cost-based explanation on its own account for the full set of experimental results.

Retrospective voting theories, as incarnated by Fiorina (1981), posit that evaluations of a party's recent performance should elicit a change in overall party evaluations. Over time, the argument follows, these evaluations shape voters' party identification. Retrospective voting, then, is conceptually associated with swings in party identification. This chapter is not well suited to test this mechanism because the data are aggregated, so I cannot test whether longer exposure to program benefits changed partisan affiliations. Yet, the fact that the program had stronger mobilizing effects, compared to persuasive effects, suggest that retrospective voting (through its effect on party identification) is not the main driver behind the findings.

A simpler explanation for the results is that from the point of view of recipients, the longer the duration of program benefits, the more desirable the program is. From the point of view of incumbents, the longer the duration of program benefits, the more opportunities exist to claim the credit for something that voters consider desirable. Following Mayhew's (1974) seminal work, "an actor who believes that a member [the incumbent] can make pleasing things happen will no doubt wish to keep him in office so that he can make pleasing things happen in the future" (53). The experimental results are consistent with this explanation.

One of the things that perhaps recipients liked about the program, and that took time to materialize, was precisely that benefits were not contingent on vote choice. In Brazil, for example, CCT recipients voted at higher rates for incumbent mayors who were perceived as managing the program less politically, and with fewer program resources going to the non-poor (de Janvry et al. 2009). This would be compatible with a credit claiming explanation, as well as with social psychology theories that suggest that unconditional gifts foster reciprocity (Landry et al. 2010).

In sum, this chapter provides evidence on the electoral returns of the Mexican CCT by analyzing a unique randomized variation in the duration of program benefits across eligible villages. The findings suggest that the targeted program led to an increase in voter turnout and incumbent vote shares. Whereas previous work focused on CCTs' persuasive effects, this chapter shows that CCTs' proincumbent effects are mainly explained by a mobilizing mechanism. Finally, this chapter finds little support for explanations based on clientelism. An explanation based on programmatic politics, and credit claiming, seems more likely to be at work. Despite the inconclusiveness in this regard, this chapter suggest one important general lesson. Programs targeted at individuals, when operated in a programmatic way, are compatible with healthy democratic habits, such as participating in elections, and have the attractive feature of fostering proincumbent support.

8

Conclusions

Some governments in Latin America are innovators in the fight against poverty. In a region where social assistance programs implemented before the 1990s were characterized by discretionary and ineffective spending, some governments have since undertaken significant reforms to their policy repertoires and have created antipoverty programs that are more effective at improving the lives of the poor. The breakthrough in this recent wave of social policy reform is that presidents in the region, to varying degrees, have adopted programs that limit the ability of politicians to manipulate programs for political gain. A central task in this book has been to explore the political processes that led some governments in Latin America to adopt CCTs with operational guidelines that suppress political discretion, some other governments to adopt CCTs without such provisions, and yet other governments not to reform their social assistance programs at all. Another central task has been to assess the implications of the variation in the design and implementation of CCT programs for efforts to eradicate poverty and improve the political capabilities of the poor in Latin America.

In this final chapter, I first summarize the results of my inquiry, and then discuss some questions that remain unanswered.

THE FACTORS THAT EXPLAIN CCT ADOPTION AND THEIR DESIGNS

The argument I present in this book integrates three strands of literature. First, I build on economic-centered theories, most clearly articulated by Carnes and Mares (2010) and Díaz-Cayeros, Estévez, and Magaloni (2007). Reflecting on the economic crisis in Latin America throughout the 1980s and 1990s, Carnes and Mares argue that "an increase in the economic insecurity of wage earners in the formal sector contributed to the formation of coalitions between this group and the poor," which led to policies with a higher pro-poor bias (2010, 108). This argument is useful for understanding why governments in Latin America decided to pursue antipoverty policies, such as CCT programs. However, the economic insecurity argument does not provide insight into the variation in the degree to which presidents included provisions that tied their hands in the operational rules of poverty alleviation programs. Díaz-Cayeros et al. (2007) argue that, in the case of Mexico, an economic crisis weakened the ruling coalition and generated demands from within the incumbent party to limit presidential authority. My argument is situated between these two accounts of the effects of economic downturns. I show that economic conditions enlarge the political coalition in favor of pro-poor policies, but that the specific operational guidelines of CCT programs depend on the degree of resistance that the president's antipoverty policy faces in congress.

My argument also borrows from state-centered explanations of policymaking, which are dominant in the literature on Latin America. These arguments posit that policies are the result of bureaucrats acting independently of underlying socioeconomic forces (Geddes 1994). This state-centered approach takes into account bureaucrats' capacity and level of professionalism, which are typically considered exogenous factors. I build on this notion, and along the lines of Geddes' (1991) model of the level of professionalism of the bureaucracy, I contend that presidents' political calculations are critical to understanding when politicians will or will not invest in their bureaucracies to increase their country's capacity to fight poverty.

Finally, my argument builds on theories of delegation, which place the strategic interaction between presidents and legislators at the core of policymaking. This literature contends that the more politicians' and bureaucrats' preferences diverge, the less likely delegation becomes.[1] My argument follows recent work within this strand of literature that distinguishes among the interests of the president, legislators, and the bureaucracy (McCarty 2004; Ting 2001). In addition, my argument presupposes that presidents initiate the process of policymaking and legislators influence policy through exercising their budgetary powers (McCarty 2004; Morgenstern and Nacif 2002). This sequence of actions is reversed in most arguments of delegation.

In sum, the argument of this book is that when facing a severe economic crisis, as many countries in Latin America were throughout the 1990s and 2000s, a democratically elected president will adopt a CCT with a design that limit his own influence over the policy, and limits other politicians' influence as well, when he faces resistance from legislators either from his own party or from the opposition. A stricter policy suppresses political discretion and is more effective at addressing poverty. In turn, these policy outcomes further strengthen democratic systems by eroding clientelism and promoting the electoral participation of program recipients. When there is no resistance to the president, which is the

[1] See Huber and Shipan (2006) for a thorough review of this literature.

case when the president's preferences are aligned with those of legislators, the president facing an economic crisis adopts a CCT with fewer provisions to tie the executive's hands. As a consequence, politicians have greater opportunities to politicize the program, and efforts to fight poverty are less effective. Needless to say, if there is no economic crisis, the president has less reason to innovate in the social sector.

Conflict between presidents and legislators has not generally resulted in the adoption of innovative social policies. Rather, conflict has often created gridlock. Take, for example, the adoption of market-oriented reforms in the telecommunication and electricity sectors. Murillo (2009) shows that "when the opposition controls the legislature, and when the preferences of legislators are ideologically distant from those of the executive, an incumbent's policy initiative declines rapidly, making reform adoption unlikely... Conversely, the larger the legislative contingent of the incumbent party, the easier policy adoption should be, as the party can impose the preferences of a fiscally constrained executive on congress" (2009, 25). In this example, conflicting preferences create policy paralysis.

Another example is the privatization of pensions. Executives' control of congress is a crucial factor to explain the privatization of pensions in Latin America (Madrid 2003). As Brooks (2002) argues, executives facing fragmented party systems "are more likely to shy away from structural reform... or to significantly reduce their reform agenda to win support for contentious reform such as pensions" (503). More generally, the welfare state literature has documented numerous cases where power dispersion prevents welfare state expansion and welfare retrenchment (Castiglioni 2005, Huber 1996). The evolution of pension systems has followed Tsebelis's (2002) argument: the more veto players there are, and the more divergent their preferences, the more stable policies are.

Why does conflict lead to different results for pensions and for CCTs? The answer to this question is three fold. First, CCTs are relatively inexpensive, especially compared to pensions. Second, CCTs target children from poor households, who are generally considered a deserving group. And, third, CCTs create a minimum safety net, which the poor and people at risk of becoming poor welcome at times of economic insecurity. Thus, governments with a sense of urgency to respond to an economic crisis can adopt a CCT without antagonizing organized interests. On the other hand, a reform of the pension systems is bound to antagonize these interests.

Still, a president without legislative support faces greater difficulty in introducing a CCT than a president who controls the legislature. As in other policy domains, conflicting preferences provide the president and legislators with incentives to counteract each other's actions. When the legislature is controlled by the opposition, the median legislator knows that if she funds a CCT with a lax design, the president can claim the credit for the welfare gains associated

Conclusions

with adopting a CCT. Moreover, the president, being the incumbent, can take more advantage from the opportunities that a CCT with a lax design offers in terms of strengthening patronage bases. If the legislator does not fund a CCT with a lax design, she can blame the president for promoting a clientelist policy in times of crisis, which can boost her political capital. Thus, if the president proposes a CCT with a weak design, a legislator from the opposition has incentives to refuse to fund it.

On the other hand, if the legislator from the opposition funds a CCT with a design that suppresses political discretion, the president can still claim the credit for innovating to fight poverty. However, the more stringent operational rules limit the opportunities for the incumbent, and other politicians, to use program resources in a clientelist fashion. If the legislator does not fund a CCT with a stringent design, she incurs the cost of rejecting a poverty relief policy that is both more effective to deal with poverty and less discretionary than the status quo policies. Thus, if the president proposes a CCT with a design that limits political discretion, a legislator from the opposition has incentives to fund it.

Anticipating the reaction of the opposition's legislator, the president opts for a CCT with a stringent design. Such a program may take longer to design and launch. Yet it is preferable to opting for a policy that will not get funded. Failing to respond to the crisis is costly, and so is promoting a clientelist policy when there is discontent associated with the economic crisis. The worse the economic crisis, the higher the cost of promoting a clientelist response or, alternatively, the cost of rejecting an insulated policy, all else being equal.

Conflict also arises when the president and median legislator are from different factions within a party. If the president's faction controls the party's machine, then the political game plays out in a similar fashion as when the legislator is part of the opposition. If the legislator's faction controls the party machine, then the president is better off opting for a CCT with stringent operational rules because such a program is more effective at fighting poverty and limits the extent to which his rival faction can use program resources for patronage. Thus, the president faced with a legislator from a different faction within his party opts for a CCT with stringent operational rules.

Harmonious preferences give the president the flexibility to design a CCT without operational rules that suppress political discretion. Such a policy appeals to the president and legislators because, as long as the CCT is better at dealing with the crises than previous policies, the president can claim credit for improving the lot of the poor, and the policy design leaves open the opportunity to use program resources for building and strengthening patronage bases.

Once the program is designed and funded, the president could implement any policy variation because he controls the policy's agency. In other words, operational guidelines are a necessary but not a sufficient condition for a robust program implementation Yet, the president implements a policy that closely mirrors its design because legislators can revise the policy's budget on a yearly basis. Thus, repeated interactions between a president and legislators have implications for both the design and the effectiveness of the policy, as well as its political neutrality and its likelihood of survival.

POLITICS BEHIND POLICY OUTCOMES

Policy outcomes are systematically different when presidents face checks on their authority and when they do not. The same factors that lead to strict operational rules also lead to a robust implementation and to the elimination of political-economic cycles that result from the expansion of CCT programs during election years. In addition, programs with weaker designs – and more flawed implementations – are more likely to be dismantled than programs with stronger designs and more exacting implementations. Thus, the arguments and evidence presented in this book offer an explanation for the heterogeneous effects of CCT programs on education and health outcomes across countries in Latin America. Ultimately, the effectiveness of poverty relief efforts can be traced back to the political dynamics explored in this book.

With respect to the effects of CCT programs on the quality of democracy, I demonstrate that programs that tie the hands of the executive affect clientelism through three mechanisms: an income effect resulting directly from the cash transfer, which raises the price of the votes of program recipients; an information effect associated with the robust implementation of the program, which encourages program recipients to resist clientelism; and an operations effect, as provisions to tie the hands of the executive also limit local brokers' ability to use the program for their political aims.

Finally, I document the proincumbent effects of the Mexican CCT program, Progresa, through downstream analysis of a unique randomized field experiment conducted in the early stages of the program. The proincumbent effects of CCT programs are primarily explained by a mobilizing mechanism, and in the case of Mexico, it is clear that voters are mobilized as a result of programmatic politics, rather than clientelism. This finding contrasts sharply with lessons drawn from developed countries, most notably from the United States, where means-tested welfare programs seem to demobilize program recipients. In the context of Latin America, when CCT programs are operated in a programmatic way, they may foster healthy democratic activities, such as participating in elections.

THE FUTURE OF CCT PROGRAMS

Conditional cash transfer programs are highly regarded by practitioners and scholars. Investments in children's education and health are in the collective interest of a country, and when programs' operational rules tie the hands of the executive, support for funding these antipoverty programs is likely to extend far

Conclusions

beyond program recipients. Yet CCT programs will likely face three challenges in the near future.

Although many countries in Latin America are close to reaching universal primary education and access to health care, concerns about the quality of education and health services, which are key components of CCT programs, are prevalent (Adato and Hoddinott 2010). A regional health director in Peru expressed his concerns about the burden that the Peruvian CCT program, *Juntos*, was placing on local clinics to the team evaluating *Juntos*: "The [health] sector was not prepared to cope with the increased demand and this compromised the quality of services offered, especially in terms of equipment, human resources and medications... we didn't have the necessary resources, neither the materials nor the manpower to respond to the demand or to the promises that were made, and many of our establishments have collapsed" (Regional Health Director, Ayachucho, in Jones et al. 2008). The education systems in many countries are under similar pressures. CCT programs have increased the demand for education, but in many countries the supply of education services – teachers, materials, and infrastructure – has lagged behind. If the quality of education and health services does not improve, it is likely that CCT programs may begin to lose support.

A second challenge is that although CCT programs are considered to be highly cost-effective transfer schemes, in many Latin American countries the budget for these programs and program coverage are insufficient. To expand coverage, governments require resources. An ambitious program expansion, however, may trigger a backlash from groups in society who do not directly benefit from CCTs. The key question is whether governments throughout the region will be able to build the political coalitions necessary to further expand their poverty relief programs. The findings in this book suggest that to form these coalitions, governments should take two factors into account: first, if the president moves an antipoverty policy too far from legislators' preferences, the program's budget may be at risk; and, second, the government is more likely to convince the middle and upper classes to fund antipoverty programs if social assistance is not implemented in a clientelistic way.

Finally, CCT programs have become a pillar of social assistance systems in Latin America. Yet the extent to which CCTs are institutionalized is unclear. In the argument that I present in Chapter 3, I list two critical factors that influence the president's policy preferences: social unrest associated with economic crises, and legislative checks. The more pressing social unrest is, the more interested the president will be in implementing a policy that effectively addresses poverty; the more resistance the policy faces in congress, the more willing the president will be to tie his own hands to secure funding for the policy. A strict CCT program deters recipients from joining protest movements. In their calculations of whether or not to protest the government, program recipients may find fewer reasons to join a protest if program benefits are of greater value than the expected value of protesting.

Over time, however, as social unrest subsides or in the event that checks on presidential authority disappear at some point, as would happen when the preferences of the president become perfectly aligned with those of legislators, how would CCT programs evolve? One possibility is that presidents would be tempted to relax CCT programs' operational rules to allow politicians to manipulate the programs for political aim at the expense of the programs' effectiveness to reduce poverty. A return to clientelist practices could shrink the size of the constituency that is currently in favor of keeping these programs in place. In fact, a digression such as this could even reverse the positive link between program enrollment and political participation, because recipients may be demoralized if they find that governments are reverting to clientelist practices.

In this book, I have shown that CCT programs can mobilize recipients to participate in elections. Beyond electoral turnout, these programs also appear to affect other forms of political participation. An evaluation of the Colombian CCT program, *Familias en Acción*, found that program recipients reported that they had opportunities to participate and express their views in their communities at higher rates than nonrecipients. Program recipients also reported that they participated more frequently than nonrecipients in initiatives to solve problems affecting their communities and were more likely to belong to civil society organizations (*Centro Nacional de Consultoría* 2008). In my interviews with program recipients in Mexico, I often heard women enrolled in Progresa talking about how program meetings had become a forum for women to discuss their communities' needs, and on various occasions those needs were communicated to municipal authorities.

Most promising for the future of CCTs is that program recipients are likely prepared to defend their benefits. It seems plausible that in places where CCT programs have been in operation for several years, there are constituencies that would defend the program in the event that the government threatens to cut benefits or chooses to revert to clientelist practices. Scholars of social policy in the United States emphasize the role of social policy in shaping political participation, broadly defined. Cambell (2003) shows how the development of Social Security transformed seniors from the least politically active age group to the most politically active age group. Seniors in the United States actively defend their programs from potential threats. Even though it is too soon to tell, there are reasons to believe that CCT programs are creating such constituencies in Latin America. In Peru, for example, during the 2006 presidential campaign, the lack of commitment to continue the Peruvian CCT program from candidates prompted women beneficiaries from the province of Ayachucho to organize and march in defense of the program (Jones et al. 2008).

In the long run, there are also reasons to be skeptical about the resilience of CCT programs. Most countries target program resources to a subgroup within the poor, which is defined according to an eligibility threshold. Although this threshold is calculated based on poverty criteria, it is arbitrary. Households

Conclusions

that are just below or just above the eligibility threshold suffer the hardship of poverty in similar ways. The group deemed ineligible is bound to wonder about the justifications for the selection process. If a government threatens to cut program benefits, it is unclear if the population of ineligible poor would join program recipients to demand the continuation and expansion of program benefits, or if they would support the dismantling of the program.

Much remains to be examined with respect to the conditions that will enable governments to further reform their poverty relief programs, and the consequences of such policy decisions for the economic and political capabilities of the poor. The evidence presented in this book suggests, however, that many countries in Latin America have taken a significant step toward pro-poor programmatic politics. This evolution has substantive implications for the effectiveness of poverty relief programs, and for the overall quality of democracy in the region. Certainly, poverty and clientelism have not disappeared in Latin America. However, in areas where CCT programs have been implemented in a programmatic way, many recipients have experienced improvements in well-being and have seen that clientelism is no longer the only game in town. This may not be a revolution, but it is certainly a transformation that has improved the lives of many of the most impoverished people in Latin America.

APPENDIX

A.1 *Robustness Check: Marginal Effects of Divided Government and Checks after Probit Models*

	CCT Above Mean		CCT Below Mean		CCT Above Mean		CCT Below Mean	
	(1)	(2)	(3)	(4)	(5)	(6)	(7)	(8)
Divided	0.200***	0.129***	−0.015	−0.091***				
	(0.029)	(0.042)	(0.020)	(0.033)				
Checks					0.062***	0.036**	−0.023***	−0.031***
					(0.012)	(0.017)	(0.008)	(0.008)
Left		−0.041		0.163***		−0.029		0.128***
		(0.043)		(0.051)		(0.046)		(0.045)
GDP		−0.015		0.007		−0.024		0.011
		(0.016)		(0.007)		(0.015)		(0.007)
Openness		0.004***		0.001***		0.005***		0.001***
		(0.001)		(0.000)		(0.001)		(0.000)
Inflation (log)		−0.022		−0.015		−0.031*		−0.007
		(0.017)		(0.011)		(0.017)		(0.011)
Population (log)		0.178***		0.009		0.183***		0.008
		(0.028)		(0.010)		(0.026)		(0.009)
Deindustrialization		0.006		−0.009***		0.007*		−0.008***
		(0.004)		(0.002)		(0.004)		(0.002)
Child labor		0.004		0.000		0.003		0.000
		(0.003)		(0.002)		(0.003)		(0.002)
Observations	580	326	580	326	572	326	572	326

Robust standard errors in parentheses.
*** p < 0.01, ** p < 0.05, * p < 0.1.

A.2 *Effects of Divided Government and Checks on CCT Duration*

	(1) Program Duration	(2) Program Duration	(3) Program Duration	(4) Program Duration
Divided	1.067**	1.042*		
	(0.545)	(0.540)		
High checks			0.954*	0.491
			(0.518)	(0.495)
Left		−0.764		−0.466
		(0.655)		(0.575)
GDP pc		0.101		0.009
		(0.122)		(0.110)
Openness		−0.002		0.001
		(0.012)		(0.011)
Inflation (log)		−0.292		−0.371
		(0.273)		(0.288)
Population (log)		0.222		0.277
		(0.404)		(0.394)
Child labor		0.013		0.017
		(0.037)		(0.037)
Constant	1.632***	1.458	1.666***	1.753
	(0.365)	(2.000)	(0.404)	(1.908)
Log gamma	−0.568*	−1.008***	−0.556*	−0.909***
	(0.292)	(0.344)	(0.293)	(0.330)
Observations	131	107	138	107

Standard errors in parentheses.
***$p < 0.01$, **$p < 0.05$, *$p < 0.1$.

References

Abers, Rebecca Neaera. 1997. "Porto Alegre and the participatory budget: Civic education, politics and the possibilities for replication." In Building Local and Global Democracy. Montreal: Carold Institute.
Accíon Ciudadana. 2010. "Informe de auditoría social al programa Mi Familia Progresa: Percepciones Cuidadanas." Transparencia Internacional.
Acedo Angulo, B. and R. Ruiz Suárez. 1995. Solidaridad en Conflicto: el Funcionamiento del PRONASOL en Municipios Gobernados por la Oposicíon. México, D.F.: Nuevo Horizonte Editores.
Adato, Michelle, and John Hoddinott (eds.). 2010. Conditional Cash Transfers in Latin America. Baltimore, MD: Johns Hopkins University Press.
Agis, Emmanuel, Carlos Cañete, and Demian Panigo. 2010. El Impacto de la Asignacíon Universal por Hijo en Argentina. Documento de Trabajo. CENDA; SID; PROFOPE; CEIL-PIETTE.
Aguilar Camín, Hector, and Lorenzo Meyer. 1993. In the Shadow of the Mexican Revolution: Contemporary Mexican History, 1910–1989. Austin: University of Texas Press.
Aguilar Zinzer, Adolfo, Cesáreo Morales, and Rodolfo F. Peña (eds.). 1986. Aún tiembla: sociedad política y cambio social: el terremoto del 19 de septiembre de 1985. México: Grijalbo.
Ahmed, Akhter, Michelle Adato, Ayse Kudat, Daniel Gilligan, and Refik Colasan. 2007. Impact Evaluation of the Conditional Cash Transfer Program in Turkey: Final Report. Washington, DC: International Food Policy Research Institute.
Alesina, Alberto, Edward Glaeser, and Bruce Sacerdote. 2001. "Why doesn't the US have a European-style welfare system?" NBER Working Paper No. 8524 (October).
Alesina, Alberto, Ricardo Hausmann, Rudolf Hommes, and Ernesto Stein. 1999. "Budget institutions and fiscal performance in Latin America." Journal of Development Economics, 59(2), 253–273.
Amorim Neto, Octavio. 2006. "The presidential calculus: Executive policy making and cabinet formation in the Americas" Comparative Political Studies 39: 415.

Angrist, Joshua D., and Jorn-Steffen Pischke. 2009. Mostly Harmless Econometrics: An Empiricist's Companion. Princeton, NJ: Princeton University Press.

Arceneaux, Kevin, Alan S. Gerber, and Donald P. Green. 2010. "A cautionary note on the use of matching to estimate causal effects: An experimental example comparing matching estimates to an experimental benchmark." Sociological Methods and Research, 39(2): 256–282.

Auyero, J. 2000. Poor People's Politics: Peronist Survival Networks and the Legacy of Evita. Durham, NC: Duke University Press.

Baldez, Lisa, and John M. Carey. 1999. "Presidential agenda control and spending policy: Lessons from General Pinochet's constitution." American Journal of Political Science 43(1): 29–55.

Bardan, Pranab, and Dilip Mookherjee. 2011. "Political clientelism and capture: Theory and evidence from West Bengal." Unpublished manuscript. University of California, Berkeley.

Barrientos, Armando. 2004. "Latin America: Toward a liberal welfare regime," in Gough, Ian, Geof Wood, Insecurity and Welfare Regimes in Asia, Africa, and Latin America. Social Policy in Developing Context. Cambridge, UK: Cambridge University Press.

Bawn, Kathleen. 1997. "Choosing strategies to control the bureaucracy: Statutory constraints, oversight, and the committee system." Journal of Law, Economics, and Organization 13:101–126.

BBC. 2009. "Trinidad government tightens social welfare programme." BBC News, September 4.

Beck, Thorsten, George Clarke, Alberto Groff, Philip Keefer, and Patrick Walsh. 2001. "New tools and new tests in comparative political economy: the Database of Political Institutions." Policy Research Working Paper, No. 2283, Development Research Group, World Bank.

Behrman, J., and John Hoddinott. 2000. "An evaluation of the impact of PROGRESA on pre-school child height." July. Washington, DC: International Food Policy Research Institute, Washington, D.C.

Behrman, Jere R., and Petra E. Todd. 1999. Randomness in the Experimental Samples of PROGRESA. Washington DC: International Food Policy Research Institute.

Bendor, Jonathan, Amihai Glazer, and Thomas H. Hammond. 2001. "Theories of delegation." Annual Review of Political Science 4: 23569.

Berry, William D., Michael B. Berkman, and Stuart Schneiderman. 2000. "Legislative professionalism and incumbent reelection: The development of institutional boundaries." The American Political Science Review 94(4): 859–874.

Bezdek, Robert R. 1995. "Democratic changes in an authoritarian system: Navismo and opposition development in San Luís Potosí," in Victoria E. Rodríguez and Peter M. Ward, Opposition Government in Mexico. Albuquerque: University of New Mexico Press.

Blair, Graeme, and Kosuke Imai. 2012. "Statistical analysis of list experiments." Political Analysis, 20(1): 47–77.

Brady, Henry E., Sidney Verba, and Kay Lehman Schlozman. 1995. "Beyond SES: A resource model of political participation." The American Political Science Review 89(2): 271–294.

Brooks, Sarah M. 2002. "Social Protection and Economic Integration. The Politics of Pension Reform in an era of Capital Mobility." Comparative Political Studies 35(5): 491–523.

Brooks, Sarah M. 2007. "When does diffusion matter? Explaining the spread of structural pension reforms across nations." The Journal of Politics 69(3): 701–715.
Brooks, Sarah M. 2009. Social Protection and the Market: The Transformations of Social Security Institutions in Latin America. Cambridge, UK: Cambridge University Press.
Bruhn, Kathleen. 1996. "Social spending and political support: The 'lessons' of the National Solidarity Program in Mexico." Comparative Politics 28(2): 151–177.
Brusco, Valeria, Marcelo Nazareno, and Susan C. Stokes. 2006. "Reditos y peligros electorales del gasto publico en la Argentina." Desarrollo Economico 46(181): 63–88.
Caldés, Natàlia, David Coady, and John A. Maluccio. 2010. "The costs of conditional cash transfer programs: A comparative analysis of three programs in Latin America," in Adato, Michelle and John Hoddinott (eds.), Conditional Cash Transfers in Latin America. Baltimore, MD: Johns Hopkins University Press.
Calvo, Ernesto, and Maria Victoria Murillo. 2004. "Who delivers? Partisan clients in the Argentine electoral market." American Journal of Political Science 48(4): 742–757.
Camacho, Adriana, and Emily Conover. 2011. "Manipulation of social program eligibility." American Economic Journal: Economic Policy, 3(2): 41–65.
Cameron, David R. 1978. "The expansion of the public economy: A comparative analysis." American Political Science Review 72(December): 124361.
Campbell, Andrea. 2003. How Policies Make Citizens: Senior Political Activism and the American Welfare State. Princeton, NJ: Princeton University Press.
Carnes, Matthew, and Isabela Mares. 2009. "Social policy in developing countries." Annual Review of Political Science 12: 91–113.
Carnes, Matthew, and Isabela Mares. 2010. Deindustrialization and the rise of non-contributory social programs in Latin America. Unpublished manuscript. Columbia University, New York.
Castiglioni, Rossana. 2005. The Politics of Social Policy Change in Chile and Uruguay: The Retrenchement versus Maintenance, 1917–1998. New York: Routledge.
Centeno, M. A. 1999. Democracy within Reason: Technocratic Revolution in Mexico. University Park, PA: Pennsylvania State University Press.
Centro Nacional de Consultoría. 2008. "Evaluacíon del Programa Familias en Accíon para la poblacíon desplazada: Informe Final." Departamento Nacional de Poblacíon, Sistema Nacional de Evaluacíon de Resultados de la Gestión Pública. Bogotá, Colombia.
Cerda, Rodrigo, and Rodrigo Vergara. 2008. "Government subsidies and presidential election outcomes: Evidence for a developing country." World Development 36(11): 2470–2488.
Cleaves, Peter S. 1974. Bureaucratic Politics and Administration in Chile. Berkeley: University of California Press.
Coady, David. 2000. Final Report: The Application of Social Cost Benefit Analysis to the evaluation of PROGRESA. November. Report submitted to Progresa. Washington, DC: International Food Policy Institute.
Coady, David, Margaret Grosh, and John Hoddinott. 2004. Targeting of Transfers in Developing Countries: Review of Lessons and Experience. The International Bank for Reconstruction and Development. The World Bank.
Consejo de Cohesión Social. 2009. "Rendición de Cuentas: Mi Familia Progresa." Working document. Government of Guatemala.

Cornelius, W. A., and A. L. Craig. 1991. The Mexican Political System in Transition. La Jolla, CA: Center for U.S.-Mexican Studies University of California San Diego.

Cornelius, Wayne. 2004. "Mobilized voting in the 2000 elections: The changing efficacy of vote buying and coercion in Mexican electoral politics," in Domínguez, Jorge I., and Chappell Lawson (eds.), Mexico's Pivotal Democratic Election. Stanford, CA: Stanford University Press.

Cortina, Jeronimo, Narayani Lasala Blanco, and Andrew Gelman. 2009. "One vote, many Mexicos: Income and region in the 1994, 2000, and 2006 presidential elections." Unpublished working paper. University of Houston.

Cox, Gary W. 2010. "Swing voters, core voters, and distributive politics," in Shapiro, Ian, Susan Stokes, E. J. Wood, and Alexander Kirshner (eds.), Political Representation. Cambridge, UK: Cambridge University Press.

de Figueiredo, R. J. P., Jr. 2002. "Electoral competition, political uncertainty, and policy insulation." American Political Science Review 96: 321–333.

de Janvry, Alain, Frederico Finan, and Elisabeth Sadoulet. 2009. "Local electoral incentives and decentralized program performance." University of California at Berkeley. Unpublished working paper.

De La O, Ana Lorena. 2013. "Do conditional cash transfers affect electoral behavior? Evidence from a randomized experiment in Mexico." American Journal of Political Science 57(1): 1–14.

Díaz-Cayeros, Alberto, and Beatriz Magaloni. 2009a. "Aiding Latin America's poor." Journal of Democracy 2(4 October): 36–49.

Díaz-Cayeros, Alberto, and Beatriz Magaloni. 2009b. "Welfare benefits, canvassing and campaign handouts." in Domínguez, Jorge, Chappell Lawson, and Alejandro Moreno (eds.), Consolidating Mexico's Democracy, the 2006 Presidential Campaign in Comparative Perspective.Baltimore, MD: Johns Hopkins University Press.

Díaz-Cayeros, Alberto, Federico Estévez, and Beatriz Magaloni. 2007. Strategies of vote buying: Social transfers, democracy and welfare in Mexico. Unpublished manuscript. Stanford University.

Dion, Michelle L. 2010. Workers and Welfare. Comparative Institutional Change in Twentieth-Century Mexico. Pittsburgh, PA: University of Pittsburgh Press.

Domínguez, Jorge I. 2012. "Mexico's campaigns and the benchmark elections of 2000 and 2006," in Roderic Ai Camp (ed.), The Oxford Handbook of Mexican Politics. New York: Oxford University Press.

Domínguez, Jorge I., and Chappell Lawson (eds.). 2004. Mexico's Pivotal Democratic Election. Candidates, Voters, and the Presidential Campaign of 2000. Stanford, CA: Stanford University Press.

Domínguez, Jorge I., and James A. McCann. 1995. "Shaping Mexico's electoral arena: The construction of partisan cleavages in the 1988 and 1991 national elections." American Political Science Review 89(1): 34–48.

Drazen, Allan, and Vittorio Grilli. 1990. "The benefits of crises for economic reforms." Working paper no. 3527. National Bureau of Economic Research.

Dresser, Denise. 1991. Neopopulist Solutions to Neoliberal Problems. La Jolla, CA: UCSD Center for U.S.-Mexican Studies.

Druckman, James N., Donald P. Green, James H. Kuklinski, and Arthur Lupia. 2011. "Experiments: An introduction to core concepts," in Druckman, James N., Donald P. Green, James H. Kuklinski, and Arthur Lupia (eds.), Handbook of Experimental Political Science. Cambridge, UK: Cambridge University Press.

Duflo, E. 2006. "Poor but rational?" in Banerjee, Abhijit V., Roland Benabou, and Dilip Mookherjee (eds.), Understanding Poverty. New York: Oxford University Press.

Dunning, Thad. 2012. Natural Experiments in the Social Sciences. New York: Cambridge University Press.

Dunning, Thad, and Susan Hyde. 2008. "The analysis of experimental data: Comparing techniques" presented at the annual meeting of APSA.

Edwards, Sebastian. 1995. Crisis and Reform in Latin America. A World Bank Book. New York: Oxford University Press.

Epstein, David, and Sharyn O'Halloran. 1994. "Administrative procedures, information and agency discretion." American Journal of Political Science 38: 697–722.

Epstein, David, and Sharyn O'Halloran. 1999. Delegation Powers. New York: Cambridge University Press.

Escobar, Cristina. 2002. "Clientelism and citizenship: The limits of democratic reform in Sucre, Colombia." Latin American Perspectives 29(5): 20–47.

Esping-Andersen, G. 1985. Politics against Markets: The Social Democratic Road to Power. Princeton, NJ: Princeton University Press.

Esping-Andersen, G. 1990. The Three Worlds of Welfare Capitalism. Cambridge, UK: Polity Press.

Fernald, Lia C., Pail J. Gertler, and Lynette M. Neufeld. 2009. "10-year effect of Oportunidades, Mexico's conditional cash transfer programme, on child growth, cognition, language and behaviour: A longitudinal follow-up study." The Lancet 374(9706): 1997–2005.

Fiorina, Morris, P. 1981. Retrospective Voting in American National Elections. New Haven, CT: Yale University Press.

Fiorina, Morris P. 1994. "Divided government in the American states: A byproduct of legislative professionalism?" The American Political Science Review 88(2): 304–316.

Fiszbein, Ariel, and Norbert Schady. 2009. Conditional Cash Transfers: Reducing Present and Future Poverty. Washington, DC: World Bank.

Fox, Jonathan, and Julio Moguel. 1995. "Pluralism and antipoverty policy, Mexico's National Solidarity Program and left opposition municipal governments," in Rodriguez, Victoria E., and Peter M. Ward (eds.), Opposition Government in Mexico. Albuquerque: University of New Mexico Press.

Fox, Jonathan. 1994. "The difficult transition from clientelism to citizenship: Lessons from Mexico." World Politics, 46(2): 151–184.

Fraga, A. 2004. "Latin America since the 1990s: Rising from the sickbed?" Journal of Economic Perspectives 18(2): 89–106.

Garland, Allison M. 2000. "The politics and administration of social development in Latin America," in Tulchin, Joseph S., and Allison M. Garland (eds.), Social Development in Latin America. The Politics of Reform. Boulder, CO: Lynne Rienner.

Geddes, Barbara. 1991. "A game theoretic model of reform in Latin American democracies." The American Political Science Review 85(2 Jun): 371–392.

Geddes, Barbara. 1994. Politician's Dilemma: Building State Capacity in Latin America. Berkeley: University of California Press.

Gertler, Paul J. 2000. Final Report: The impact of Progresa on Health. Washington, DC: International Food Policy Research Institute.

Gertler, Paul J. 2004. Do conditional cash transfers improve child health? Evidence from Progresa's controlled randomized experiment. American Economic Review 94: 33136.

Gertler, Paul J., and Simone Boyce. 2001. "An experiment in incentive based welfare: the impact of Progresa on health in Mexico." Unpublished manuscript, University of California at Berkeley.

Gil Díaz, Francisco, and Agustín Carstens. 1996. Some Hypotheses Related To The Mexican 1994–95 Crisis. Mexico City: Banxico.

Gonzalez-Ocantos, Ezequiel, Chad Kiewiet de Jonge, Carlos Melendez, Javier Osorio, and David Nickerson. 2012. "Vote buying and social desirability bias: Experimental evidence from Nicaragua." American Journal of Political Science 56(1): 202–217.

Green, Donald P., Terence Y. Leong, Holger L. Kern, Alan Gerber, and Christopher W. Larimer. 2009. "Testing the accuracy of regression discontinuity analysis using experimental benchmarks." Political Analysis 17(4): 400–417.

Green, Tina. 2006. "Do social transfer programs affect voter behavior? Evidence from Progresa in Mexico." Unpublished manuscript. University of California, Berkeley.

Grindle, Merilee. 1977. Bureaucrats, Politicians, and Peasants in Mexico: A Case Study in Public Policy. Berkeley: University of California Press.

Grindle, Merilee. 1996. Challenging the State: Crisis and Innovation in Latin America and Africa. London: Cambridge University Press.

Grzymala-Busse, Anna. 2007. Rebuilding Leviathan: Party Competition and State Exploitation in Post-Communist Democracies. New York: Cambridge University Press.

Haggard, Stephan, and Robert R. Kaufman. 2008. Development, Democracy, and Welfare States: Latin America, East Asia, and Eastern Europe. Princeton, NJ: Princeton University Press.

Hibbings, John. R. 1999. "Legislative careers: Why and how we should study them." Legislative Studies Quarterly 24(May): 149–171.

Hicken, Allen. 2011. "Clientelism." Annual Review of Political Science 14: 289–310.

Hirschman, A. 1985. "Reflections on the Latin American experience," in Lindberg, L. and C. Maier (eds.), The Politics of Inflation and Economic Stagnation. Theoretical Approaches and International Studies. The Brookings Institution.

Hoddinott, John, and Emmanuel Skoufias. 2004. "The impact of PROGRESA on food consumption." Economic Development and Cultural Change, 53(1): 37–61.

Hoddinott, John, Emmanuel Skoufias, and Ryan Washburn. 2000. The impacts of Progresa on consumption: A final report. September. Report submitted to Progresa. Washington, DC: International Food Policy Research Institute.

Huber, Evelyn, François Nielsen, Jennifer Pribble, and John D. Stephens. 2006. "Politics and inequality in Latin America and the Caribbean." American Sociological Review 71(6):943–963.

Huber, Evelyn, Thomas Mustillo, and John D. Stephens. 2008. "Politics and social spending in Latin America." The Journal of Politics 70(2): 420–436.

Huber, Evelyn. 1996. "Options for social policy in Latin America: Neoliberal versus social democratic models," in Gøsta Esping-Andersen (ed.), Welfare States in Transition: National Adaptations in Global Economies. London: Sage.

Huber, John D., and N. McCarty. 2001. "Legislative organization, bureaucratic capacity and delegation in Latin American democracies." Unpublished manuscript. Prepared for the Conference on Brazilian Political Institutions in Comparative Perspective. St. Antony's College, Oxford University, 28–29 May.

Huber, John D., and N. McCarty. 2004. "Bureaucratic capacity, delegation and political reform." American Political Science Review 98: 481–494.

References

Huber, John D., and Charles R. Shipan. 2006. "Politics, delegation, and bureaucracy," in Weingast, Barry R. and Donald Wittman (eds.). The Oxford Handbook of Political Economy. New York: Oxford University Press.

Humphreys, Macartan, and Jeremy Weinstein. 2009. Annual Review of Political Science 12: 36778.

Hunter, Wendy, and Natasha Borges Sugiyama. 2011. "Documenting citizenship: Contemporary efforts toward social inclusion in Brazil." Paper presented at APSA Annual Meeting, Seattle, WA.

Hytrek, Gary. 2002. "Introduction: Globalization and social change in Latin America." Latin American Perspectives 29(5): Clientelism and Empowerment in Latin America, 7–19.

IDIES. 2009. "Evaluacíon Programa Mi Familia Progresa: Estudio de percepcíon incluyendo procesos." Instituto de Investigaciones Económicas y Sociales. Universidad Rafael Landívar.

Inter-Parliamentary Union reports. Various years. http://www.ipu.org/english/home.htm

Iversen, Torben, and Thomas R. Cusak. 2000. "The causes of welfare state expansion: Deindustrialization or globalization?" World Politics 52(3): 313–349.

Jones, Mark P., Sebastian Saiegh, Pablo T. Spiller, and Mariano Tommasi. 2002. "Amateur Legislators – Professional Politicians: the Consequences of Party-Centered Electoral Rules in a Federal System." American Journal of Political Science 46(3): 656–669.

Jones, Nicola, Rosana Vargas, and Eliana. 2008. "Cash transfers to tackle childhood poverty and vulnerability: An analysis of Peru's Juntos program." Environment and Urbanization 20: 255–273.

Kalaycioglu, Ersin. 2010. "Democracy, Islam, and secularism in Turkey," in Brown, Nathan J., and Emad El-Din Shanin (eds.), Struggle over Democracy in the Middle East: Regional Politics and External Policies. New York: Routledge.

Kaufman, Robert R., and Alex Segura-Ubiergo. 2001. "Globalization, domestic politics, and social spending in Latin America: A cross-sectional time series analysis, 1973–1997." World Politics 53(4): 553–587.

Kaufman, Robert R., and Guillermo Trejo. 1997. "Regionalism, regime transformation, and PRONASOL: The politics of the National Solidarity Programme in four Mexican states." Journal of Latin American Studies 29(3).

Kaufman, Robert R., and Joan M. Nelson. 2004. Crucial Needs, Weak Incentives: Social Sector Reform, Democratization, and Globalization in Latin America. Baltimore, MD: Johns Hopkins University Press.

Keefer, Philip, and David Stasavage. 2003. "The limits of delegation: Veto players, central bank independence and the credibility of monetary policy." American Political Science Review 97(3): 407–423.

Keefer, Philip. 2002. Clientelism, Credibility and Democracy. Unpublished manuscript. World Bank.

Keefer, Philip. 2010. DPI2010. Database of Political Institutions: Changes and Variable Definitions. Development Research Group, World Bank.

Keeler, John T. S. 1993. "Opening the window for reform: Mandates, crises and extraordinary policy-making." Comparative Political Studies 25(4): 433–486.

Kitschelt, Herbert. 2000. "Linkages between citizens and politicians in democratic polities." Comparative Political Studies 33(6–7): 845–879.

Kitschelt, Herbert. 2007. "The demise of clientelism in affluent capitalist democracies." 2007. In Kitschelt, Herbert, and Steven I. Wilkinson. 2007. Patrons, Clients, and Policies. Cambridge, UK: Cambridge University Press.

Kitschelt, Herbert, and Steven I. Wilkinson. 2007. Patrons, Clients, and Policies. Cambridge, UK: Cambridge University Press.

Klesner, Joseph L., and Chappell Lawson. 2001. "Adios to the PRI? Changing voter turnout in Mexico's political transition." Mexican Studies/Estudios Mexicanos 17(1): 17–39.

Korpi, W., and M. Shalev. 1979. "Strikes, industrial relations and class conflict in capitalist societies." British Journal of Sociology 30(2): 164–187.

Landry, Craig E., Andreas Lange, John A. List, Michael K. Price, and Nicholas G. Rupp. 2010. "Is a donor in hand better than two in the bush? Evidence from a natural field experiment." American Economic Review 100(3): 958–983.

Lawson, Chappell, and Joseph L. Klesner. 2004. "Political reform, electoral participation, and the campaign of 2000," in Jorge Domínguez and Chappell Lawson (eds.), Mexico's Pivotal Democratic Election, Candidates, Voters, and the Presidential Campaign of 2000. Stanford, CA: Stanford University Press, Center for U.S.-Mexican Studies, UCSD.

Lemarchand, Rene, and Keith Legg. 1972. "Political clientelism and development: A preliminary analysis." Comparative Politics 4(2): 149–178.

Levitt, Steven D. and James M. Snyder, Jr. 1997. "The impact of federal spending on House election outcomes." Journal of Political Economy 105: 30–53.

Levy, Santiago. 2006. Progress Against Poverty. Sustaining Mexico's Progresa-Oportunidades Program. Washington, DC: Brookings Institution Press.

Lindert, Kathy, and Vanina Vincensini. 2008. "Bolsa Familia in the headlines: An analysis of the media's treatment of conditional cash transfers in Brazil. Preliminary results." Unpublished manuscript. The World Bank.

Lopez-Calva, Luis F., and Nora Lustig (eds.). 2010. Declining Inequality in Latin America: A Decade of Progress? Washington, DC: Brookings Institution and UNDP.

Lust, Ellen, and Tarek Masoud. 2011. "Cash or kinship? Voting and social order in the developing world." Unpublished manuscript. Yale University. http://tarekmasoud.squarespace.com/storage/research/Lust_Masoud.pdf

Madrid, Raul L. 2003. Retiring the state. The politics of pension privatization in Latin America and beyond. Stanford, CA: Stanford University Press.

Magaloni, Beatriz, Alberto Díaz-Cayeros, and Federico Estevez. 2007. "Clientelism and portfolio diversification: A model of electoral investment with applications to Mexico," in Kitschelt, Herbert, and Steven I. Wilkinson (eds.), Patrons, Clients, and Policies. Cambridge, UK: Cambridge University Press.

Mainwaring, Scott. 1993. Presidentialism, multipartism, and democracy: The difficult combination. Comparative Political Studies 31(6): 714–739.

Maldonado Trujillo, Claudia Vanessa. 2012. The political economy of conditional cash transfers in Mexico and Brazil. 1997–2006. Ph.D. Dissertation. University of Notre Dame.

Manacorda, Marco, Edward Miguel and Andrea Vigorito. 2011. "Government Transfers and Political Support." American Economic Journal: Applied Economics 3(3):1–28.

Mares, Isabela. 2005. "Social protection around the world: External insecurity, state capacity and domestic political cleavages." Comparative Political Studies 38(6): 623–651.

Martínez Dobronsy, José, and José A. Rosero Moncayo. 2007. "Impacto del Bono de Desarrollo Humano en el trabajo infantil." Documento de investigación. Programa Internacional para la Erradicación del Trabajo Infantil. Organización Internacional del Trabajo.

Mayhew, David. 1974. Congress, The Electoral Connection. New Haven, CT: Yale University Press.

McCarty, Nolan. 2004. "The Appointments Dilemma." American Journal of Political Science 48(3): 413–428.

McCubbins, M. D., R. G. Noll, and B. R. Weingast. 1987. "Administrative procedures as instruments of political control." Journal of Law, Economics and Organizations 3: 243–277.

Mesa-Lago, Carmelo. 1989. Ascent to Bankruptcy. Financing Social Security in Latin America. Pittsburgh, PA: University of Pittsburgh Press.

Mesa-Lago, Carmelo. 1997. "Social welfare reform in the context of economic-political liberalization: Latin American cases." World Development 25(4): 497–517.

Mettler, Suzanne. 2002. "Bringing the state back into civic engagement: Policy feedback effects of the G.I. Bill for World War II veterans." American Political Science Review 96(2): 351–365.

Mettler, Suzanne, and Joe Soss. 2004. "The consequences of public policy for democratic citizenship: Bridging policy studies and mass politics." Perspectives on Politics 2(1): 55–73.

Moe, T. M. 1989. "The politics of bureaucratic structure," in Chubb, J. E., and P. E. Peterson (eds.), Can the Government Govern? Washington, DC: Brookings Institution.

Molinar, Juan, and Jeffrey A. Weldon. 1994. "Electoral determinants and consequences of national solidarity," in Cornelius, Wayne, Anne L. Craig, and Jonathan Fox (eds.), Transforming State-Society Relations in Mexico: the National Solidarity. La Jolla, CA: UCSD, Center for U.S.-Mexican Studies.

Mookherjee, Dilip. 2006. "Poverty persistence and design of antipoverty policies," in Banerjee, Abhijit V., Roland Benabou, and Dilip Mookherjee (eds.), Understanding Poverty. New York: Oxford University Press.

Morales, Natasha. 2010. "La Politica Social en Bolivia. Un Análisis de los Programas Sociales (2006–2008)." Inter-American Development Bank, División de la Protección Social y Salud, Notas Técnicas, IDB-TN-139, May.

Moreno, Alejandro. 2003. El Votante Mexicano: Democracia, Actitudes Políticas y Conducta Electoral. México D.F.: Fondo de Cultura Económica.

Morgan, Stephen L., and Christopher Winship. 2007. Counterfactuals and Causal Inference. New York: Cambridge University Press.

Morgenstern, Scott, and Benito Nacif. 2002. Legislative Politics in Latin America. New York: Cambridge University Press.

Murillo, V. 2009. Political Competition, Partisanship and Policymaking in Latin America. New York: Cambridge University Press.

Nichter, Simeon. 2008. "Vote buying or turnout buying? Machine politics and the secret ballot." American Political Science Review 102(1): 19–31.

O'Donnell, Guillermo. 1973. Modernization and Bureaucratic-Authoritarianism: Studies in South American Politics. Institute of International Studies, University of California.

O'Donnell, Guillermo. 1996. "Poverty and inequality in Latin America." Working Paper No. 225–July. Kellogg Institute for International Studies.

Parker, Susan W., and Graciela M. Teruel. 2005. "Randomization and social program evaluation: The case of Progresa." Annals of the American Academy of Political and Social Science 599: 199–219.

Pérez Yarahuán, Gabriela. 2005. "Policy choice and electoral politics in social welfare programs in Mexico: From PRONASOL to OPORTUNIDADES." Unpublished manuscript. University of Chicago.

Poder Ejecutivo Federal. 1997. Progresa: Programa de Educación, Salud y Alimentación. Mexico City: Office of the President.

Ponce, Juan. 2006. "The impact of a conditional cash transfer on school enrollment: The Bono de Desarrollo Humano of Ecuador." Working paper 06-302. Facultad Latinoamericana de Ciencias Sociales. Sede Ecuador.

Ponce, Juan, and Bedi, Arjun S., 2010. "The impact of a cash transfer program on cognitive achievement: The Bono de Desarrollo Humano of Ecuador." Economics of Education Review 29(1): 116–125.

PROGRESA. 1998. Método de selección de las localidades. Unpublished manuscript. Mexico City.

Putnam, Robert D. 1993. Making Democracy Work: Civic Traditions in Modern Italy. Princeton, NJ: Princeton University Press.

Ravallion, Martin. 2006a. "Transfers and Safety Nets in Poor Countries: Revisiting the Trade-offs and Policy Options." in Banerjee, Abhijit V., Roland Benabou, and Dilip Mookherjee (eds.), Understanding Poverty. New York: Oxford University Press.

Ravallion, Martin. 2006b. Evaluating Anti-Poverty Programs. Policy Research Working Paper 3625. Washington, DC: World Bank, Development Economics Research Group.

Riker, William H., and Peter Ordeshook. 1968. "A theory of the calculus of voting." American Political Science Review 62(1): 25–42.

Rodrik, Dani. 1997. Has Globalization Gone Too Far? Washington, DC: Institute for International Economics.

Rogers-Dillon, Robin. 2004. The Welfare Experiments: Politics and Policy Evaluation. Stanford, CA: Stanford University Press.

Romer, Paul. 1996. "Preferences, promises and the politics of entitlements," in Victor R. Fuchs, Victor R. (ed.), Individual and Social Responsibility: Child Care, Education, Medical Care and Long Term Care in America. The National Bureau of Economic Research. Chicago: University of Chicago Press.

Rosenthal, Alan. 1996. "State legislative development: observations from three perspectives," Legislative Studies Quarterly 21(May): 169–198.

Ross, Michael. 2006. "Is democracy good for the poor?" American Journal of Political Science 50(4): 860–874.

Rubio-Freidberg, Luis. 1998. "Coping with political change," in Kaufman Purcell, Susan, and Luis Rubio-Freidberg (eds.), Mexico Under Zedillo. Boulder, CO: Lynne Rienner Publishers.

Rueda, David. 2005. "Insider–outsider politics in industrialized democracies: The challenge to social democratic parties." American Political Science Review 99(1): 61–74.

Schady, Norbert, and Maria Caridad Araujo. 2006. "Cash transfers, conditions, school enrollment, and child work: evidence from a randomized experiment in Ecuador." World Bank Policy Research Working Paper 3930, June.

Schedler, Andreas. 2000. "The democratic revelation." Journal of Democracy 11(4): 5–19.

References

Schneider, Ben R. 1991. Politics within the State: Elite Bureaucrats and Industrial Policy in Authoritarian Brazil. Pittsburgh, PA: University of Pittsburgh Press.

Schultz, Paul. 2001. "School subsidies for the poor: Evaluating a Mexican strategy for reducing poverty." FCND Discussion Paper No. 102, International Food Policy Research Institute.

Scott, James C. 1969. "Corruption, machine politics, and political change." The American Political Science Review 63(4): 1142–1158.

Scott, John. 2001. "Distributive incidence of social spending in Mexico." DECIDE, México.

Segura-Ubiergo, Alex. 2007. The Political Economy of the Welfare State in Latin America. Globalization, Democracy, and Development. New York: Cambridge University Press.

Shipan, Charles, and Craig Volden. 2008. "The mechanisms of policy diffusion." American Journal of Political Science, 52(4): 840–857.

Shugart, Matthew S., and John M. Carey. 1992. Presidents and Assemblies: Constitutional Design and Electoral Dynamics. Cambridge, UK: Cambridge University Press.

Skocpol, Theda. 1991. "Targeting within universalism: Politically viable policies to combat poverty in the United States," in Jencks, Christopher, and Paul E. Peterson (eds.), The Urban Underclass. Washington, DC: Brookings Institution.

Skocpol, Theda. 1992. Protecting Soldiers and Mothers: The Political Origins of Social Policy in the United States. Cambridge, MA: Belknap Press of Harvard University Press.

Skocpol, Theda, and E. Amenta, 1986. "State and social policies." American Review of Sociology, 12:131–157.

Skoufias, E. 2005. PROGRESA and Its Impacts on the Welfare of Rural Households in Mexico. Washington, DC: International Food Policy Research Institute.

Skoufias, Emmanuel, and Bonnie McClafferty. 2001. Is PROGRESA Working? Summary of the results of an evaluation by IFPRI. Washington, DC: International Food Policy Research Institute.

Skoufias, Emmanuel, Benjamin Davis, and Jere Behrman. 1999. Final Report: An Evaluation of the Selection of Beneficiary Households in the Education, Health, and Nutrition Program (PROGRESA) of Mexico. June. Washington, DC: International Food Policy Research Institute.

Skoufias, Emmanuel, Benjamin Davis, and Sergio de la Vega. 2001. "Targeting the poor in Mexico: Evaluation of the selection of beneficiary households into PROGRESA." World Development (10): 1769–1784.

Snyder, Richard. 2001. Politics after Neoliberalism. Reregulation in Mexico. New York: Cambridge University Press.

Sobrado Chavez, Miguel, and Richard Stoller. 2002. "Organizational empowerment versus clientelism." Latin American Perspectives 9(5): Clientelism and Empowerment in Latin America, 7–19.

Sobrado Chavez, Miguel. 2000. "Clodomir Santos de Morais: The origins of the large scale *Capacitacíon* theory and method," in Carmen, R., and M. Sobrado (eds.), A Future for the Excluded. London: Zed Books.

Soederberg, Susanne. 2001. "From neoliberalism to social liberalism: Situating the National Solidarity Program within Mexico's passive revolutions." Latin American Perspectives 28(3): 104–123.

Soss, Joe. 1999. "Lessons of welfare: Policy design, political learning and political action." American Political Science Review 93(2): 363–380.
Soss, Joe, Jacob Hacker, and Suzanne Mettler (eds.). 2007. Remaking America. Democracy and Public Policy in an Age of Inequality. Russell Sage Foundation.
Staiger, D., and J. H. Stock. 1997. Instrumental variables regression with weak instruments. Econometrica 65(May): 557–586.
Stein, Ernesto, and Mariano Tommasi (eds.). 2008. Policymaking in Latin America: How Politics Shape Policies. Washington, DC: Inter-American Development Bank.
Stein, Ernesto, Ernesto Talvi, and Alejandro Grisanti. 1999. "Institutional arrangements and fiscal performance: The Latin American experience," in Poterba, James M. (ed.), Fiscal Institutions and Fiscal Performance. Chicago: University of Chicago Press.
Stock, J. H., and M. Yogo. 2002. "Testing for weak instruments in linear IV regression." NBER Working Paper No. T0284.
Stokes, Susan C. 2001. Mandates and Democracy: Neoliberalism by Surprise in Latin America. Cambridge, UK: Cambridge University Press.
Stokes, Susan C. 2005. "Perverse accountability: A formal model of machine politics with evidence from Argentina." American Political Science Review 99(3) 315–325.
Stokes, Susan C. 2007. "Is vote buying undemocratic?." in Frederic C. Schaffer (ed.), Elections for Sale: The Causes and Consequences of Vote Buying. Boulder, CO: Lynne Rienner.
Stokes, Susan, Thad Dunning, Marcelo Nazareno, and Valeria Brusco. 2012. Brokers, Voters, and Clientelism. Unpublished manuscript. Yale University and Universidad Nacional de Córdoba.
Tendler, Judith. 2000. "Why are social funds so popular?" in Yusuf, Shahid, Weiping Wu, and Simon Evenett (eds.), Local Dynamics in an Era of Globalization. Oxford University Press.
Thatcher, Mark and Alec Stone Sweet. 2002. "Theory and practice of delegation to non-majoritarian institutions." Western European Politics 25(1): 1–22.
The Economist. 2011. "All in the family: Guatemala's presidential election." March 15. http://www.economist.com/blogs/americasview/2011/03/guatemalas_presidential_election
The Washington Post. 2006. "Cash aid bolsters Lula's reelection prospects; Incentives for families to help themselves spreads beyond Brazil." October 29.
Ting, M. 2001. "The power of the purse and its implications for bureaucratic policy-making." Public Choice 106(3,4): 243–274.
Todd, Petra E., and Kenneth I. Wolpin. 2006. "Assessing the impact of a school subsidy program in Mexico: Using a social experiment to validate a dynamic behavioral model of child schooling and fertility." The American Economic Review 96(5): 1384–1417.
Trejo, Guillermo and Claudio Jones. 1998. "Political dilemmas of welfare reform: Poverty and inequality in Mexico," in Susan Kaufman and Luis Rubio (eds.), Mexico under Zedillo. Boulder, CO: Lynne Rienner.
Tsebelis, George. 2002. Veto Players. Princeton, NJ: Princeton University Press.
Udry, Christopher. 2006. "Child labor," in Banerjee, Abhijit V., Roland Benabou, and Dilip Mookherjee (eds.), Understanding Poverty. New York: Oxford University Press.
United Nations Children's Fund (UNICEF). 2010. The State of the World's Children. http://www.unicef.org/rightsite/sowc/statistics.php
Valenzuela, Arturo. 2004. "Latin American presidencies interrupted." Journal of Democracy 15(4): 5–19.

References

Van de Walle, Dominique. 1998. "Targeting revisited." World Bank Research Observer 13(2): 231–248.
Volden, C. 2002. "Delegating power to bureaucracies: evidence from the states." Journal of Law, Economics and Organizations 18: 187–220.
Wantchekon, L. 2003. "Clientelism and voting behavior: Evidence from a field experiment in Benin." World Politics Vol. 55: 399–422.
Weitz-Shapiro, Rebecca. 2012a. Curbing Clientelism. Politics, Poverty, and Social Policy in Argentina. Unpublished manuscript. Brown University.
Weitz-Shapiro, Rebecca. 2012b. "What wins votes: Why some politicians opt out of clientelism." American Journal of Political Science 56(3): 568–583.
Weyland, Kurt. 1996. Democracy without Equity. Failures of Reform in Brazil. Pittsburgh, PA: University of Pittsburgh Press.
Weyland, Kurt. 1999. "Neoliberal populism in Latin America and Eastern Europe." Comparative Politics 31(4): 379–401.
Weyland, Kurt. 2006. Bounded Rationality and Policy Diffusion. Social Sector Reform in Latin America. Princeton, NJ: Princeton University Press.
Williams, H. L. 2001. Social Movements and Economic Transition: Markets and Distributive Conflict in Mexico. New York: Cambridge University Press.
Wood, B. D., and J. Bohte. 2004. "Political transaction costs and the politics of administrative design." Journal of Politics, 66: 176–202.
Wooldridge, J. 2002. Econometric Analysis of Cross Section and Panel Data. Cambridge, MA: MIT Press.
World Bank. 2001. "Crisis management in Mexico 1994–1995" (June). http://www1.worldbank.org/finance/assets/images/Crisis_Man.pdf
World Bank. 2009. "Financial crisis highlights needs for more social safety nets, including conditional cash transfers." Press Release No. 2009/220/DEC.
World Bank. 2010. World Development Indicators. http://data.worldbank.org/data-catalog/world-development-indicators
World Bank. Various years. Poverty and Inequality Database. http://databank.worldbank.org/data/views/variableselection/selectvariables.aspx?source=Poverty-and-Inequality-Database
Yaschine, Iliana, and Mónica Orozco. 2010. "The evolving antipoverty agenda in Mexico," in Adato, Michelle, and John Hoddinott (eds.), Conditional Cash Transfers in Latin America. Baltimore, MD: Johns Hopkins University Press.
Zucco, Cesar. 2008. "The President's New Constituency: Lula and the Pragmatic Vote in Brazil's 2006 Presidential Elections." *Journal of Latin American Studies* 40(1): 29–49.
Zucco, Cesar. 2011. "On redistribution and backlash: Are conditional cash-transfers more acceptable than other public transfers?" Unpublished manuscript. Princeton University.
Zucco, Cesar. 2013. "When Payouts Pay Off: Conditional Cash Transfers and Voting Behavior in Brazil 2002–2101." American Journal of Political Science 57(4): 810–822.
Zuckerman, Alan S. 1983. "Review of S. N. Eisenstadt and Rene Lemarchand, Political Clientelism, Patronage and Development." The American Political Science Review 77(4).

Index

Africa, 19
American Popular Revolutionary Alliance, 84, 87
Antipoverty programs, 3, 24
Appointment powers, 11, 48, 53, 82
Argentina, 11, 12, 17, 18, 22, 24, 28, 41, 43, 57, 59, 95, 99, 101, 109, 110, 111, 134
  parliamentary debates, 93, 95
Armed rebellion, 46
Asignación Universal por Hijo, Arg., 17, 28, 41, 57, 95, 110. See Argentina
Avancemos, Costa Rica, 28

Belize
  child labor, 26
Bolsa Familia, Brazil, 16, 28, 62
Bono de Desarrollo Humano, Ecuador, 28
  conditionalities, 34
  evaluation, 38, 39
  evolution, 40
  targeting, 32
  transparency, 37
Bono Juancito Pinto, Bolivia, 5, 27, 28, 29, 110
  conditionalities, 33
  targeting, 33
  transparency, 37
Bono Solidario, Ecuador, 28, 72
  conditionalities, 33
  targeting, 32
  transparency, 36

Brazil, 3, 5, 8, 11, 16, 28, 36, 43, 48, 83, 112, 137, 148
Bureaucratic insulation, 8

Checks on governments
  and program design
    bivariate correlations, 43
    multivariate regression, 60
  and program implementation
    bivariate correlations, 43
    multivariate regression, 101
  definition, 60
Child labor
  and poverty, 27
  and program adoption, 64
  and program design, 61, 64, 67
  and program implementation, 100, 101, 103
  effects on, 39
  statistics, 26
Chile Solidario, Chile, 28
Clientelism, 2, 10, 12, 13, 15, 46, 56, 133, 147
Colom, Alvaro, 17, 89
Colombia, 11, 16, 17, 18, 22, 24, 28, 31, 33, 34, 36, 39, 40, 47, 57, 58, 65, 114, 117, 118, 119, 120, 156
  child labor, 26
  parliamentary debates, 80–2
Com. Solidarias, El Salvador, 28
Concertación Parlamentaria (CP), 85
Conditional cash transfers
  and clientelism, 112

Conditional cash transfers (*cont.*)
  causes of, 9
  consequences of, 14
  definition, 3
  description, 27
  future of, 154
  list of, 27
Corruption, 15, 18, 19, 48, 53, 55
Credit claiming, 12

Da Silva, Lula, 3
Debt crisis, 6, 46
Deindustrialization, 6, 46, 61, 100, 101, 103
  and program design, 61
Diffusion, 8, 65
Divided government
  and program design
    multivariate regression, 60
  and program implementation
    multivariate regression, 101
  definition, 59

Economic crisis, 9, 10, 13, 20, 45, 50, 51, 53, 62, 150, 151, 152, 153
  and program design, 61
Ecuador, 3, 4, 5, 11, 28, 32, 33, 34, 36, 37, 38, 39, 40, 58, 72
Electoral behavior, 16, 136
Electoral bonus, 16, 134
Electoral turnout, 7, 135
Encuentro por Guatemala, 91
Entitlements, 4, 8, 44, 72, 98
Experimental evidence, 138

Familias en Acción, Colombia, 16, 17, 28, 57, 58, 65, 119, 156. *See* Colombia
  conditionalities, 33
  evaluation, 39
  targeting, 31
  transparency, 36
Fernández de Kirchner, Cristina, 17, 93
Fixed effects models
  electoral behavior, 142
  political-economic cycles, 102
  program design, 61
  program implementation, 99
Fox, Vicente, 119

Gómez de León, José, 79
Gómez Hermosillo, Rogelio, 119
García, Alan, 3, 82, 87

GDP
  and program design, 61
Guatemala, 16, 17, 18, 22, 28, 33, 36, 39, 47, 57, 92, 114, 118, 123
  child labor, 26
  parliamentary debates, 89–93

Ideology, 3, 7, 61, 101
ILAE, Dom. Rep., 28
Inequality, 5
inflation, 9, 61, 62, 65, 67, 100, 101, 103
Informal economy, 10, 47
Institutional Revolutionary Party (PRI), 73, 75, 76, 78, 121, 122, 143, 144, 146
Inter-American Development Bank, 8, 39, 43, 80, 93, 109
International Food Policy Research Institute, 5, 19, 37
International Labor Organization, 26

Juntos, Peru, 17, 28, 57, 84, 85, 86, 87, 88, 111, 123, 155. *See* Peru
  conditionalities, 33

Kirchner, Néstor, 17, 93

Levy, Santiago, 29, 79
Liberal Party, Colombia, 80
Lost decade, 9

Mahuad, Jamil, 32
Malawi, 19
Mexican National Institute for Public Health, 92
Mexico, 2, 3, 7, 8, 10, 11, 16, 17, 18, 22, 24, 28, 29, 31, 37, 38, 39, 40, 46, 57, 58, 59, 99, 107, 109, 111, 114, 115, 116, 118, 120, 121, 122, 123, 133, 135, 136, 138, 139, 147, 151, 154, 156
  child labor, 26
  parliamentary debates, 72–80
MIFAPRO, Guatemala, 16, 17, 28, 34, 57, 89, 90, 91, 92, 93, 123, 124. *See* Guatemala
  conditionalities, 33
  evaluation, 39
  transparency, 36
Morales, Evo, 6

National Action Party (PAN), 27, 75, 76, 77, 78, 127, 143, 146

Index

National Unity of Hope (UNE), 89, 93
Neoliberalism, 46

Oportunidades, Mexico, 5, 16, 27, 28, 29, 109, 111, 114, 115, 116, 117, 118, 119, 120, 121, 122, 123, 124, 126, 127, 128, 129, 130, 131, 132, 133. *See* Progresa, Mexico
  targeting, 31
  transparency, 36

PANES, Uruguay, 28
Parliamentary debates, 70–95
Partisanship, 7. *See* Ideology
Party of the Dem. Rev. (PRD), 75, 76, 77, 127, 143, 146
Pastrana, Andrés, 17, 80
PATH, Jamaica, 28
Patrana, Andrés, 80
Pension privatization, 8
Peru, 3, 11, 17, 18, 22, 24, 28, 33, 47, 57, 59, 99, 109, 111, 114, 117, 123, 155, 156
  child labor, 26
  parliamentary debates, 82–9
Peru Posible, 84
Philippines, 18
Plan Colombia, 80
Plan Equidad, Uruguay, 28
Plan Familias, Argentina, 17, 28, 57, 93, 94, 110
Plan Jefes y Jefas de Hogar, Arg., 93
Plan Pro-Peru, 82
Policy convergence, 5
Policy implementation, 96–102
Policy survival, 15, 54, 104–7
Political game
  actions, 45
  cases, 50
  decision tree, 48
  hypotheses, 53–6
  players, 44
  status quo, 46
Political-economic cycles, 15, 102–4
Popular Action (PAP), 85
Population
  and program design, 61
Poverty alleviation, 1
Power resource theory, 6
PRAF, Honduras, 28
Preferences for antipoverty policies
  median legislator, 48

  president, 48
  voters, 108
Pro-Peru, 83
PROCAMPO, 76
Program design, 30
  conditionalities, 33
  evaluation, 37
  recertification, 35
  targeting, 30
  transparency and monitoring, 35
Program implementation, 30
Progresa, Mexico, 3, 5, 17, 27, 28, 29, 37, 38, 40, 57, 72, 73, 75, 76, 77, 78, 79, 80, 135, 136, 137, 138, 139, 141, 142, 143, 144, 145, 146, 147, 148, 154, 156. *See* Oportunidades, Mexico
  conditionalities, 33
  evaluation, 37, 38
PRONASOL, 75, 77, 121, 122
PRONASOL, Mexico, 73
Propais, Paraguay, 28
Proyecto 300, Uruguay, 28

Red de Oportunidades, Panama, 28
Red de Protección Social, Nicaragua, 28
Red Solidaria, El Salvador, 28
Regression discontinuity design
  program design, 67
Rent-seeking, 15

Samper, Ernesto, 80
SISBEN, 80
Sistema de Atención a Crisis, Nicaragua, 28
Social assistance, 25
Social insurance, 25
Social policy reform, 1, 3
Social protection, 2, 4, 6, 25
Social unrest, 46
Solidaridad, Dom. Rep., 28
State capacity, 8
Subsidio Único Familiar, Chile, 27, 28

Tarjeta de Asistencia Escolar, Dom. Rep., 28
Technocrats, 7
Tekopora, Paraguay, 28
Toledo, Alejandro, 82
Torres de Colom, Sandra, 90, 92
Trade openness, 61, 64, 67, 100, 101, 103
Turkey, 18

Unconditional Cash Transfers, 19
UNICEF, 19, 26

Unions, 6, 46
United States, 6
Uribe, Alvaro, 16, 17, 80, 81
USAID, 93

Veto players, 11

Welfare state, 6, 7, 10
Western Europe, 6
World Bank, 4, 8, 10, 18, 19, 38, 43, 62, 80, 81, 88, 89, 100

Zedillo, Ernesto, 17, 72, 79

For EU product safety concerns, contact us at Calle de José Abascal, 56–1°,
28003 Madrid, Spain or eugpsr@cambridge.org.

www.ingramcontent.com/pod-product-compliance
Ingram Content Group UK Ltd.
Pitfield, Milton Keynes, MK11 3LW, UK
UKHW011314060825
461487UK00005B/71